CHARLES OPPENHEIMER

FROM CRAFTSMAN TO ARTIST

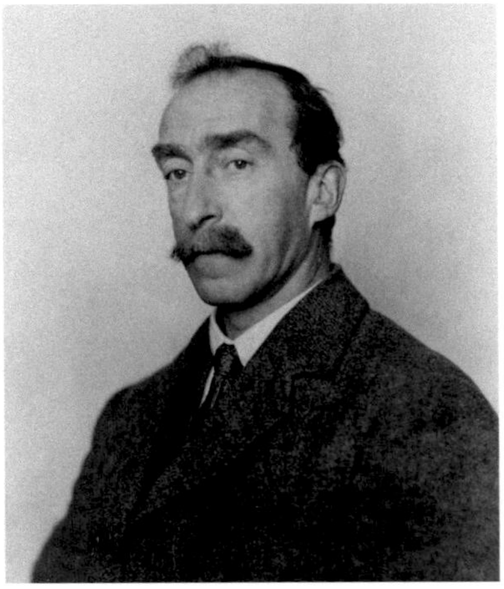

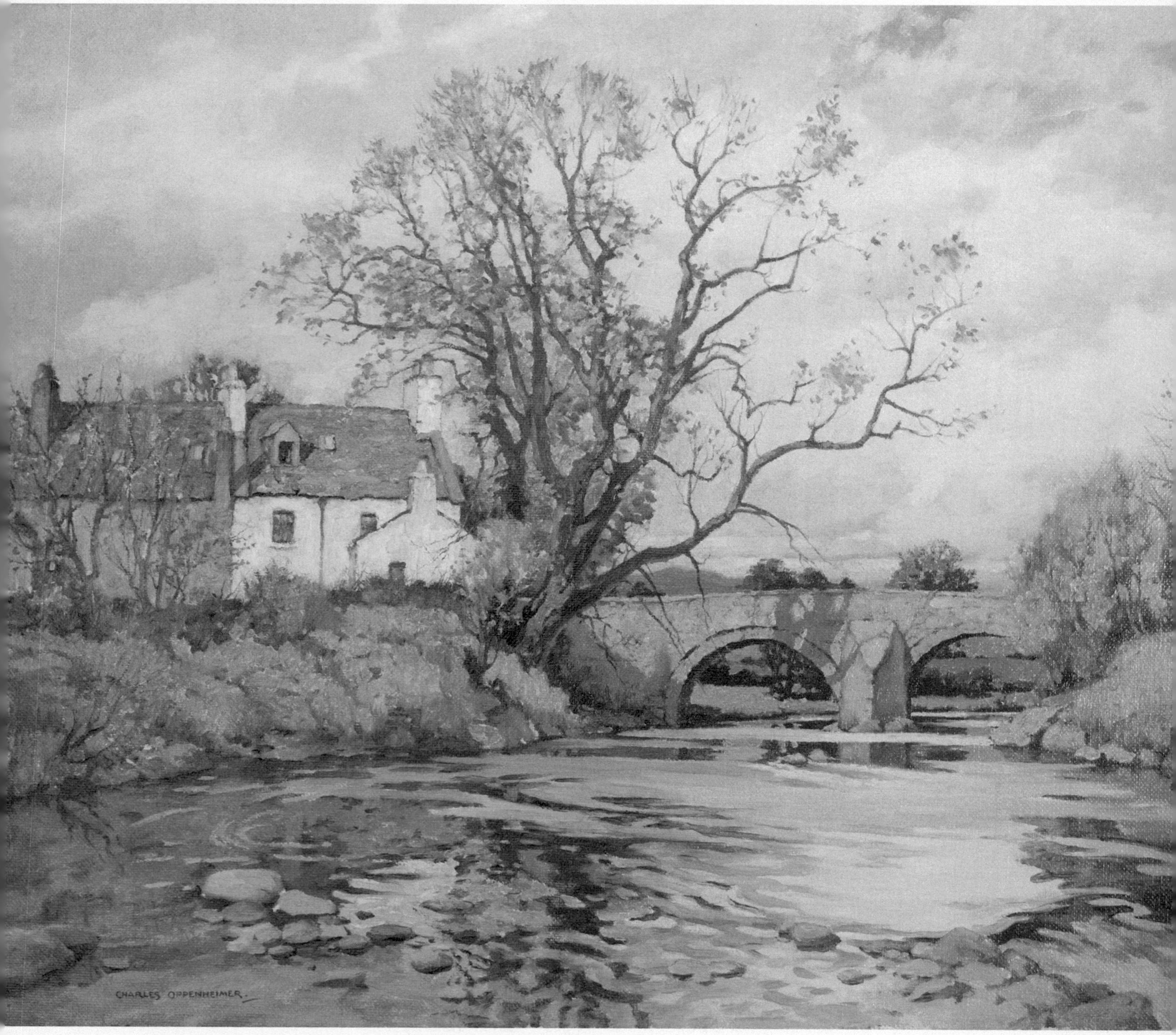
CHARLES OPPENHEIMER

Euan Robson

CHARLES OPPENHEIMER

FROM CRAFTSMAN TO ARTIST

Atelier Books · Edinburgh

for Mum and Dad

First published in Great Britain in 2012
by Atelier Books, 6 Dundas Street
Edinburgh EH3 6HZ
an imprint of The Fine Art Society, London

ISBN 978 1 873830 25 3

Frontispiece: *The Old Bridge, Gatehouse of Fleet*, c.1940, Private Collection, 25 x 34¼ inches

Designed and typeset in Fournier by Dalrymple
Printed in Belgium by DeckersSnoeck

Unless stated otherwise, all works illustrated are by Charles Oppenheimer

CONTENTS

Preface and Acknowledgements 7

1 Manchester 11

2 Mosaics – the Pattern of Life 15

3 To Kirkcudbright 23

4 An Artist's Town 33

5 War 43

6 Back Home 51

7 The Fusion of Colour 61

8 'A Student of Art' 81

9 'A Gentle Painter' 89

10 'Once there were Great Men' 103

Appendix: Ludwig Oppenheimer Ltd 115

Chronology 121

Bibliography 127

Works Exhibited by Oppenheimer 123

Index 127

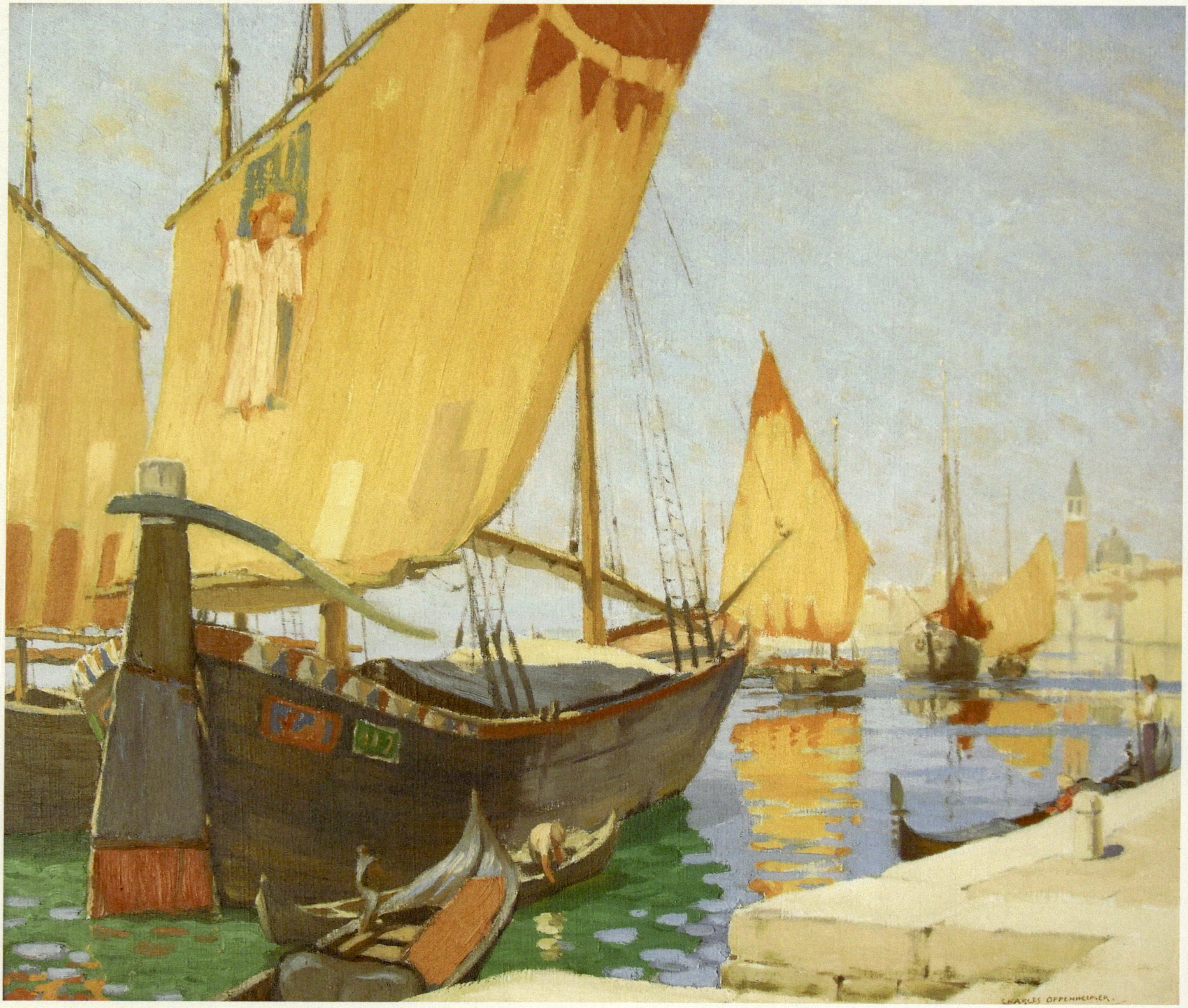
CHARLES OPPENHEIMER.

PREFACE & ACKNOWLEDGEMENTS

Plate 1 | *Venetian Barges*, c.1936, Private Collection, oil on canvas, 20 × 24 inches

CHARLES OPPENHEIMER was born and brought up in Manchester. The aim of this book is to explain how he came to be considered as a Scottish artist of the foremost rank. It is true that his mother was a Free Presbyterian from Montrose but other than holidays with her family in Angus, he had little connection with Scotland until a chance meeting suggested the small town of Kirkcudbright in Galloway as a new place in which to make his home and a career as a professional artist.

Oppenheimer trained as a designer for his German Jewish immigrant father's mosaic business in Manchester. He was destined for an obscure but comfortable and worthy career in commerce. A natural talent and enthusiasm for drawing and painting, a dedication to his work and the inspiration of professional artists who lived and worked nearby took him on a journey from a craftsman and designer to an artist.

His early career in mosaics and in illustration and design followed study at Manchester Municipal School of Art under Walter Crane. After breaking free from commercial constraints his painting style especially in oils changed over the years. At first his work was more painterly and expressive. He chose light and colour over form. Fred Jackson in Manchester and WS MacGeorge in Kirkcudbright were strong influences. Later, after they had gone, there was more emphasis on line and structure.

One of the reasons that very little has been written about Oppenheimer's life and work is that, although distinct among his Scottish contemporaries in the 1930s and 1940s, he founded no movement or school nor had any particular followers. Furthermore, of a naturally modest character, he was never a self publicist. Lack of self promotion was in turn partly caused in the years around the First World War by vulnerability due to his German ancestry.

Oppenheimer was a man of principle and courage. He supported free trade and women's suffrage, great issues of their day. He enlisted as a private in the Royal Artillery at the age of forty in the service of his king and country and went to the Western Front. After the war he advocated the causes of ex-servicemen and spoke up for the protection of the built heritage and environment with tenacity and distinction.

His was a fascinating and full life of many achievements and his paintings are a wonderful legacy much sought after today. My hope is that this book does Charles Oppenheimer justice and gives him a proper place amongst artists both north and south of the border. Perhaps it may also give the reader and collector a better understanding of the man himself.

This book would not have been possible without the advice and encouragement of the Oppenheimer family who generously gave me access to their memories, papers and records. I wish particularly to thank Professor Stephen Oppenheimer, Niki Hein, Jo Hammond, Isabel Nirula and Mairi Oppenheimer for their help.

Charles Oppenheimer's wife Connie's family have made an similar contribution to my understanding of their uncle by marriage. My particular appreciation goes to Robert Taylor and David Taylor whose boyhood instamatic camera made the only visual record of the pictures exhibited at the Oppenheimer exhibition in Broughton House in Kirkcudbright in 1981.

Parts of this book would have been infinitely the more poor without the memories of the late Mary Evans, Connie Oppenheimer's niece. I will be forever grateful for our long talks about the Oppenheimers and her first-hand insights into their life in Kirkcudbright. She also opened entirely new lines of enquiry about her uncle's war service. We shared an interest in education which may have diverted our attention from the artist from time to time.

I also wish to thank Elizabeth Burn, Beryl Moultrie and Peter Holmes for their enthusiasm and for sharing their reminiscences. I am greatly indebted to Joe Campbell for his generous assistance born of his acquaintance with Oppenheimer and his wife and a passion for the artist's work. David Devereux was very generous with his time. His knowledge of the archives in the Stewartry Museum was invaluable in piecing together parts of Charles Oppenheimer's life in Kirkcudbright. Caroline McGee and Michael Holland shared information with me about Ludwig Oppenheimer Ltd's mosaic and decorative work in Irish religious buildings.

My thanks go to many private collectors who have shown me their Oppenheimer paintings. Some are reproduced on the pages that follow. I also greatly appreciated the efforts of curators of galleries who went to some trouble to let me see works. Especial gratitude is due to everyone at The Fine Art Society in London, Bourne Fine Art in Edinburgh and the Niall Duncan Gallery in Castle Douglas for their advice and assistance.

I am also grateful to Joanna Soden and Nicola Ireland of the Royal Scottish Academy for their help with references and for making material available from the Academy's archives. Jeremy Parrett of the All Saints Library of Manchester Metropolitan University went to a great deal of trouble finding information about the Manchester Metropolitan School of Art for me including the lists of student prizes in the School's Annual Reports. We intend to establish an archive about Ludwig Oppenheimer Ltd in the library. I am similarly in the debt of the staff at the National Archives in Kew, Richmond, the National Library of Scotland, the City Library in Edinburgh, the Central Library in Manchester, the National Archives of Scotland and the National Trust for Scotland in Broughton House. Special mention ought to be made of Leonie O'Dwyer who helped carry several of the dustiest volumes of press cuttings that I have ever seen up from the basement store to the Reading Room in the Walker Institute and Art Gallery in Liverpool. Sheila Dewsbury the archivist of the Manchester Academy of Fine Arts spent a great deal of time looking through the Academy's archives for me.

Many individuals contributed in different ways. They include David Collin, Margaret Shamash, Elizabeth Gladstone, Pat and Jim Campbell, Niall Duncan, Cordelia Bourne, Selina Skipwith, Dan Shackleton, Joe Craig, Dawn Hendersby, Michael Moore MP and Ian and Kathleen Howie.

John McKenzie and Leo Blamire's photographic skills and professionalism have ensured the quality of the illustrations. Robert Dalrymple's design has brought the pages that follow to life. Rona Stevenson was ever patient and assiduous in typing the early manuscript and making sense of changes and alterations through the various drafts. Bill Smith offered me invaluable advice on the first draft text and a later version focusing my attention on the structure of the book and pointing out necessary changes. Patrick Bourne similarly put his immense experience and expertise into guiding me along the way.

Thanks are due to my family and my wife Valerie in particular who have supported me throughout.

This book offers a chance to expand upon my essay in *Kirkcudbright 100 Years of an Artists' Colony* published in 2000. It corrects errors and misunderstandings and benefits from ten or more years of additional research. However there will be things yet to learn about the life and times of Charles Oppenheimer. Anyone who would like to share information or memories is invited to get in touch via the publishers. There is much to be done to discover the full achievement of Ludwig Oppenheimer Ltd's mosaic business and that is of equal interest.

Any mistakes or omissions in what follows are mine; any credit belongs to the artist.

EUAN ROBSON
Kelso, May 2012

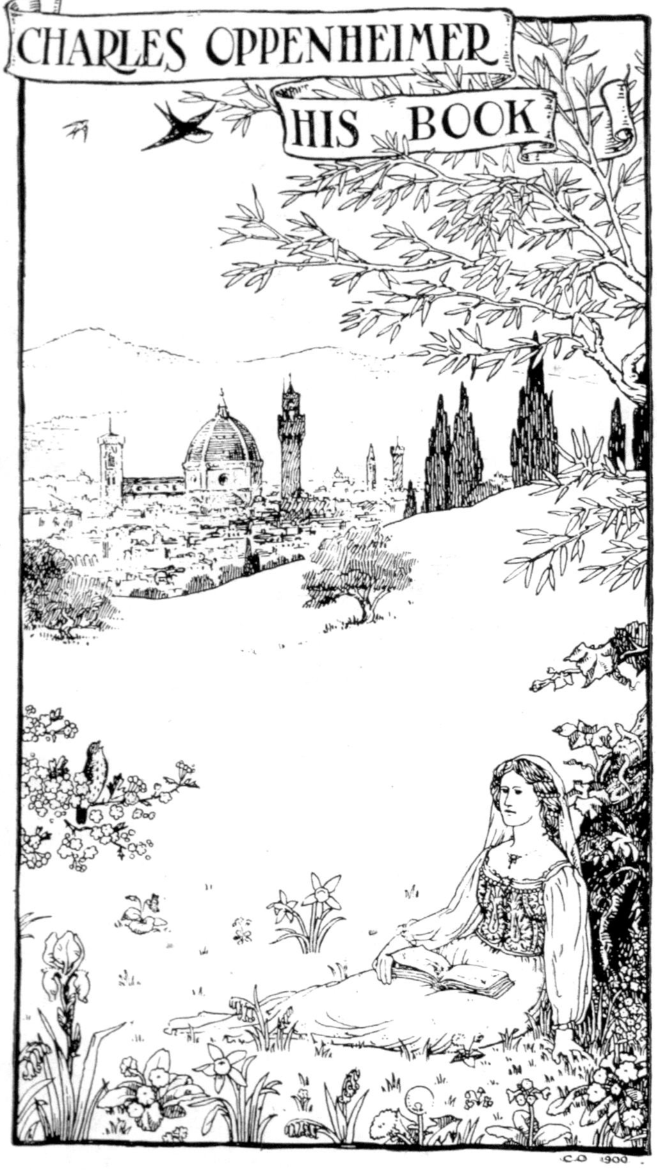
CHARLES OPPENHEIMER
HIS BOOK
C.O 1900

1 MANCHESTER

Plate 2 | Bookplate, 1900, from a private library

ON A CLEAR NIGHT many years ago in his native Lancashire, a young man was thrilled to see one of the moons of Saturn without the aid of a telescope. At least that was the often repeated family tale about Charles Oppenheimer's eyesight. The Royal Astronomical Society confirms that it is not actually possible to see the rings of the planet with the naked eye and so perhaps it was another planet's moons or maybe just the features of the moon itself that Oppenheimer could see. Whatever the truth he employed his fine vision throughout his life, first in his family's mosaic business in Manchester, then as a professional artist, later during military service in the Great War and again on return to a life of painting and drawing in his adopted home town of Kirkcudbright. He had vision of another kind and it was his aspiration to express what he saw before him on canvas and paper that led to a transition in his thirties from master craftsman to artist. He left legacies from both periods of his life of which anyone would be proud.

Oppenheimer's family background had a profound influence upon his professional development. His father, Ludwig, was born in 1830 in Brunswick not far from Hanover in Germany, the son of a Jewish family of merchant bankers. He may have first journeyed to Britain in 1849 as a letter dated 1914 suggests this. Moreover a family of Oppenheimers from Brunswick are recorded in Lancashire in the 1851 Census although Ludwig was not among them. Years later a grandson of Ludwig recorded in an unpublished autobiography that Ludwig was a self taught engineer. He went to Australia in the gold rush of the 1850s to sell mining equipment to the prospectors. He was successful and prospered but on travelling back to Europe to replenish his stock, the sea voyage made him so unwell that he never returned. Ludwig Oppenheimer next served in the Schleswig Holstein war of 1864 but after its conclusion decided that he did not wish 'to be involved in any more of Bismarck's military exploits'.

At some moment in these years a quarrel developed with his brothers over an inheritance from his parents. He was the youngest in a large family. It is unclear whether the argument was resolved but one of the consequences, according to one of his granddaughters, was that Ludwig left Germany to lodge with a Scottish couple in Manchester in order to improve his English but also to make a start in business under the wing of an Oppenheimer relation. Not long after his arrival family lore claims that he was asked by his hosts to go to Manchester's Piccadilly station to meet their niece from Montrose who was to visit for a holiday.

In Victorian and Edwardian Britain railways connected not only the great cities but almost all towns of any significant size and many a village as well. They were the engines of prosperity and social mobility. The plume of smoke, the hiss of steam, the taste of soot, the rattle of carriages, the whistles of train and guard were a part of everyone's life. The connecting service from York brought Susan McCulloch Findlay, the daughter of James Findlay a Montrose grain merchant, to the city.

Susan was petite, had a mass of auburn hair and blue eyes set in delicate features. Ludwig was enchanted and Susan must have been taken with her escort. A courtship began. Susan eventually overcame doubts about marrying a German Jew who spoke broken English. A tenacious lady, she made Ludwig agree to desert Judaism before she would consent to be his wife. He eventually became a Unitarian. They were married on 3 September 1867 at Susan's home in Balmain Street in Montrose by the local Free Presbyterian Minister, William Nixon.

According to the marriage certificate, both Ludwig's parents, Lehmann and Betty had died by that time as had Susan's mother. Susan's father was at the wedding and two brothers were witnesses. Ludwig's family allegedly now finally disowned him as a result of his change of religion. Whether family memory on this particular point is true or not, what is certain is that Ludwig never returned to Brunswick.

The marriage certificate also records Ludwig's occupation as an importer of parquetry at 52 Brown Street in Manchester. Indeed the 1868–69 *City Trade Directory* describes him as a tile merchant whose business premises were at the same address. His home was at 58 Park Street, Greenheys in the Parish of Chorlton-upon-Medlock in Manchester. Park Street, now called Encroft Way, lies a short distance to the west of Oxford Road, the latter a main thoroughfare to and from the city centre. The Oppenheimers were to have six sons. Five were raised in this neighbourhood in which, at 5 York Place, off Hargreaves Street, was the birthplace of David Lloyd George.[1]

The suffragette, Emmeline Pankhurst,[2] lived locally for a number of years. In December 1894 Mrs Pankhurst was elected to the Chorlton-upon-Medlock Board of Guardians (the Poor Law Board), one of the few offices then open to women and won re-election before resigning in August 1898. The cause of votes for women was to be a part of Charles

1 17 January 1863

2 Emmeline Goulden (1858–1928) was born at Seedley close to Pendleton on the western side of Salford. She married Richard Marsden Pankhurst (1834–1898) in 1878. They had three daughters who were near contemporaries of Charles Oppenheimer. Christabel Hariette (1880–1958), Estelle Sylvia (1882–1960) and Adela Constantia (1885–1961) together with their mother became leading suffragettes and social campaigners. Richard and Emmeline's sons Francis Henry (1884–1888) and Henry Francis (1889–1910) died in early life. Richard Pankhurst stood unsuccessfully for Parliament in Manchester at a by-election in 1883 and later at Rotherhithe (1885) and Gorton (1895)

Oppenheimer's later life. Whether the Oppenheimers and Pankhursts knew one another is not recorded.

Charles Oppenheimer was born on 10 October 1875 at 58 Park Street. Lehmann James, Ludwig's and Susan's eldest child had arrived in 1869. Ludwig Junior (Louis in later life) and Albert followed in 1871 and 1874 respectively. A younger brother, William Renwick, was born in 1877 in the same house. The youngest of the six brothers, Frank, came ten years later in 1888, his mother's forty third year, by which time the family had moved to the adjoining Burlington Street. The boys grew up in an area squeezed between Hulme and Moss Side to the west and south, with the present day campus of the University of Manchester immediately to the east. Whitworth Park and the Whitworth Art Gallery were a stone's throw to the south east.

Victorian and Edwardian Manchester had a radical reputation. Professor Martin Pugh has described it as 'the shock city of mid-nineteenth century Britain.'[3] It had nearly doubled in population to over a quarter of a million in thirty years from 1830 to 1860. The increase was fuelled by the immigration of Irish, Welsh and Jewish people. The cotton trade and related textile industries grew at a remarkable rate. 'Cottonopolis' as the city was nicknamed, was darkened by the smoke of innumerable chimneys, its unplanned streets crowded with horse drawn vehicles of all shapes and sizes, its alleys, hastily built homes and lodgings crowded with the human material that fuelled the industrial revolution.

'Yet it was not simply size that seemed to contemporaries to make Manchester a phenomenon, but the combination of economic change, social tension and political innovation that it represented.'[4] Disraeli talked of the Manchester School of political thought. The *Manchester Guardian* became a national newspaper. Aspiring politicians sought constituencies in the city which to many contemporaries, was more the political cockpit of the nation than London. What happened in Manchester in terms of economic growth, coping with population growth, class and social relations and political change was thought to presage the same or similar in the rest of the country.

The Oppenheimer brothers grew up in a household dedicated to business, in a city of commerce and political agitation. Ludwig senior dominated the household. Described in later life when he had mellowed as 'an old bear', he planned that his sons would join his business. Business-like was the highest accolade that Ludwig would bestow. His son Charles became imbued with a work ethic that never left him and translated the disciplines and routines of the family business to his later life as an artist.

As prosperity grew, the commercial and industrial elite of Manchester, just as in Glasgow, sought to spend their wealth on the arts. It was from this environment that the young Oppenheimer would flourish and eventually develop from a craftsman and designer into an artist.

3 *The Pankhursts* by Professor Martin Pugh, Allen Lane The Penguin Press, 2001, chapter 1, Radical Manchester (1858–78)

4 Ibid

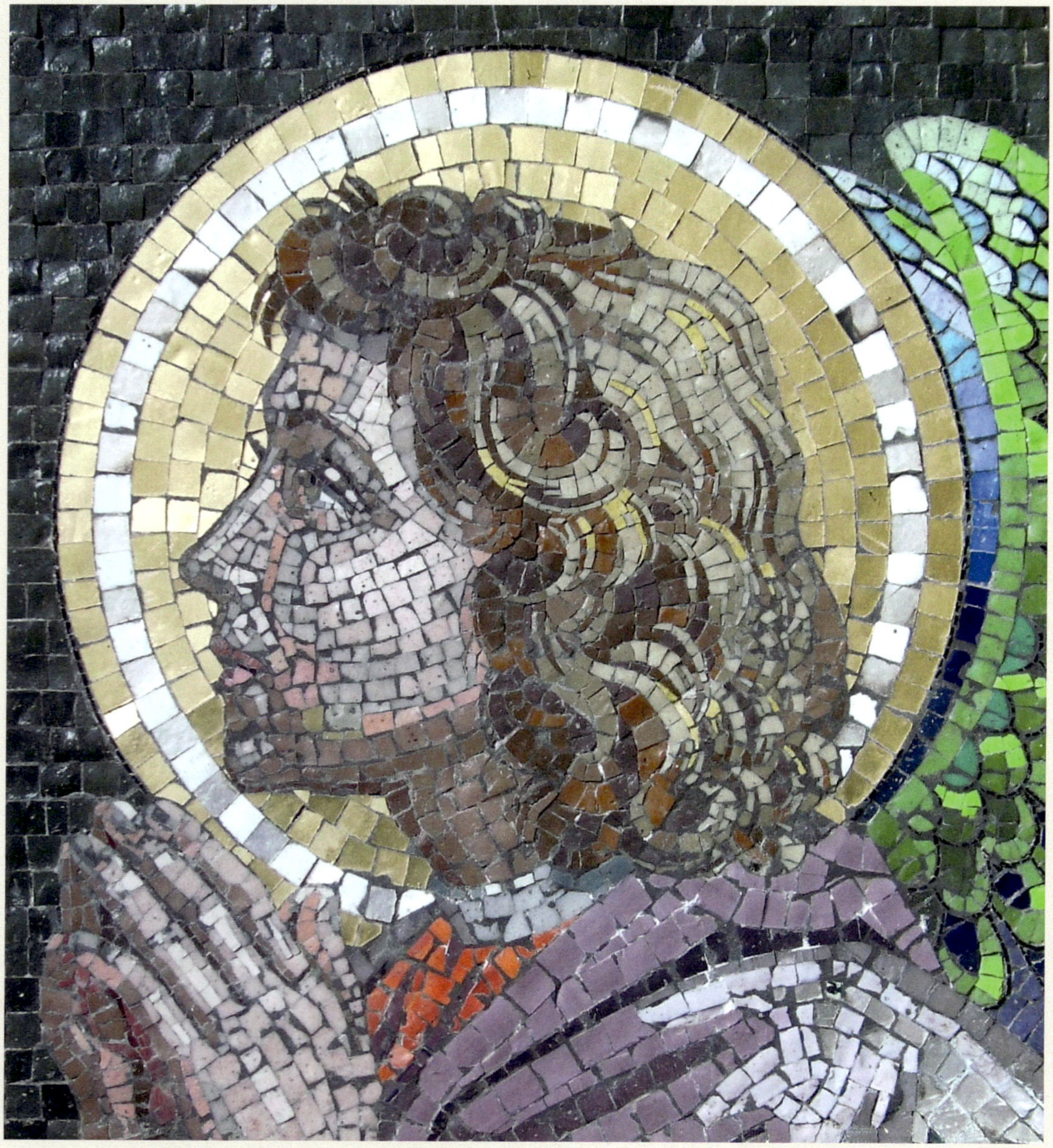

2 MOSAICS – THE PATTERN OF LIFE

Plate 3 | Ludwig Oppenheimer Ltd, sample mosaic design, Private Collection, 13 × 12 inches

WHEN CHARLES OPPENHEIMER was three, the family moved home to 102 Burlington Street. The old buildings in the street have been demolished but it is safe to assume that the house was more spacious than Park Street as the family remained there for the whole of the next decade moving for a final time in 1892 or 1893.

Oppenheimer's childhood was passed in relatively comfortable circumstances. Evidence from the 1881 Census reveals that the family employed a resident servant, Elizabeth Evans from Staffordshire. In 1891 the household at 102 Burlington Road included two employees in their twenties, Maggie Marry, a nurse, possibly for three year old Frank, and Hannah Johnson, a general domestic.

By Oppenheimer's early teenage years his elder brothers had already entered the family firm either as a result of inclination, assumption or persuasion. The 1891 Census describes Lehmann as a designer of mosaics and Ludwig Junior and Albert as mosaic workers. Nevertheless the *Manchester Trade Directory* in 1895 referred to Ludwig Senior as a parquet floor manufacturer which may of course have been accurate in so far that parquet flooring may have formed a complementary or subsidiary commercial activity. It was not until 1897 that he was deemed to be a 'mosaic tile manufacturer'.

Personal details from Oppenheimer's earliest years are now scant. He did intimate some highlights in discussion with F G Mories of *The Artist* for an article in that magazine's issue of August 1947. Oppenheimer attended a local elementary day school close to his home. On his twelfth birthday he enrolled in Manchester School of Art, the very first moment that he was permitted to do so, entering it full time just before his fifteenth birthday in the academic year 1890/91. 'He now studied everything connected with the craft of mosaic in order to equip himself for his father's business.' That was not all. 'Besides design he took painting and modelling, while his later studies were chiefly in the life class.'

Oppenheimer followed his brothers Lehmann, Ludwig and Albert into the School of Art together with his future sister in law, Edith Newton, Lehmann's wife in later years. Lehmann in particular had a glittering

Plate 4 | Ludwig and Susan Oppenheimer, 1890s, Oppenheimer family photograph

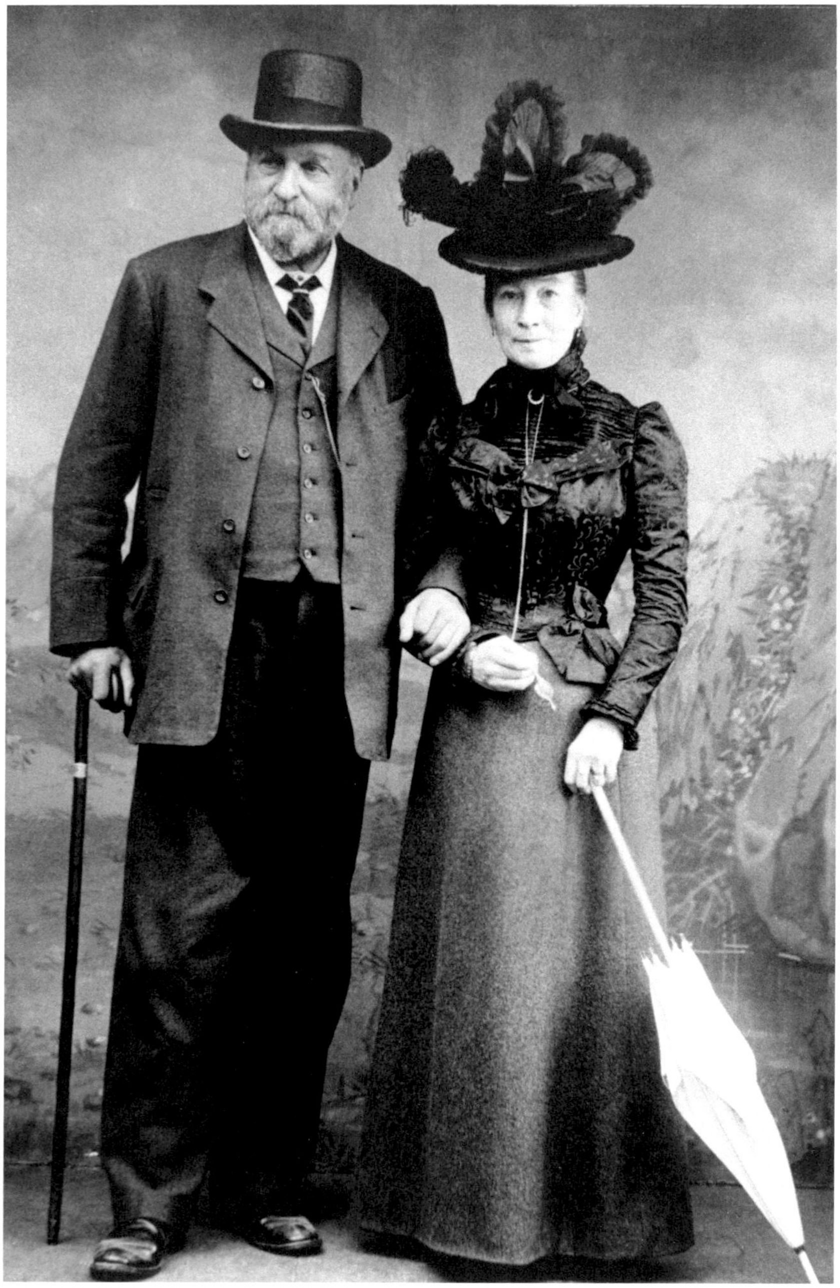

career at the School and is mentioned continuously in its Annual Reports both achieving excellent examination results and winning national prizes. In 1886 for instance, he won a Local Exhibition of £50 in the annual National Competition held at South Kensington and a Silver Medal for a design for the decoration of a mineral spring well.

The first mention of Oppenheimer's work came in 1888, the year after his enrolment when aged thirteen he achieved a Second Class in the Second Grade Examination in Freehand Drawing. In 1892 he was awarded a Free Studentship. The family must have taken some pride from the Annual Report of that year in which Albert, Charles and Lehmann won six prizes, three for Charles in hand-painted tiles, mosaic pavement and design for painted tiles.

The family firm could justifiably feel that its annual subscription of £2 to the Manchester School of Art had been worthwhile. The fifth brother, William was by now also in attendance. Later in 1892 Oppenheimer won a National Book prize. In 1893 he collected two Goadsby prizes, one specially awarded for a drawing of a head from the cast in light and shade and in 1894 a third prize in the School's Heywood Prizes for the best design in filling an arched headed panel in mosaic, sgraffito, faience or carving.

His tutors included RHA Willis,[5] the Irish painter and sculptor who was head of the School from 1882 to 1892 and the renowned Walter Crane. Crane's influence was particularly important upon Oppenheimer's career. Crane believed that there was little distinction between what was then described as fine art and decorative art. The traditional view of a strict dichotomy between the two was in his view obsolete. The supposed superiority of fine art painting to decoration was false; the artist could and should be a craftsman and the craftsman, an artist. He rejected exclusivity and believed that training in art and design should include a thorough grounding in core skills such as drawing, modelling, carving, sculpting and design work.

Crane was appointed the Director of Art and Design at the Manchester School of Art in 1892 in succession to Willis. His years as head of the School in the remainder of the decade coincided with some of Oppenheimer's time there. Crane's main task was to sweep away the stultifying, restrictive curriculum of the government sponsored South Kensington system. *The Studio* claimed that in making the appointment 'Manchester has committed itself to what is very like incipient revolt against excessive domination of the central authority at South Kensington.'[6] Crane revolutionised the syllabus at Manchester broadening it, making it more relevant to the needs of local businesses but doing this without restricting the development of those students who wished to paint or to become full time artists.

Oppenheimer not only gained a modern and thorough education in a range of skills but he also absorbed Crane's philosophy of the unified nature of art. Oppenheimer was given the intellectual foundation for his career move in the first decade of the twentieth century from mosaic craftsman and designer to full time professional artist.

Oppenheimer never forgot his roots. As an artist he chose the frames for his pictures with great care and often asked to place them in a client or patron's home. Oppenheimer's habit may have been inspired by the

5 Richard Henry Albert Willis, 1853–1905, born at Dingle in County Kerry, he won a scholarship to the National Art Training School at South Kensington, head of the Manchester School of Art from 1882 to 1892, then a professional painter and sculptor in London until 1904 when he became the head of the Dublin Metropolitan School of Art

6 *The Studio*, Volume XV, 1898–99, page 104

thoughts in a footnote in Crane's essay in the *Art Journal* of 1881 *On the Position and Aims of Decorative Art* which said:

> *In fact, every picture and statue declares its original decorative purpose and architectural origin by the frame which surrounds the one, and the plinth or pedestal which supports the other; and in these adjuncts, so necessary to their completion and due setting, we may see the connecting links, not only with the surrounding structural characteristics of the room or gallery where they are placed, but also with that mural art and architecture of which they are the offshoots, and of which they once formed an integral part.*

Oppenheimer most probably attended the series of lectures which Crane gave at the School which formed the basis of his illustrated books *The Bases of Design* and *Line and Form* published by George Bell and Sons in 1898 and 1900 respectively. Oppenheimer may have absorbed some of Crane's more radical political philosophy as well as Crane had declared himself a socialist in 1884. Oppenheimer was to be found on the progressive side of many political and social debates at least until his very senior years.

The Oppenheimer brothers would have studied lettering at the School. A bookplate dated 1900 [pl.2] inserted into a volume from Oppenheimer's personal library although somewhat lacking in technique, demonstrates Crane's influence and the Florentine back drop in the image underscores the evidence of his early visits to Italy. In 1901, Oppenheimer accomplished a prodigious piece of work in the form of an illuminated, handwritten manuscript of the poem *The Eve of Saint Agnes*, by John Keats [pl.5]. The bound volume is of thirteen pages of vellum and demonstrates Oppenheimer's craftsmanship and skill and improving drawing. Its purpose, whether commission, academic exercise or business sample is presently unknown.

Plate 5 | cover and three pages from *The Eve of Saint Agnes*, 1901, illuminated manuscript on vellum of John Keats's poem, courtesy of Barrie Marks

For many years the Oppenheimers spent summer and other holidays in Scotland. The long train journey to escape the smoke and grime of Manchester for the sea air of Montrose was undertaken at least once a year to visit Findlay relatives. Lehmann Oppenheimer recalled one of the earliest journeys when he was six or seven trying to spot the Cheviots on the old Waverley railway line, the part of the journey from Carlisle to Edinburgh:

> *Very cautiously I clear the moisture from the glass at intervals, for my mother, though tired out and dozing, with one of my brothers (Charles) asleep in her arms, is easily disturbed, and the least noise will make her sit up with a start and tell me to lie back and shut my eyes.*[7]

It is certain from what is known of Oppenheimer's formative years that his eldest brother was both an influence and an example. Both were

7 *The Heart of Lakeland* by Lehmann Oppenheimer, 1908

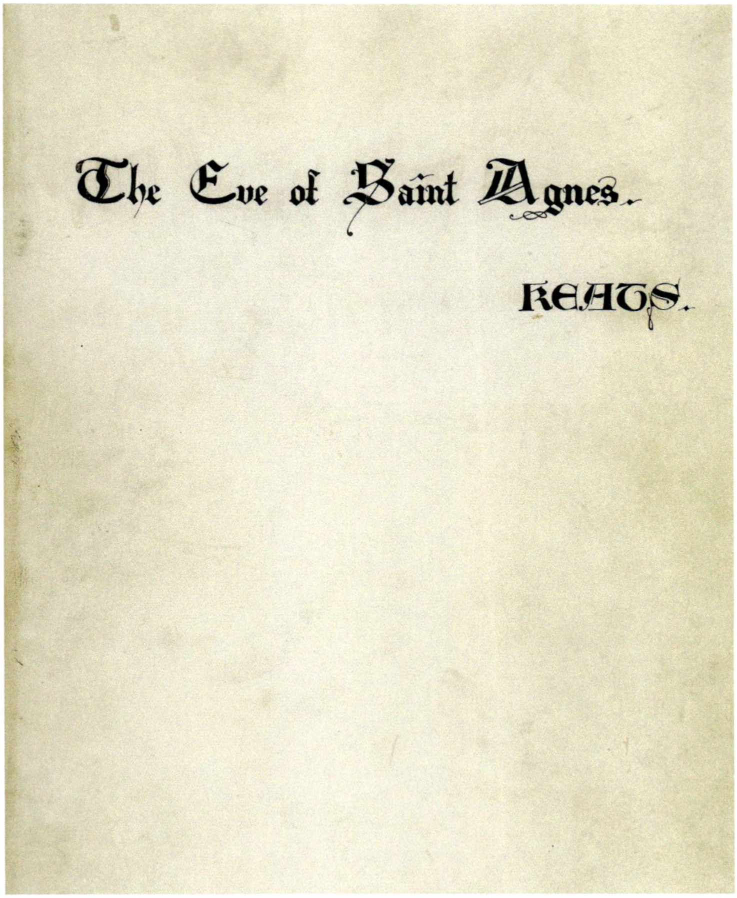
The Eve of Saint Agnes.

KEATS.

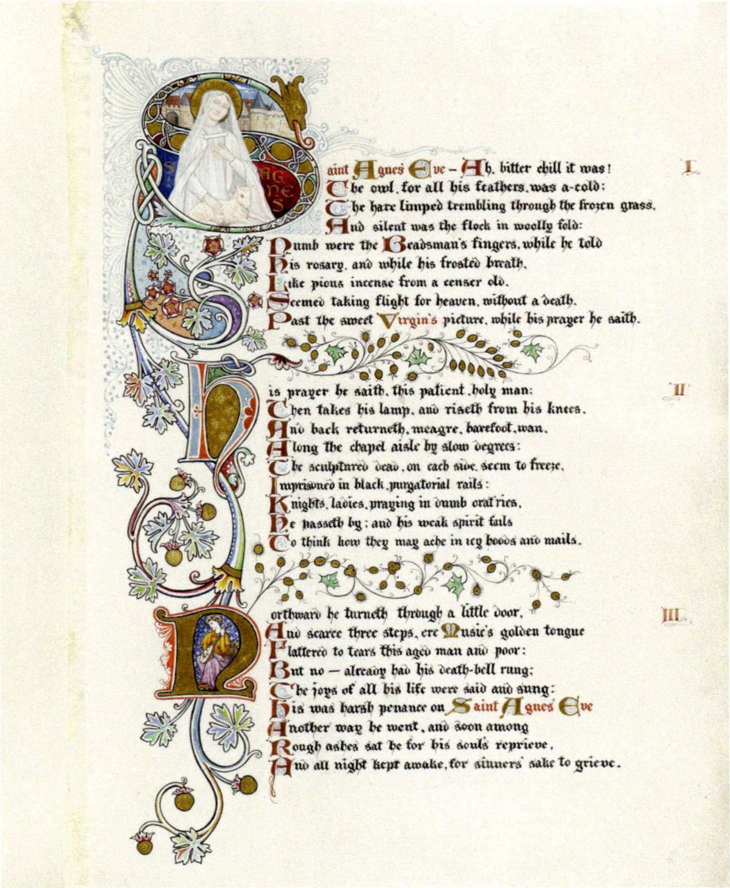
Saint Agnes Eve – Ah, bitter chill it was! I.
The owl, for all his feathers, was a-cold;
The hare limped trembling through the frozen grass,
And silent was the flock in woolly fold:
Numb were the Beadsman's fingers, while he told
His rosary, and while his frosted breath,
Like pious incense from a censer old,
Seemed taking flight for heaven, without a death,
Past the sweet Virgin's picture, while his prayer he saith.

His prayer he saith, this patient, holy man; II
Then takes his lamp, and riseth from his knees,
And back returneth, meagre, barefoot, wan,
Along the chapel aisle by slow degrees:
The sculptured dead, on each side, seem to freeze,
Imprisoned in black, purgatorial rails:
Knights, ladies, praying in dumb orat'ries,
He passeth by; and his weak spirit fails
To think how they may ache in icy hoods and mails.

Northward he turneth through a little door, III.
And scarce three steps, ere Music's golden tongue
Flattered to tears this aged man and poor;
But no – already had his death-bell rung;
The joys of all his life were said and sung:
His was harsh penance on Saint Agnes Eve
Another way he went, and soon among
Rough ashes sat he for his soul's reprieve,
And all night kept awake, for sinners' sake to grieve.

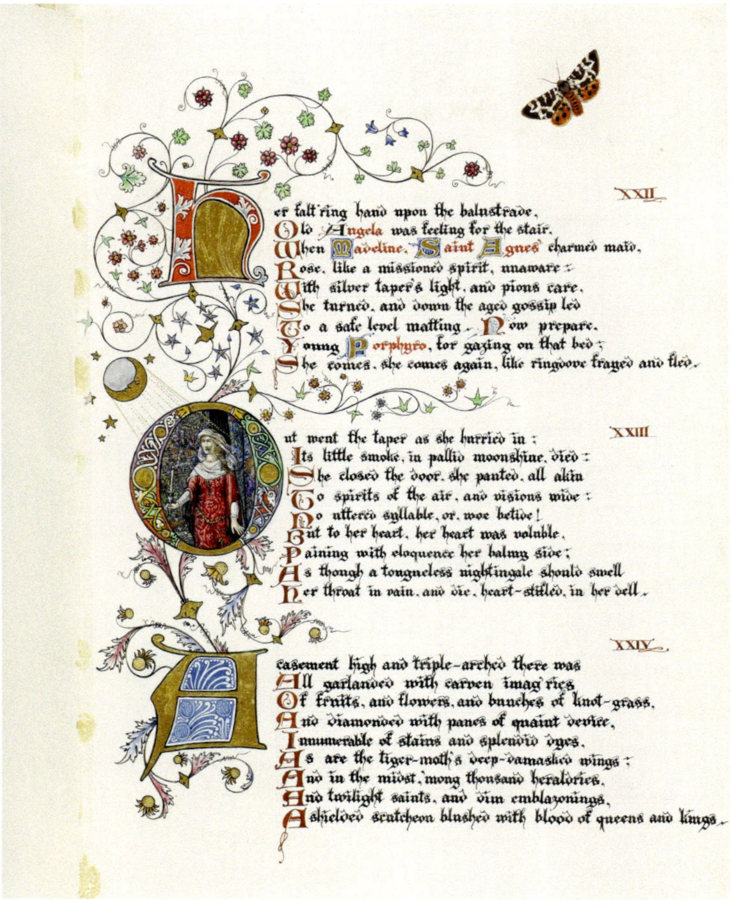
Her falt'ring hand upon the balustrade, XXII.
Old Angela was feeling for the stair,
When Madeline, Saint Agnes' charmed maid,
Rose, like a missioned spirit, unaware:
With silver taper's light, and pious care,
She turned, and down the aged gossip led
To a safe level matting. Now prepare,
Young Porphyro, for gazing on that bed;
She comes, she comes again, like ringdove frayed and fled.

Out went the taper as she hurried in; XXIII
Its little smoke, in pallid moonshine, died:
She closed the door, she panted, all akin
To spirits of the air, and visions wide:
No uttered syllable, or, woe betide!
But to her heart, her heart was voluble,
Paining with eloquence her balmy side;
As though a tongueless nightingale should swell
Her throat in vain, and die, heart-stifled, in her dell.

A casement high and triple-arched there was XXIV.
All garlanded with carven imag'ries
Of fruits, and flowers, and bunches of knot-grass,
And diamonded with panes of quaint device,
Innumerable of stains and splendid dyes,
As are the tiger-moth's deep-damasked wings;
And in the midst, 'mong thousand heraldries,
And twilight saints, and dim emblazonings,
A shielded scutcheon blushed with blood of queens and kings.

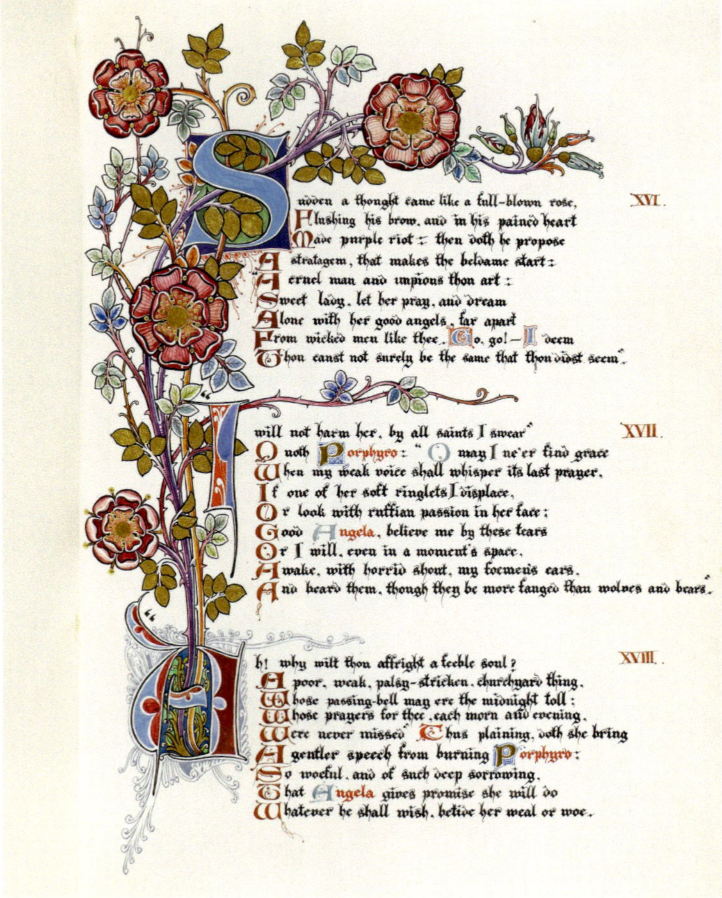
Sudden a thought came like a full-blown rose, XVI.
Flushing his brow, and in his pained heart
Made purple riot: then doth he propose
A stratagem, that makes the beldame start:
"A cruel man and impious thou art:
Sweet lady, let her pray, and dream
Alone with her good angels, far apart
From wicked men like thee. Go, go! – I deem
Thou canst not surely be the same that thou didst seem."

"I will not harm her, by all saints I swear" XVII.
Quoth Porphyro: "O may I ne'er find grace
When my weak voice shall whisper its last prayer,
If one of her soft ringlets I displace,
Or look with ruffian passion in her face;
Good Angela, believe me by these tears
Or I will, even in a moment's space,
Awake, with horrid shout, my foemen's ears,
And beard them, though they be more fanged than wolves and bears."

"Ah! why wilt thou affright a feeble soul? XVIII.
A poor, weak, palsy-stricken, churchyard thing,
Whose passing-bell may ere the midnight toll;
Whose prayers for thee, each morn and evening,
Were never missed." Thus plaining, doth she bring
A gentler speech from burning Porphyro;
So woeful, and of such deep sorrowing,
That Angela gives promise she will do
Whatever he shall wish, betide her weal or woe.

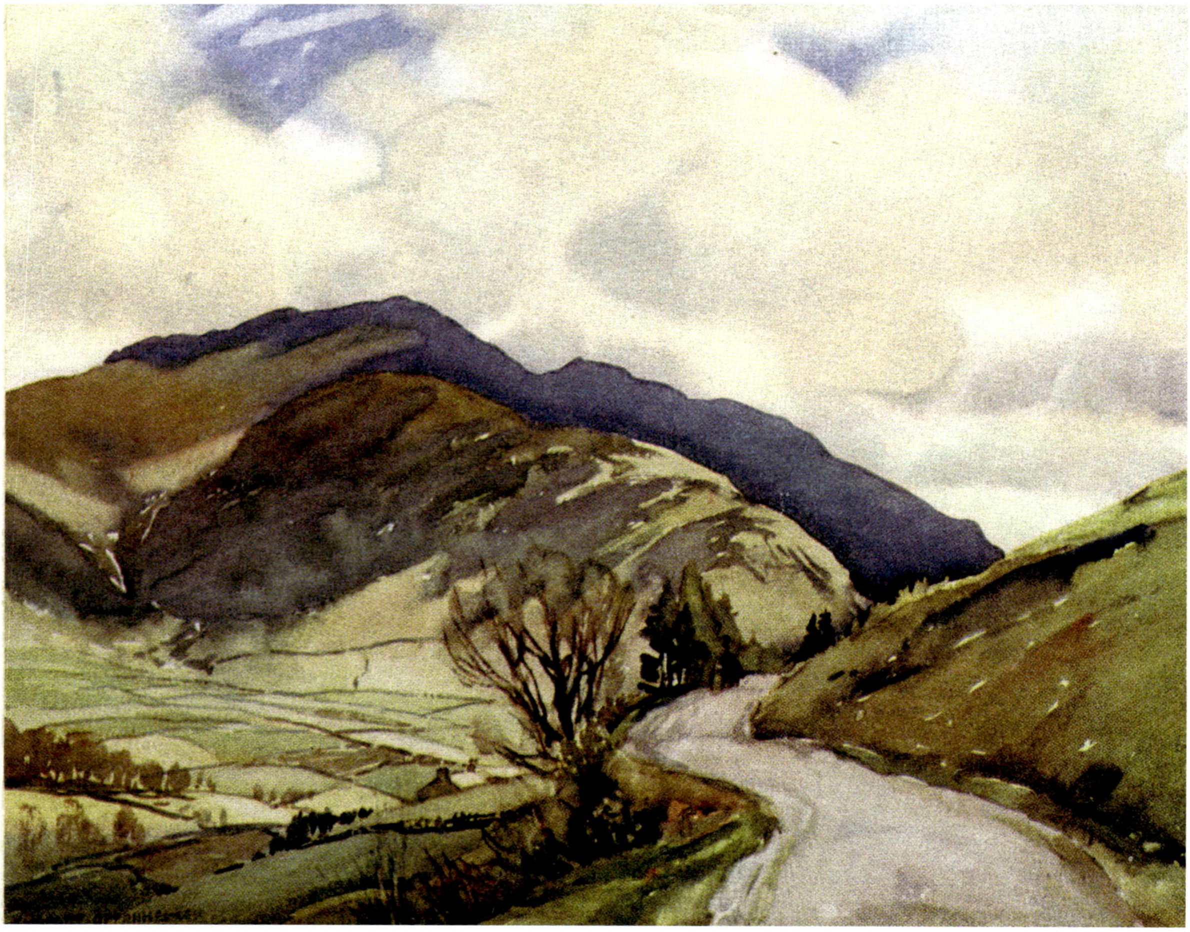

Plate 6 | *The Road to Buttermere*, watercolour, reproduced from a print, courtesy of the Stewartry Museum, Kirkcudbright

talented and artistic. Lehmann's grand-daughter confirms Census entries that show that after art school both his sibling and he went into the family business on the creative and design side. Ludwig Junior, Albert and William looked after the commercial activities of the firm travelling to Europe and Ireland from whence most of the orders originated. Oppenheimer said as much himself many years later when interviewed for an article in the *Manchester Guardian*.[8]

Lehmann and Charles shared an interest in outdoor activities and climbing. In 1908 Lehmann published a book about climbing in the Lake District. *The Heart of Lakeland* is a forerunner of later twentieth century guide books and hill walking and mountaineering companions. More Wainwright than Poucher,[9] the text is a mixture of anecdote with topographical description and route finding. An 'unconventional but charmingly intimate record', the book found 'a large circle of readers'. Lehmann had a deep affection, amounting almost to a passion, for the English Lake District. 'Buttermere district was (Lehmann's) favourite playground. He was a keen and tireless rock climber, and took part in a

8 *Manchester Guardian*, 1 July 1959

9 Alfred Wainwright (1907–1991) fell walker, television personality and author of pictorial guides with anecdotes, to the Lakeland Fells. Walter Arthur Poucher FRPS (1891–1988) mountain photographer and guide book writer

considerable number of first ascents. Stack Gill, Bowfell Buttress and the north-west climb on the Pillar Rock are perhaps most closely associated with his name'.[10]

As Mary Evans, Oppenheimer's niece by marriage recalled, Oppenheimer accompanied his elder brother on climbing expeditions.[11] Indeed he was possibly 'my brother' mentioned on page 116 of *The Heart of Lakeland* 'setting out to climb The Pillar'. It is thus no surprise to find Lakeland paintings in Oppenheimer's oeuvre. *The Studio* in April 1927 declared that *The Road to Buttermere* [pl.6] 'illustrates uncommonly well one of his direct renderings of many equally successful watercolour memories of a sketching trip amongst the Cumberland hills'.[12]

Oppenheimer, as will be described in chapter 7, travelled widely on the Continent as did Lehmann. The brothers achieved a notable distinction when in 1906 they both exhibited debut pictures at the Royal Academy. Oppenheimer's work was entitled *Old Mills, Montreuil* which was to be the first of the sixty paintings which he showed there over forty four years until 1952.

From surviving accounts it is clear that Oppenheimer and his eldest brother were alike, not in height (Oppenheimer was taller) but in appearance, and in talent, interests and temperament. Lehmann Oppenheimer's obituary notice in the *Manchester Guardian*[13] describes him as 'a shy and reserved man but a delightful field companion. He had a chivalrous ideal of conduct, and his unfailing generosity of heart endeared him to all his friends.' The words could equally have been written about his younger brother.

In 1890, at the age of fifteen Oppenheimer was at Manchester City Municipal Art School and was on the threshold of a career in his family's business. He had the family background and circumstances, the example, the opportunity and, most important, the talent to make mosaics the pattern of his life.

10 *Manchester Guardian*, 13 November 1916

11 In conversation with Mary Evans, 19 February 2006

12 *The Studio*, April 1927

13 *Manchester Guardian*, 13 November 1916

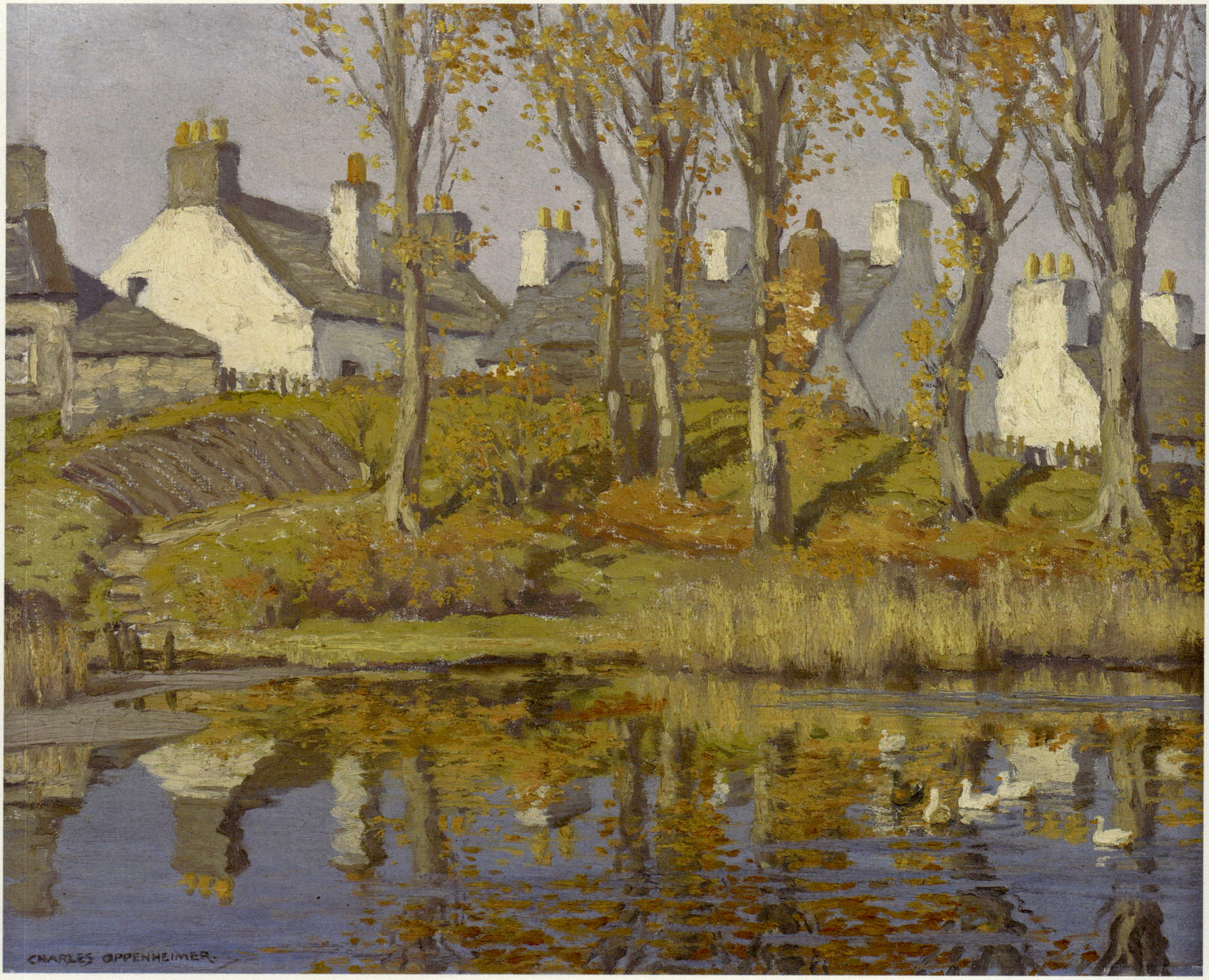
CHARLES OPPENHEIMER.

3 TO KIRKCUDBRIGHT

Plate 7 | *Barlochan Pool, Galloway*, c.1930, Private collection, oil on canvas, 15¾ x 19½ inches

IN HIS OWN ESTIMATION Oppenheimer spent much of his youth doodling and drawing to develop his latent talent for his own pleasure and satisfaction and for practical application in his chosen career. He sketched obsessively in later life as well. Connie, his wife, would send him on domestic errands in Kirkcudbright only to find him returning much later than the task required without some of her shopping but with a sketch usually of the harbour on the back of her list.[14] Mary Evans recalled her uncle regularly holding his hands before him, squaring off a part of the landscape in a frame made of his palms and fingers, saying, now that would make a good picture and scribbling notes on colours and the exact location.

In his early years Oppenheimer's first public recognition came at nineteen when, in 1894, he first had a picture, the title of which is now lost,[15] exhibited at the annual exhibition of Manchester Academy of Fine Arts. He would have qualified to do so as a student. Until 1931 only students, associates and members could exhibit in the annual exhibition. The Manchester Academy's records show that his next successfully entered works were shown in 1898. *Blencathra from the Druid's Circle*, price ten guineas and *The Lion of St Mark, Venice* presumably an oil at the higher price of £31 and ten shillings are untraced. The latter picture was clearly, either a fruit of his three weeks in Italy paid for by winning 'a money prize' in 1896,[16] or a return visit to the south of that country which took place two years later.

Oppenheimer's two journeys were mostly for his own artistic stimulation and progress but he combined this with some study of mosaic work. The family business remained his career and the business prospered.

Important changes in family circumstances occurred in the early to mid 1890s. The Oppenheimers moved to a more spacious house at 144 Withington Road, Whalley Grange in 1892 or 1893. [pl.8] Lehmann and Ludwig junior, by now both married, had set up their own homes close to the business which had also moved from a group of buildings at 54 to 64 Mulberry Street to premises in Blackburn Street off Stamford Street in Old Trafford. The Blackburn Street business premises remain outwardly

14 *The Artist*, August 1947

15 Mentioned in a newspaper obituary in the archives of Manchester Academy of Fine Arts, this work was probably an unrecorded student effort that found a space on the walls

16 The exact nature of this prize is not known but it was probably awarded by the Manchester School of Art although it seems to have been unrecorded.

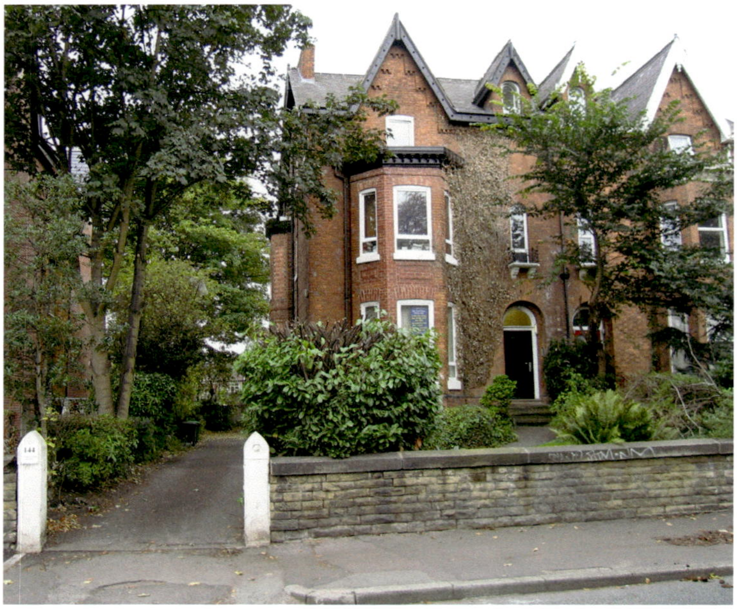

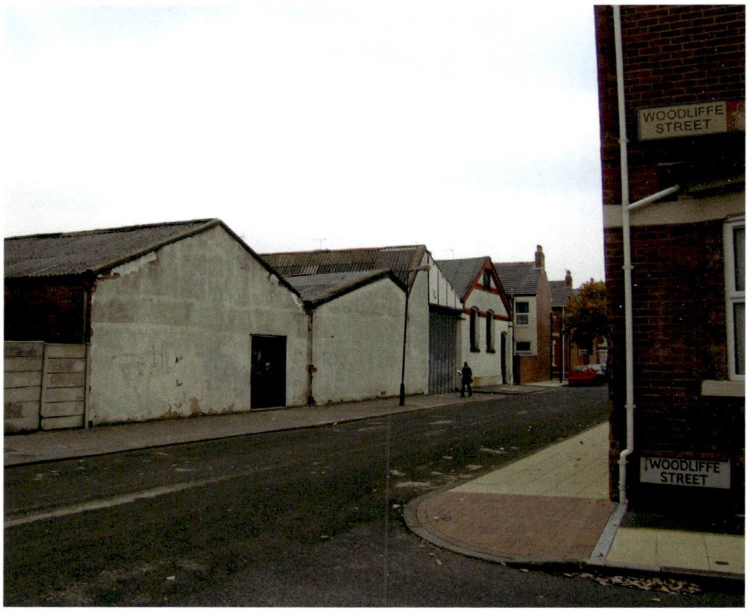

Plate 8 | 114 Withington Road, Manchester (2005)

Plate 9 | Blackburn Street, Manchester (2005)

much as they were in the late 1890s [pl. 9]. In discussion with the author in 2005, elderly residents recalled that when children they would search round the perimeter for 'jewels'. These were of course small coloured mosaic pieces accidentally discarded or of second quality that had been meant for disposal but instead became the home made jewellery, the fashion accessory of the moment, in the local junior school.

The last year of Queen Victoria's reign found the Oppenheimers industriously engaged upon their business activities, all living within a few miles of one another, with Ludwig senior presiding over what must have been his proud achievement. However on 8 January 1901 he died after a short illness thus just missing inclusion in the Census of that year whereas Victoria, the monarch of his adopted country, survived him by a fortnight and was therefore included.[17] Ludwig's death was the immediate precursor of and is most likely to have precipitated, a further period of change for the Oppenheimers. The business was incorporated as a limited liability company later in 1901.The Articles of Association prove that this was a family firm. The eight subscribers of £1 each were five Oppenheimer brothers and three wives, Edith, Jessie and Grace respectively Lehmann, Louis and Albert's spouses. Before the end of the decade Oppenheimer was to sever his day to day connections with the company because of his intention to leave Manchester and to become a full time professional artist.

Oppenheimer had developed other interests in his twenties. He served for a time in the 2nd Volunteer Battalion of the Manchester Regiment of Mounted Infantry. Mounted infantry was a novel part of the British

17 The 1901 Census was taken in the middle of the month and there was hence no entry for Ludwig Oppenheimer. Queen Victoria died on 22 January and was consequently recorded at Osborne House on the Isle of Wight.

Army. Controversy surrounded its role and effectiveness as a rapid mobile force of high fire power as opposed to the traditionalist shock tactics of the cavalry charge. Boer War engagements under commanders such as Sir John French fuelled the debate but there is no record or family anecdote that explains why Oppenheimer chose the then cutting edge of the Army compared to other branches or regiments of the service [pls 10 and 11].

One day in 1902, Oppenheimer was on parade with his Battalion in Manchester. He cut an impressive figure mounted on a horse resplendent in his uniform with gleaming saddle and polished metal insignia. He was about six feet tall, lean but square shouldered with red brown hair and a typically full Edwardian moustache. He caught the attention of Constance Emily Taylor, the twenty five year old daughter of a science teacher, Robert Llewellyn Taylor FIC, FCS. An engagement followed not long thereafter.

Connie, as she was known to all, had attended Newnham College in Cambridge University from 1897 to 1901. Women were not at that time permitted to be members of the University or allowed to graduate but they could sit examinations. Connie read Natural Sciences and gained a First in Part 1 in 1900 and a Second in Part 2 a year later. Thereafter she taught maths and physics at Cheltenham Ladies' College from September 1901 to December 1902.

Connie was in some ways a contrast to her fiancé. Elegant and a breathless talker, she was considered by many to be very much the academic. She was an accomplished musician who in later years taught children in

Plate 10 | Charles Oppenheimer, Mounted Infantryman, c.1900, courtesy of the Stewartry Museum, Kirkcudbright

Plate 11 | Charles Oppenheimer on horseback, c.1900, courtesy of the Stewartry Museum, Kirkcudbright

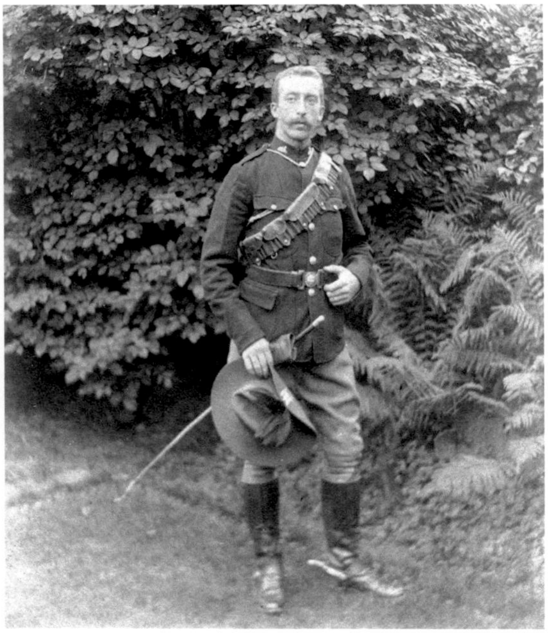

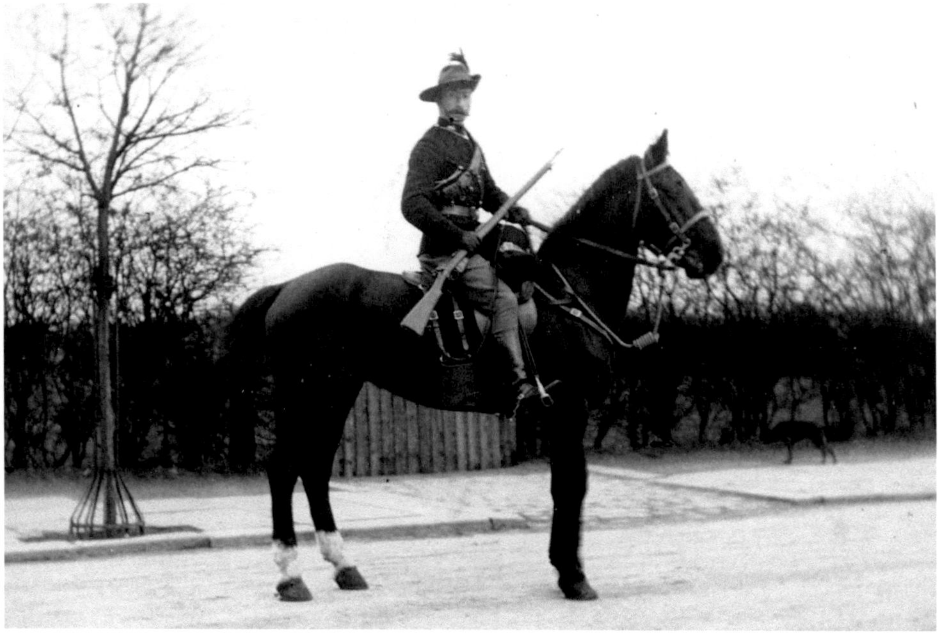

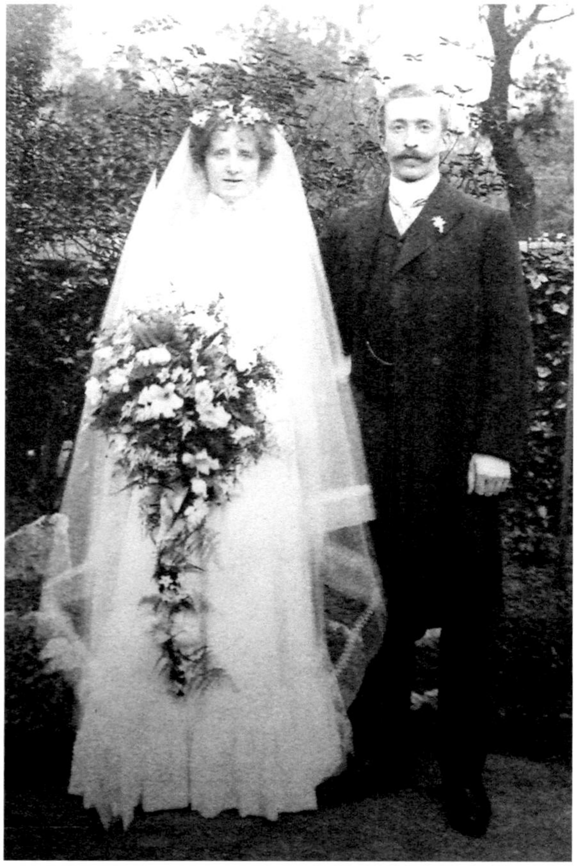

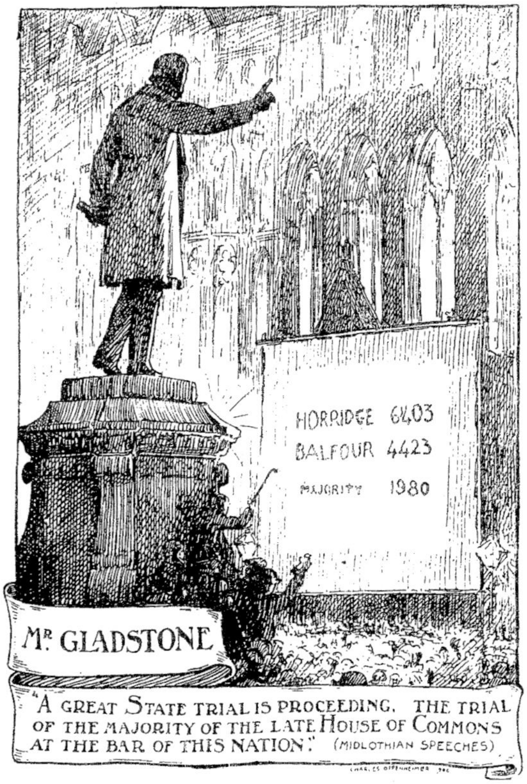

Plate 12 | Charles and Connie Oppenheimer's Wedding Day, 28 May 1903, Oppenheimer family photograph

Plate 13 | General Election cartoon, January 1906, courtesy of *The Guardian*

Kirkcudbright and arranged and participated in concerts, musicals and plays. Her instruments were the viola, violin, cello and piano. She played daily, hummed tunes and filled her homes with music to the delight of her family and later her husband who was enthusiastic, although less accomplished, in that branch of the arts. Joe Campbell remembers her recalling Oppenheimer's resolution to play the piano less frequently or maybe even to stop altogether as playing made his fingers ‘too supple for painting.’

Connie and Charles married in St Margaret's Parish Church in Whalley Grange on 28 May 1903. He was twenty seven and she twenty five [pl.12]. A devoted couple, they remained childless. Undoubtedly they were both fond of children and there is testament aplenty to their kindness and hospitality to nephews and nieces and to the offspring of friends in Kirkcudbright. Mary Evans remembered as a young girl paddling in a duck pond and getting much wetter than had been intended. No towel to hand, she was dried by Aunt Connie's hastily removed petticoat. Beryl Moultrie recalls being shown the goldfish in the lily pond at 14 High Street by Oppenheimer and then as an older child of teenage years his offering her a small sherry making her feel special and grown up.

It has been said that Oppenheimer severed his connections with Ludwig Oppenheimer Ltd not long after his marriage. This is not supported by the available evidence. The marriage certificate describes him as a mosaic manufacturer. Furthermore in the summer of 1903, the newly married Oppenheimer left his family home at 144 Withington Road for 197 Stamford Street, Old Trafford, much closer to the company's factory premises in Blackburn Street, in fact less than five minutes' walk away. The Manchester Trade Directories record his move and repeat the identical entry in 1905 and 1906 although the Royal Academy's records suggest that he had moved in the later part of 1906. In the next three editions his address is recorded as 24 Athol Road, Alexandra Park, but the phrase, mosaic tile manufacturer, is still next to Oppenheimer's name. Moreover the business' Articles of Association were altered on 14 February 1908 to say that any subscriber leaving the business would have to offer his or her share to the remaining shareholders. This would at least suggest that the ground was being prepared in case Oppenheimer decided to leave.

There is no reference to Oppenheimer in the Trade Directories from 1910 and so the truth of his leaving the family business is more complex than has hitherto been understood. As far as is known neither he nor Connie made a written record of their five married years in Manchester but further evidence of Oppenheimer's continuing links with the business after his marriage comes from the *Manchester Guardian* of 16 January 1906 in the form of a cartoon. It also sheds light on Oppenheimer's progressive social and political outlook.

The Prime Minister, Arthur Balfour, and his Unionist government resigned on 4 December 1905 beset by a series of crises. They had long outstayed their welcome. Oppenheimer's daily newspaper, the *Manchester Guardian* quoting King Lear, expressed the mood of the city and, as it turned out, the nation declaring 'when beggars die, there are no comets seen'. Polling in General Elections at that time took place over a period of a fortnight or more with results announced on different days. The Liberals led by Campbell Bannerman swept to a landslide victory primarily but not exclusively by promoting free trade rather than tariff reform. Results in Oppenheimer's Manchester were the focus of national attention because of Manchester's reputation as a political hotbed and the personalities involved in local constituencies. Winston Churchill, a recent defector to Liberal ranks took a hitherto Unionist seat in the city on 13 January 1906 and on the same day sensationally, Balfour lost East Manchester to his opponent.

Oppenheimer's line drawing [pl.13] of the declaration of the result on 13 January with the statue of Gladstone looking on, was one of the first political cartoons to be published in the *Manchester Guardian*.

It is not at all surprising that the Oppenheimers preferred free trade to tariffs and protectionism or to use the contemporary description, Imperial Preference. Imperial Preference was designed to protect home industries from cheap imports by imposing tariffs on imported goods with lower duties on those from the Empire than from the rest of the world. The Oppenheimers' business would have been compromised by tariff walls especially its import and export connections with France, Belgium and Italy. Admittedly trade with Ireland and other parts of the then British Empire would have been less disturbed but a free trade policy would have been regarded as commercially far better for businesses such as Ludwig Oppenheimer Ltd.

The nature of Oppenheimer's involvement with the mosaic business therefore clearly changed in the period from 1903 to 1908. He made up his mind to leave the business and Manchester but took time to do so. Perhaps he felt he needed to be sure he could succeed as an artist before severing his ties completely. Also it took time to find the right place to which to move. He and his wife travelled a good deal in these years. It is clear that at some stage after their marriage the couple journeyed to Italy probably through France, possibly on honeymoon. A watercolour of Venice dated 1904 in the family's possession and *Old Mills, Montreuil*, Oppenheimer's 1906 Royal Academy exhibit, prove the point. It is conceivable that they lived in Venice for a short while. It would have been relatively inexpensive to do so.

That Oppenheimer painted extensively between 1903 and 1908 and sold works is certainly the case and the balance of evidence is that he continued to work for Ludwig Oppenheimer Ltd at least in some capacity until early 1908. Oppenheimer had clearly decided that the constraints of working life in the mosaics business were restricting opportunities to express himself as an artist. The work may also have been repetitive. A fourth edition of the business' pattern book dating from 1904 from which the illustrations in the appendix about the business are taken, shows the standard types of designs that Ludwig Oppenheimer Ltd could produce. Special commissions allowed more scope for design but nothing could quite match the freedom of oil on canvas or watercolour on paper.

Oppenheimer was undoubtedly encouraged into his preferred profession by his acquaintance with the well-established and respected artist, Frederick William Jackson (1859–1918). Jackson was as much a friend as a mentor. Born at Middleton Junction, near Oldham, Jackson was sixteen years Oppenheimer's senior. Another product of the Manchester Municipal School of Art, he was a well connected member of the Manchester school or circle of artists. In his early career Jackson decorated tiles which may have been how he first came to meet Oppenheimer, in a business rather than a social context. His brother, Charles Arthur Jackson was an art dealer and owned a gallery at 7 Police Street in Manchester where early Oppenheimer pictures were framed.

Their friendship was evidently close. Mary Evans related that one day in Connie's company Jackson and Oppenheimer were passing a second hand shop in Manchester. In the window, Jackson spotted an oval ornamental frame and promptly went in to buy it. He described it as ideal for Connie's portrait which was soon completed and remains in her family's possession in the duly restored frame to this day.

Jackson clearly influenced Oppenheimer's early painting style. Jackson's work is painterly and expressive and was predominantly carried out en plein air. He is said to have worked out of doors in all weathers, an example that Oppenheimer followed to some extent. Laura Knight wrote that under the winter mittens which Jackson habitually wore, 'his hands were swollen, stiff and chapped as were the edges of his ears and the wings of his nostrils.'[18] There were supposedly up to twenty or more of Jackson's sketches and small oils in Oppenheimer's studio and home at the time the latter's death. Knight said of Jackson that picture making was 'the whole world' to him. It was that passion that Jackson inspired in Oppenheimer adding to the younger man's desire to move to a place more conducive to his art.

Two of the earliest public references to Oppenheimer's paintings occurred in 1908. Oppenheimer exhibited a watercolour *A Whitby View* and an oil *The End of the Day* at the 1908 Liverpool exhibition. The *Sheffield Daily Telegraph* reporting on pictures of Yorkshire on 7 September declared that 'four sketches of that district (sic) are shown, all of them worth seeing, but none so delightful as Mr Charles Oppenheimer's *A Whitby View*. Another critic recorded his impressions in a review eight days later in the *Liverpool Courier*:

> *In Gallery No VIII we meet some of the most interesting, if not the most striking examples of landscape art. For instance, there is Mr Charles Oppenheimer's unobtrusive canvas* The End of the Day *whose soft subdued tones and dim outlines so well convey the feeling of the quiet, lingering twilight hours.*

By 1908, aged 33, Oppenheimer was an aspiring professional artist. He was confirmed in his view that he had a future as a painter but not in the grimy city of his birth. Evidently he had been looking for somewhere to which to move where he could immerse himself in a new career. Whilst he remained in Manchester he would always be tied in whole or in part to the family business and would remain a craftsman and designer but not develop as an artist. He would also have to travel to where the landscape stimulated and inspired his art. As George Bernard Shaw put it in his

18 *Oil and Grease Paint*, by Laura Knight DBE, Ivor Nicholson and Watson Ltd, London, 1936.

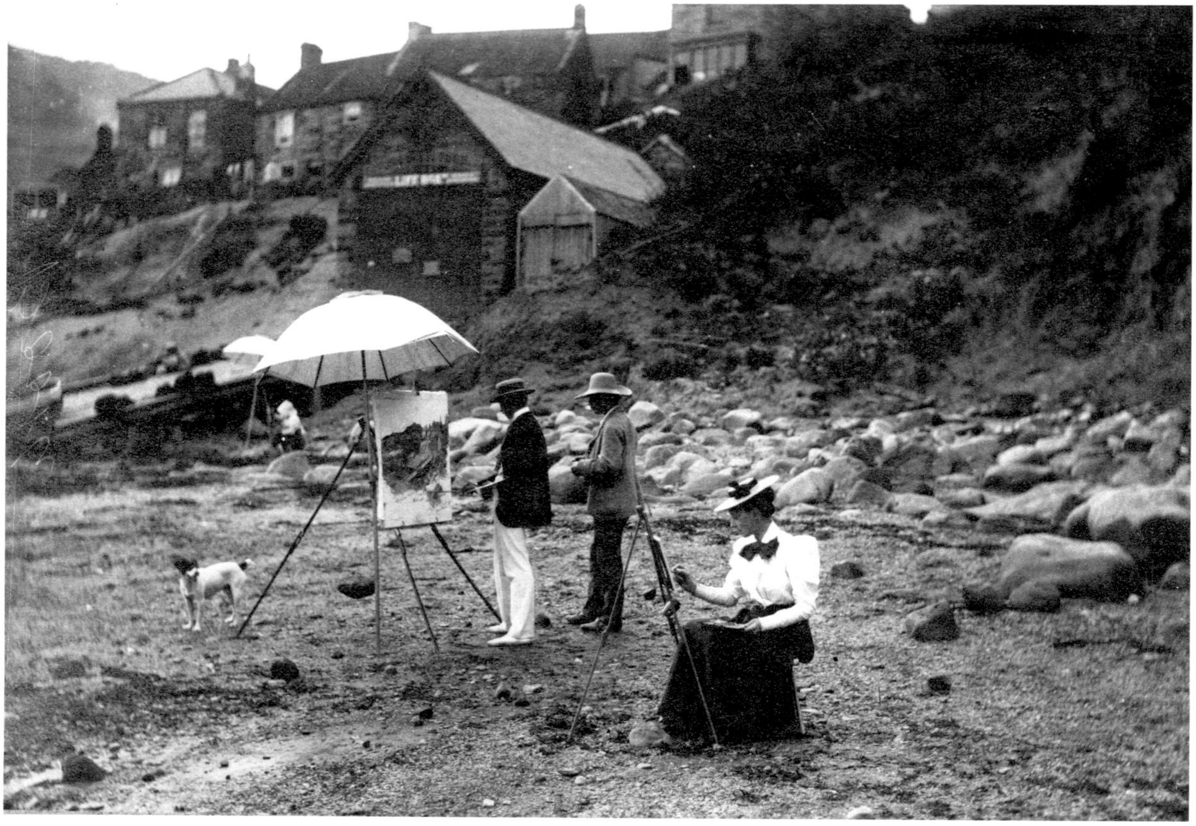

Plate 14 | Fred Jackson, Laura Knight and Charles Oppenheimer on the beach at Runswick Bay, c.1907, courtesy of the Stewartry Museum, Kirkcudbright

deliberately provocative way, Edwardian and early Georgian Manchester was an 'ugly' town. It had only really become involved in the arts 'out of the mere necessity of getting some relief from the horrors of its own surroundings'.[19]

The Oppenheimers were now determined to escape from these 'horrors'. Oppenheimer himself said in later years that he and his wife looked far and wide, visiting artists' colonies often by bicycle or a combination of train and bicycle. Yorkshire and the Staithes School of artists were nearby. The couple spent some time at Runswick Bay near Whitby in the company of Fred Jackson who had a home at Hinderwell. They were photographed on the beach together in the company of Laura Knight, Oppenheimer watching Jackson at work. [pl.14].[20] It was an area to which Oppenheimer returned from time to time throughout his life and which continued to inspire works such as *A Grey Morning, Runswick Bay* [pl.15]. It was not however where the Oppenheimers chose to settle.

Nor was Blewbury in Berkshire near Didcot where they rented accommodation for six weeks and where Jackson joined them for a while. A Jackson painting from this time is in the collection of the Whitworth Art Gallery collection in Manchester but as yet work by Oppenheimer from Berkshire has not emerged. Blewbury is on the edge of the Berkshire

19 George Bernard Shaw lecture at Walker Art Gallery, Liverpool, December 1911, as reported by the *Liverpool Courier*. Art according to Shaw was 'not an elegant superfluity but a social necessity – a thing essential in a great modern community.'

20 Laura Johnson had moved with her sister Eva to Staithes in 1900, marrying Harold Knight, in times past a fellow student at Nottingham School of Art, three years later.

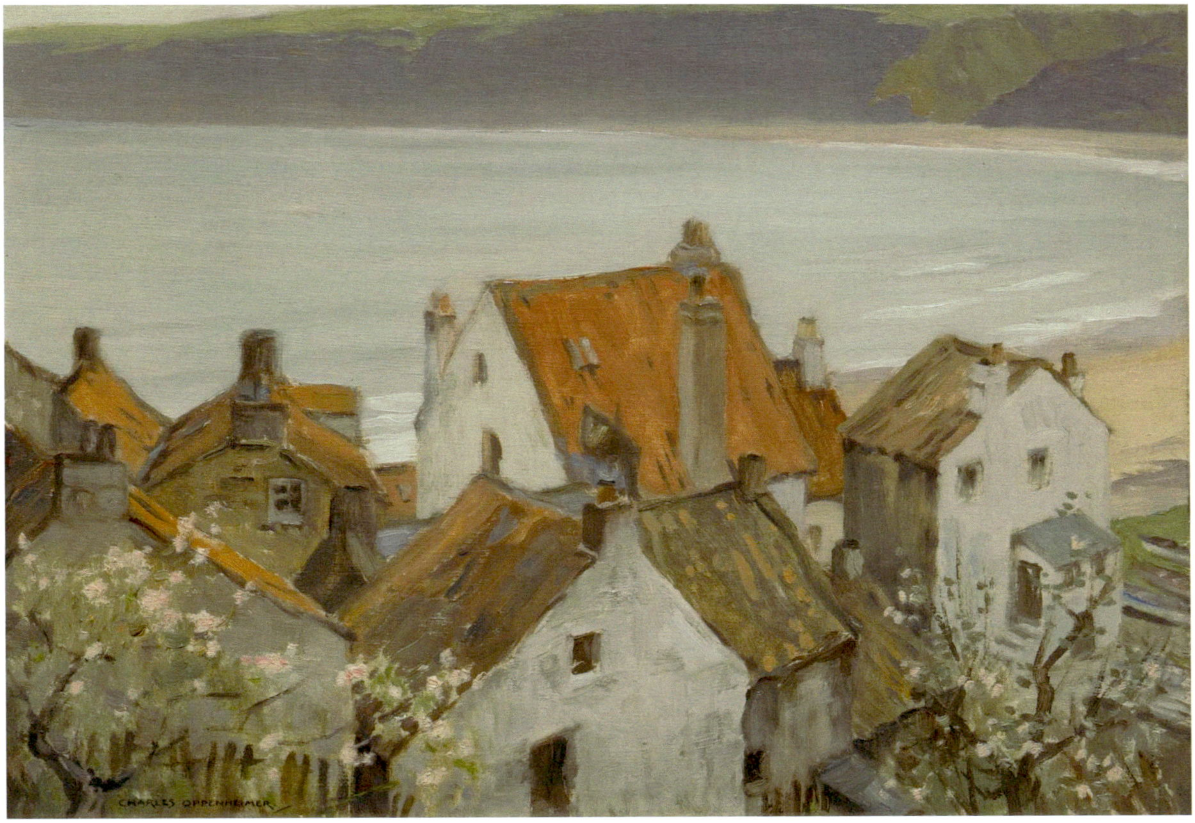

Plate 15 | *A Grey Morning, Runswick Bay*, c.1939, Aberdeen Art Gallery and Museums Collections, oil on canvas, 14 × 18 inches

Downs where military manoeuvres took place for many years around the turn of the century. It is therefore highly likely that Oppenheimer knew the area well from his time in the 2nd Volunteer Battalion of the Manchester Regiment of Mounted Infantry.

Newlyn was distant and crowded with artists, as were St Ives and Lamorna. The Knights moved there at the end of 1907 to join Lamorna Birch, Stanhope Forbes and many others. The artist colonies of Cornwall were not places in which prominence and distinction might be earned just by endeavour. Making a living among the competition would require good fortune too. It was far from family and friends in Manchester.

The east coast was not what Oppenheimer was looking for as in particular, the dull light of bleak winters would yield little inspiration. Oppenheimer himself said in 1947 for the 'Artists of Note' profile in the August edition of *The Artist*, he had tried several 'districts' without success. 'It was a chance meeting with E.A.(Ernest Archibald) Taylor, a well known Scottish designer and painter, at the Graphic Club in Manchester that fixed his habitat for life.' Taylor mentioned an old town 'where for many years a group of native painters had been working, and which had [first] become a favourite spot of Taylor's when on holiday. Oppenheimer went at once to spy out the land and Kirkcudbright won his heart . . . '

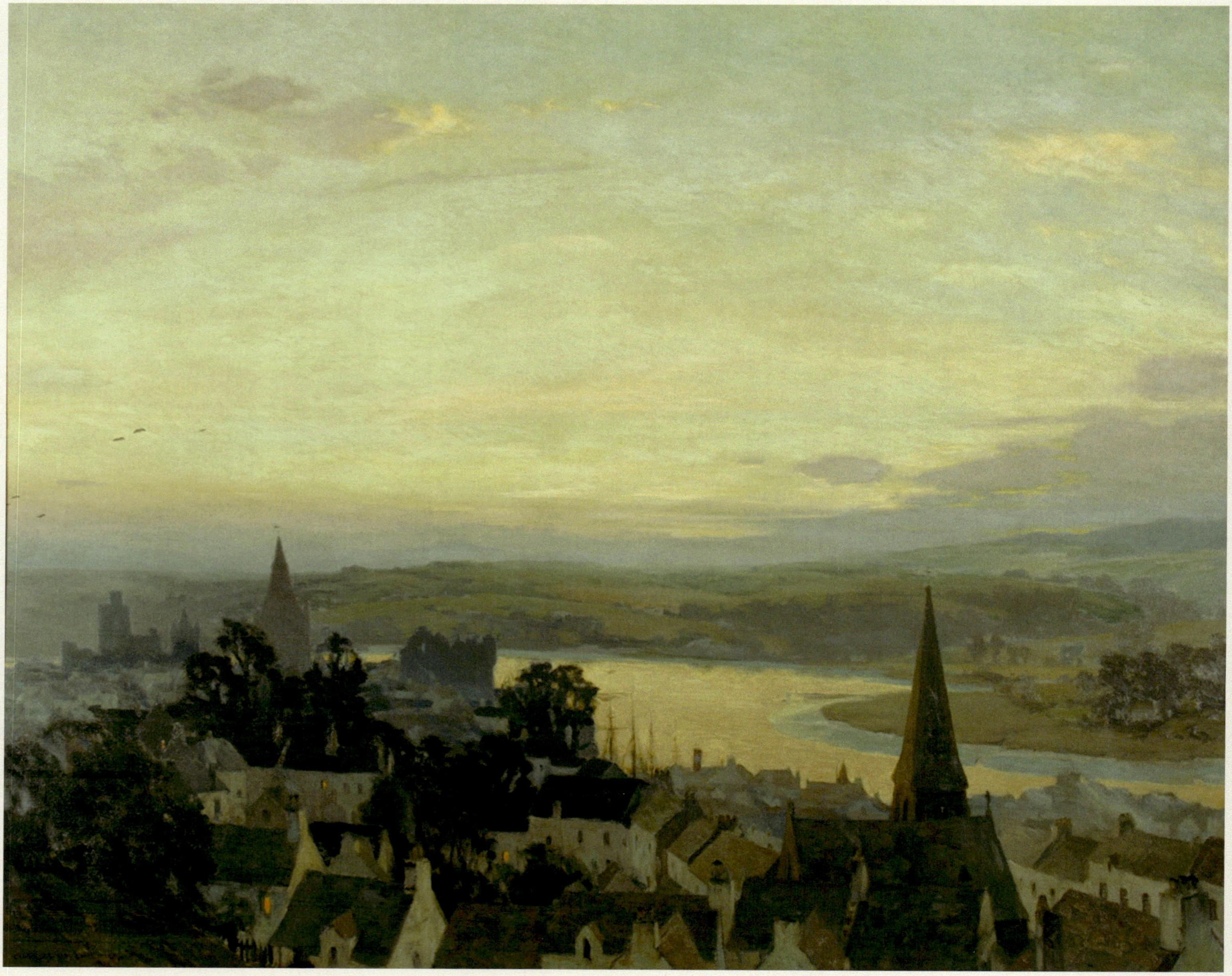

4 AN ARTIST'S TOWN

Plate 16 | *Kirkcudbright: Evening*, 1914, Manchester Art Gallery, oil on canvas, 47½ × 60 inches

OPPENHEIMER ARRIVED in Kirkcudbright by train, probably bringing his bicycle with him, in late 1908. Whether Connie accompanied him on the visit is not recorded. He may have been given local introductions by Taylor and his wife, Jessie King, with whom apparently he stayed at their newly acquired part-time home at Greengate off High Street. He would have found a ready welcome and much to relate to in the town.

Here was the light and many a subject to paint whether around the harbour, by the estuary or beside the lochs and rivers or in the nearby undulating Galloway countryside and hills. Kirkcudbright was smaller than the artists' colonies in Cornwall. It was well placed, not overly distant from Manchester with a change of train at Carlisle. To the north lay the Royal Glasgow Institute of Fine Arts and in Edinburgh, the Royal Scottish Academy, both with their prestigious annual exhibitions, as well as other institutes and societies and a throng of galleries, artists and patrons. Beyond that commercial axis which nurtured and supported the arts, there were municipal galleries and collectors on the east coast main railway line at Kirkcaldy, Dundee and Aberdeen. Oppenheimer's mother's family was still resident in and around Montrose. There was fishing and hill walking both locally and throughout Scotland.

At the start of the century Kirkcudbright was already well known as an artists' town. At that time, apart from the Taylors who became permanent residents in 1915, there were other notable painters living locally or who were regular visitors. Kirkcudbright's and the surrounding district's reputation had grown from the 1880s. The Faed family lived and worked in nearby Gatehouse of Fleet. William Stewart MacGeorge, William Mouncey, Thomas Bromley Blacklock and lesser lights such as John Copland illuminated the local scene and sold their work to an appreciative Scottish public. William Robson moved to Kirkcudbright in 1904. However, by far the most distinguished artist was Edward Atkinson Hornel. Born in Bacchus March in Australia in 1864, Hornel came to Kirkcudbright with his parents at the age of two to what was their home town. By 1909 Hornel was of international renown. He had accumulated a considerable fortune partly invested in local property. It was from Hornel that the Oppenheimers leased their new home at 14 High Street, just next door to Broughton House, Hornel's own residence. Hornel had bought no.14 in 1909 from the surviving of two elderly spinsters who had lived there.

The Oppenheimers left Manchester in the late summer or early autumn of 1909 (Oppenheimer first appears as the tenant in the 1910–1911 Valuation Roll compiled in the autumn of 1909) to begin their new life. It was not however to be Oppenheimer's last involvement with the mosaic business or his final period of residence in his home city. He would also return regularly over the years to the annual exhibitions of Manchester Academy and for family visits.

The new arrivals quickly settled into their home and surroundings. Oppenheimer's artistic career now free from constraint, moved forward apace. He purchased a studio in Millburn Street which had previously belonged to another artist Henry Ivan Neilson who had emigrated to Canada. Of wooden construction, it appears to have been purpose built and not insubstantial. Its rateable value in the 1911–12 valuation rolls (the first yearly entry with Oppenheimer as owner) was recorded as £6; his home was £25.

Oppenheimer exhibited a watercolour entitled *Whitby* at the Royal Glasgow Institute in 1910 for the time. Three other watercolours marked his debut in the same year at the Royal Scottish Academy. *The Scotsman*'s critic remarked on 13 October 1910 that *A Galloway Water and a Quiet Harbour* at the Dundee Fine Art Exhibition was 'a promising work by Mr Charles Oppenheimer of Kirkcudbright'. *Kirkcudbright Harbour* [pl.19] is almost certainly that work. Oppenheimer was even mentioned in the Glasgow's *The Bailie* of 9 November, which reported his exhibition of selected pictures at the Fine Art Galleries of George Davidson Ltd at 123 Sauchiehall Street, Glasgow, remarking that he 'is one of the Kirkcudbright School of artists'.

It was this exhibition, his first one man show, which brought Oppenheimer to the attention of the Scottish public and secured his early reputation. The *Glasgow Herald* extended considerable praise to the newcomer describing him as 'one of the most recent and already one of the most promising of that goodly company of artists who have found their happiest inspirations amid the mountains and streams of Galloway.'[21] The critic continued 'Their names are too familiar even to be recalled to the connoisseur, and no higher compliment could be paid to Mr Oppenheimer than to state that his work entitles him to rank with some at least of the leading men who have immortalised on canvas the romantic beauties of the Stewartry.' Discussing the nature of his work, the *Herald* suggested that Oppenheimer had 'the not too familiar faculty of being

21 *Glasgow Herald*, 9 November 1911

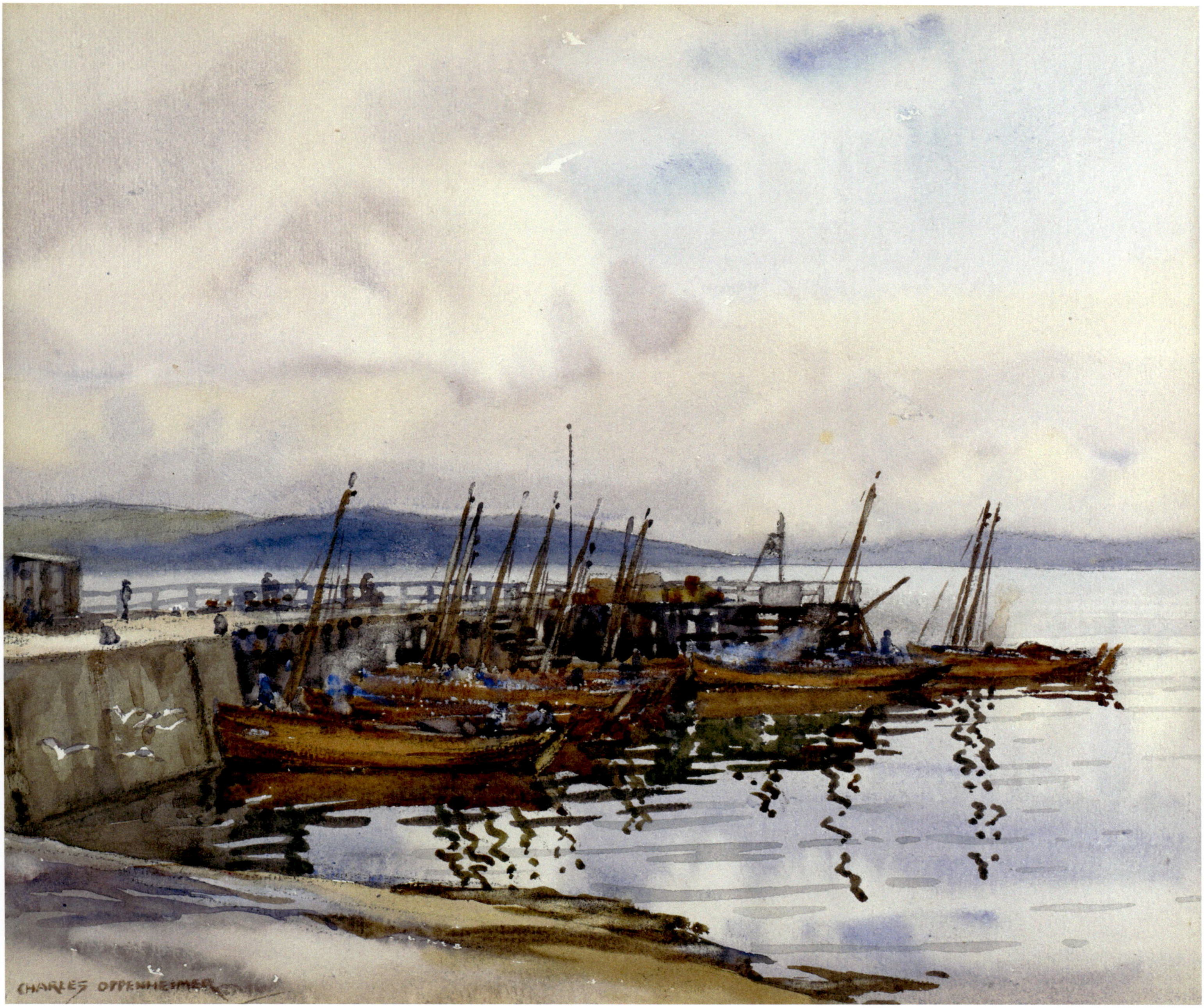

Plate 17 | *A Loch Ranza Sketch*, c.1912, Private Collection, watercolour, 10½ x 12¾ inches

able to indulge his artistic talents with equal success either in oils or in watercolours. He seems quite happy working in both media, and the pictures on view are an admirable index to his abilities'.

Oppenheimer exhibited thirty works, the majority of scenes from around Kirkcudbright. We do not know how many were sold but the assumption must be that a number acquired purchasers. *Evening Glow* and *Whitby*, both untraced, were singled out for praise as evidence of Oppenheimer's 'quiet virility' of style. 'The artist's abilities as a pure colourist are admirably shown too in *Water Lilies* and *September*

Garland, both of which attractively emphasise the riotous pageantry of the flower.'[22] *A Loch Ranza Sketch* [pl.17] dates from this period and may have been amongst the exhibits.

1911 was a similarly busy and productive year. Manchester saw five new works, the Royal Scottish Academy two, and Glasgow one. Oppenheimer also sent three to the Walker Art Gallery at Liverpool. He was perhaps fortunate to have the latter paintings hung as a railway strike meant that a hundred or more from prospective exhibitors were missing or delayed by opening day. The *Liverpool Courier*[23] commenting on the two lesser priced works described them as 'quiet pictures … which are characterful'. *The Scotsman* perhaps marking Oppenheimer's transition north of the border recorded his paintings at Liverpool as among works of 'Scots' abroad.

1911 was crowned by election to full membership of the Manchester's Academy but 1912 proved even more fruitful. Clearly by now a far more than proficient watercolourist, Oppenheimer was elected to membership of the Royal Scottish Society of Painters in Watercolours. The annual vote was held in the Glasgow Art Club in Bath Street in March. The meeting comprised a good attendance of artists from both the east and west of Scotland. Of the eight candidates for membership only Oppenheimer was successful. His work was now to attract more attention. Mentions in the reviews of that year's RGI and RSA exhibitions prove the point. *The Scotsman* critic[24] at the RSA wished to intimate that 'a mild protest might be entered against the high hanging of so excellent a picture as Mr Charles Oppenheimer's *Galloway River*, with its carefully drawn banks, its impetuous rush of water and its crisp and pure colour'. '*Kirkcudbright*', said *The Scotsman* critic at the RSW annual exhibition in Edinburgh in September 'gives Mr Charles Oppenheimer, one of the latest recruits of the Society, an opportunity of sharing his power of vigorous sky treatment and his command of spacious feeling'.[25] [pl.18] may have been this watercolour.

Oppenheimer's work was steadily drawing favourable critical attention. The praise was not however undiluted. In March 1912 the *Manchester City News* used several paragraphs to cover Oppenheimer's three paintings in the Manchester Academy's exhibition that year to describe the standard that he had obtained. 'Two of our younger landscapists challenge attention and make good their position successfully', it recorded. Herbert Royle[27] had 'arrived', whilst Oppenheimer 'is coming and will soon be there.'

The anonymous critic then concentrated upon a description and critique of *The Last Hours of Toil* (untraced) which he described as Oppenheimer's most important and ambitious work yet exhibited. The painting

22 Ibid

23 *Liverpool Courier*, 27 September 1911

24 *The Scotsman*, 14 June 1912

25 *The Scotsman*, 28 September 1912

26 *Kirkcudbright Advertiser*, 10 May 1912

27 Herbert Royle, 1870–1958, born in Manchester, a landscape and figure painter, who exhibited mainly in Liverpool and Birmingham between 1892 and 1940.

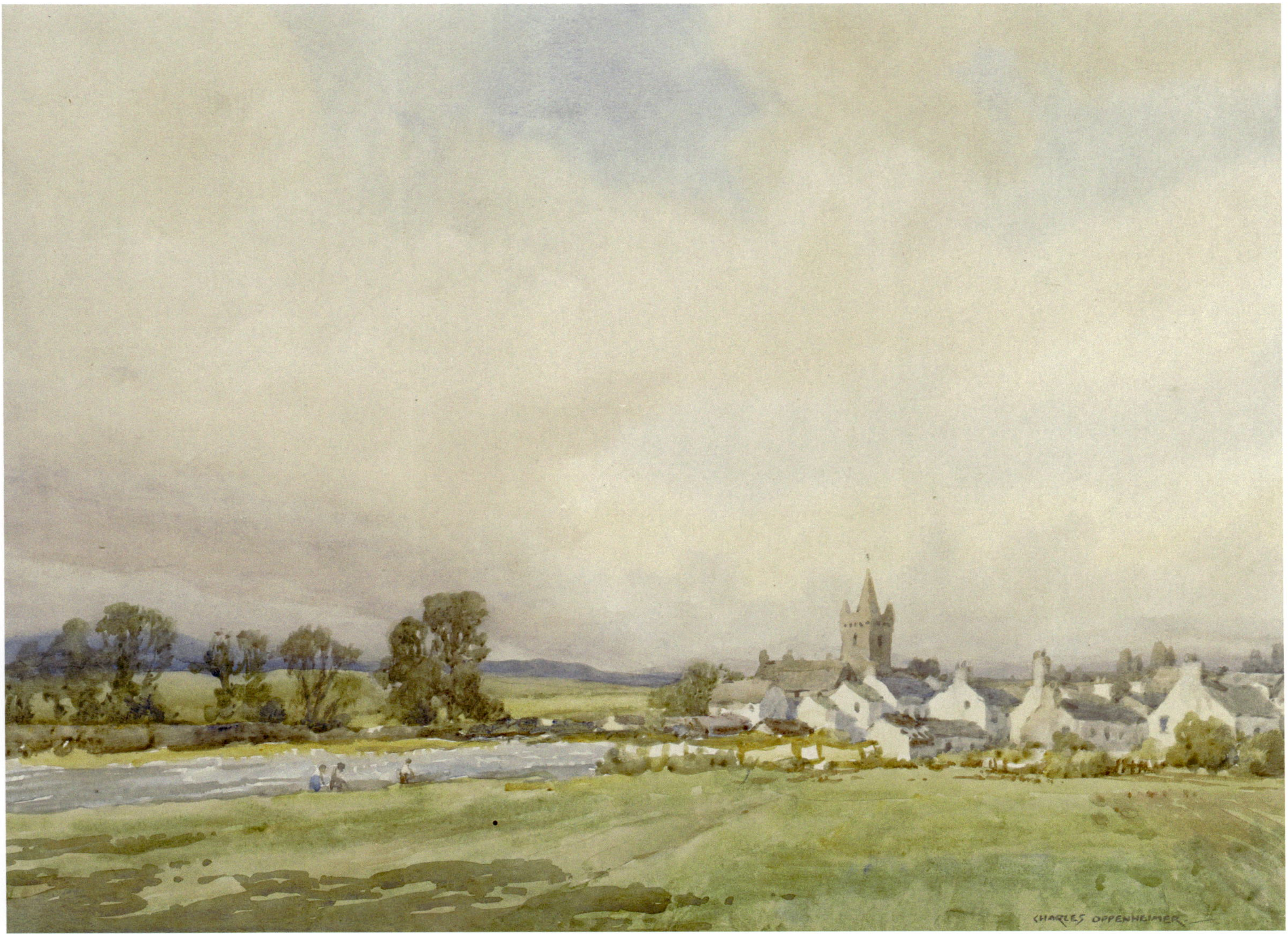

Plate 18 | *Kirkcudbright*, c.1913, Bourne Fine Art, watercolour, 13¾ x 19 inches

depicted 'a flat expanse of bare brown soil stretching to a little hamlet with a quaint old church. The white walls are washed a pale yellow in a watery sunshine of a late autumn evening. In the foreground a stalwart farm hand, with a pitch fork, and a young woman of the field labouring class are getting potatoes'. The description suggests a favourite painting ground of both resident and visiting artists, the Crofts in Kirkcudbright and the 'quaint old church', the Tolbooth. However it is the next set of observations that really matter as they inform us as to some contemporary opinion of Oppenheimer's achievement:

> *There is a good deal wanting in the picture; a want of colour and a want of quality. But the root of the matter is there. The work is conceived somewhat in the manner of H.H. La Thangue*[28] *in his earlier and more sombre period. There is no doubt that the arrangement of the picture is*

> *founded on J. F. Millet's* Angelus. *The influence of the great French peasant painter does not extend beyond the superficial arrangement. There is no trace of the profound melancholy of Millet, the pessimism induced by brooding over the hopeless, endless toil of his inarticulate fellows. The* Angelus *is the heart's cry of the poor, whose dreary lives are sustained but not brightened by their simple faith and devotion.*

Oppenheimer's star was to outshine that of Royle in later years. The *Manchester City News* critic's assessment, if over-elaborate to a twenty first century reader, was essentially accurate both as to Oppenheimer's then standard in oils and the prediction of greater achievements in years to come. He continued:

> *Our Manchester painter strikes a note of cheerful optimism. The end of the day's toil means to him a quiet evening's rest and the warm fireside. Do not mistake our drift. We are not bringing Oppenheimer into comparison with one of the world's master painters. We do not suggest that his picture even approaches greatness. But it is by earnest and ambitious efforts such as this that the way to greatness lies.*

By the close of 1912 Charles Oppenheimer RSW could look forward by contemporary reckoning to fruitful and prolific years building upon his prodigious talent. The exhibition season that lay ahead in 1913 would allow him to display a diversity of work. His painting grounds included northern Italy about which more will be related in chapter seven.

Oppenheimer held a second successful one man show in Glasgow in January and February 1913. At the Royal Academy in London in May three Oppenheimers were hung, one or more 'on the line'.[29] Later that month *Old Whitby*, a watercolour, was sold at the Royal Scottish Academy at which *Piazza Erbe, Verona* also attracted much attention, *The Scotsman* declaring it 'a well rendered view of a market place at Verona'. Charles Oppenheimer had 'taken a step forward in his art'.[30]

In the four years since his move to Kirkcudbright, Oppenheimer had made the transition from a craftsman and designer in the mosaic industry and part time painter to an accomplished professional artist. He had settled into Kirkcudbright life. Kirkcudbright had accepted him. Now claimed as one of their own in artistic circles, the townsfolk additionally elected him to their local Council in November 1913. Oppenheimer's candidacy was encouraged and indeed formally proposed by Hornel who had himself been a member until an obscure dispute about town pavements had led to his resignation some years beforehand.

At the hustings' meeting on 3 November, Oppenheimer declared that the amenity of the town, of which all were rightly proud, was something which he had taken to his own heart since his arrival in Kirkcudbright. More and more visitors were being attracted to Kirkcudbright by its

28 Henry Herbert La Thangue, 1859–1929

29 *The Scotsman*, 3 May 1913

30 *The Scotsman* 9 May 1913

31 By 30 October he had in fact attended nine out of fifteen having been given leave of absence for the other six.

natural and historic beauties. If elected he would be strongly opposed to any scheme unless it was absolutely for the good of the town. He also opposed a reduction in the membership of the Town Council from six as this would impede the dispatch of business. The Town Council was larger than most through ancient right. To the applause of his audience, Oppenheimer concluded that once a right had been given up, it would be difficult to retrieve.

The poll was not as heavy as in the previous election. 414 voted out of 567, a very respectable turnout compared to late twentieth and early twenty first century municipal elections! Voting was reportedly steady until noon, slackened in the afternoon and then picked up after five with nearly all the candidates in attendance. Polling day was uneventful save for two men in sandwich boards urging people to 'Vote for Good Water' and to 'Vote for a Watering Trough'.

The count was conducted expeditiously and the result declared to 'loud cheers':

Walter Wallace, builder 291
James McMurray, posting master [sic] 257
John Kerr Melbourn, stationer 246
Robert Craik Mitchell, flesher 215
John Chalmers, retired stationmaster 198
Charles Oppenheimer, artist 197
John Telford, grocer 127
Alexander Henry, baker 97

The last of the six Councillors to be elected, the wisdom of his view on reducing the Council in size, would not have been lost on Oppenheimer. One may also perhaps be permitted to speculate on the quality or price, or both, of produce in at least two of the town's shops given the margin of defeat of the two unsuccessful candidates. Although to be a short-lived representative career, Oppenheimer was an assiduous Councillor attending the majority of meetings until late 1914.[31] The pages of the *Kirkcudbright Advertiser* record his interest in lighting in the Town Hall, maintenance of footways, and the purchase of spraying equipment to tar certain streets to reduce dust nuisance.

More interesting than parish pump issues and reflective of his progressive political outlook was Oppenheimer's interest in women's suffrage. Admirer and occasional student of his last years, Joe Campbell, believes that Connie would have 'put Charles up to it' but there was nonetheless a genuine commitment to what was a controversial cause. As previously recorded Oppenheimer had lived close by the Pankhursts in Manchester. He would undoubtedly have known of them. Richard Pankhurst had been a Parliamentary candidate in Manchester and Emmeline had held

Plate 19 | *Kirkcudbright Harbour*, c.1910, Private Collection, oil on canvas, 9½ x 11½ inches

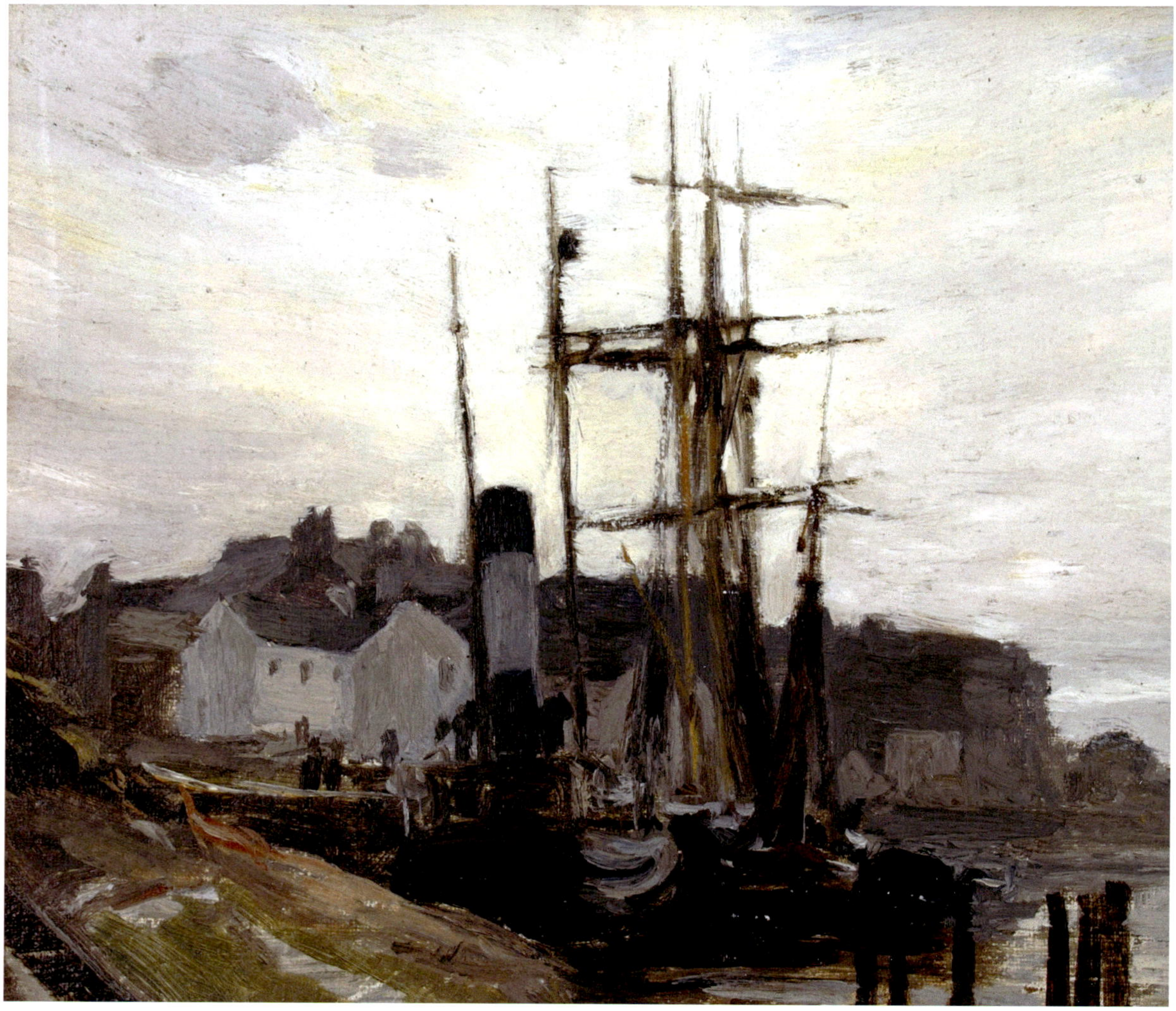

elective office for a short while in Chorlton-upon-Medlock. Christabel and Sylvia were contemporaries of Oppenheimer and his younger brothers. Intriguingly, Sylvia, an accomplished artist in later life, trained at the Manchester Municipal School of Art and in 1902 won the Proctor Memorial prize for mosaic design and another prize to travel to Venice to study mosaics and drawing. However to date research has not yet uncovered a direct link between the families.

Oppenheimer would in any event not have approved of the militants among the suffragettes. When Miss Geraldine Cooke of the non-violent National Union of Women's Suffrage Societies came to address local branches at Castle Douglas and Kirkcudbright in 1913, Oppenheimer seconded the motion from the platform at the latter meeting on Tuesday 18 November. He said that there were a certain number of empty chairs in the hall and 'everyone represented a man or woman in Kirkcudbright who had missed a great intellectual treat'. Praising Miss Cooke's

32 *Kirkcudbright Advertiser*, 21 November 1913

33 *The Bailie*, Glasgow, 3 June 1914

'eloquent' address, he endorsed her argument that 'the giving of the vote was not only a matter of faith, but was just and right'. This was not the direct action of the Pankhursts' Women's Social and Political Union. Indeed Cooke herself answering a question on militancy was reported by the local press[32] as saying that for its first two or three years the militant movement had advanced the cause but that, in the last three or four years 'everything they had done was absolutely injurious'.

The Oppenheimers were not just armchair supporters of women's suffrage. In February 1914 they took part in the local Women's Suffrage Society's presentation of the then well known play *How the Vote was Won*. Two very successful productions in Castle Douglas and Kirkcudbright saw fellow artist Bill Robson taking the lead part as Horace Cole, Connie playing his sister. Oppenheimer won praise as the stage manager and for a walk-on part.

The militants chose different means of involving the arts in their cause. In May 1914 Maude Edwards produced a hatchet from under her cloak in the RSA gallery on the Mound smashing the glass and cutting the canvas of John Lavery's half length portrait of King George V. The Glasgow Bailie was moved to suggest that the actions of the militant ladies might be turned in the 'right direction'.

> *'For instance, there are several pictures in the Kelvingrove Galleries which would be none the worse of the application of an axe of a sword or other lethal instrument. Were they slashed, the probability is that repairs would not be attempted and the wounded offences might be happily stowed in the coal cellar or utilised to light the civic fire when such a conflagration is thought necessary'.*[33]

The Bailie's satire doubtless prompted a chuckle but women's suffrage supporters like Oppenheimer roundly condemned these and other outrages such as Janet Arthur, alias Fanny Parker's attempt to blow up Burns' cottage in Alloway in July 1914. Hostilities between the militants and civil society were suspended just after the outbreak of the Great War when, on 10 August, all suffragettes were released from prison. Janet Arthur's trial did not proceed.

The Oppenheimers' cause was won in principle during the war years. On 8 January 1918 the Lloyd George coalition government's Representation of the People Bill giving votes to women of thirty years and older was passed by the House of Lords and sent for Royal Assent. It was not of course until the Equal Franchise Act of 1928 that women over twenty one were enfranchised.

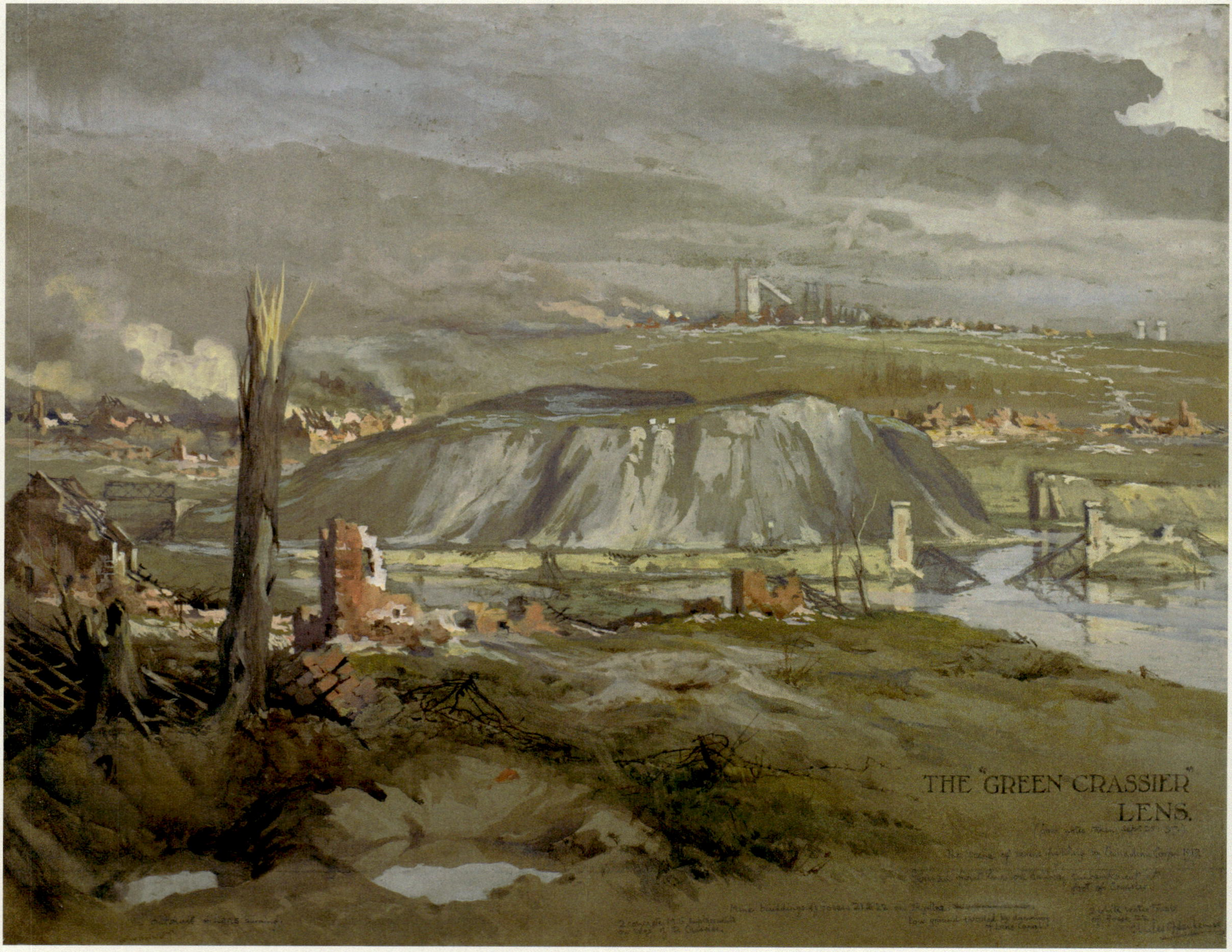

INSCRIPTIONS: THE 'GREEN CRASSIER', LENS

(from notes taken Sept. 25: 1917.)

The scene of severe fighting by Canadian Corps 1917.

German front line at railway embankment at foot of Crassier.

Mine buildings of Fosse 21 & 22 on skyline.

Low ground flooded by damming of Lens Canal.

2 concrete M.G. emplacements on edge of the Crassier

2 white water towers of Fosse 22

Charles Oppenheimer

5 WAR

Plate 20 | *The 'Green Crassier', Lens*, 1919, Imperial War Museums [Art. IWM ART 1202] watercolour, 17½ × 22¾ inches

OPPENHEIMER BEGAN 1914 with the now familiar preparations for the annual round of exhibitions. Plans for visits to painting grounds beyond Galloway were made including to the continent. Commissions were undertaken and progressed. The exhibitions at Manchester and at the RGI contained continental but no Scottish subject. [pl.16] *Kirkcudbright: Evening* was however painted in 1914 according to records in Manchester. It is likely to be the painting of the same name exhibited at Liverpool and the Royal Academy in 1921.

By the outbreak of war in August 1914 Oppenheimer's reputation had risen further so much so that the Bailie hailed him as an artist from Glasgow and the west of Scotland. Had the war been over by Christmas, as was the popular prediction, little might have changed. If the Allied offensives of 1915 had driven the Germans back and not ground to a bloody halt in the stalemate of trench warfare on the Western Front, the lives of so many, Oppenheimer included, may have been spared or unaltered.

As the war dragged on it brought a real and present danger not in France but at home for the Oppenheimer family. Not a common name, its German origin was obvious and irrefutable and became a target of the unthinking from the early days of the conflict. Windows were smashed by stones at Ludwig Oppenheimer Ltd's business premises in August 1914 and its sign defaced. The directors went to the length of writing to customers in November 1914 to stress their patriotism [pl.21] This may have been because a concurrent, well-publicised case of trading with the enemy brought anti-German sentiment uncomfortably close to home. Julius Oppenheimer (no relation) and Thomas William Colbeck were found guilty of so doing in late 1914. Julius Oppenheimer, a British subject since 1889, ran a business selling lithographic transfers which were printed in Nürnberg and imported. One such cargo had been intercepted after war had been declared. Quite how such pre-purchased material affected the war effort might now seem unclear but what shot the case to prominence was that Julius Oppenheimer and Colbeck were unsuccessfully defended, including at appeal, by the renowned barrister

Plate 21 | Ludwig Oppenheimer Ltd's letter, November, 1914, courtesy of the Oppenheimer family

Plate 22 | 1 Corps Intelligence Section, Western Front, 1917–18, courtesy of the Stewartry Museum, Kirkcudbright (Oppenheimer is the central figure in the back row).

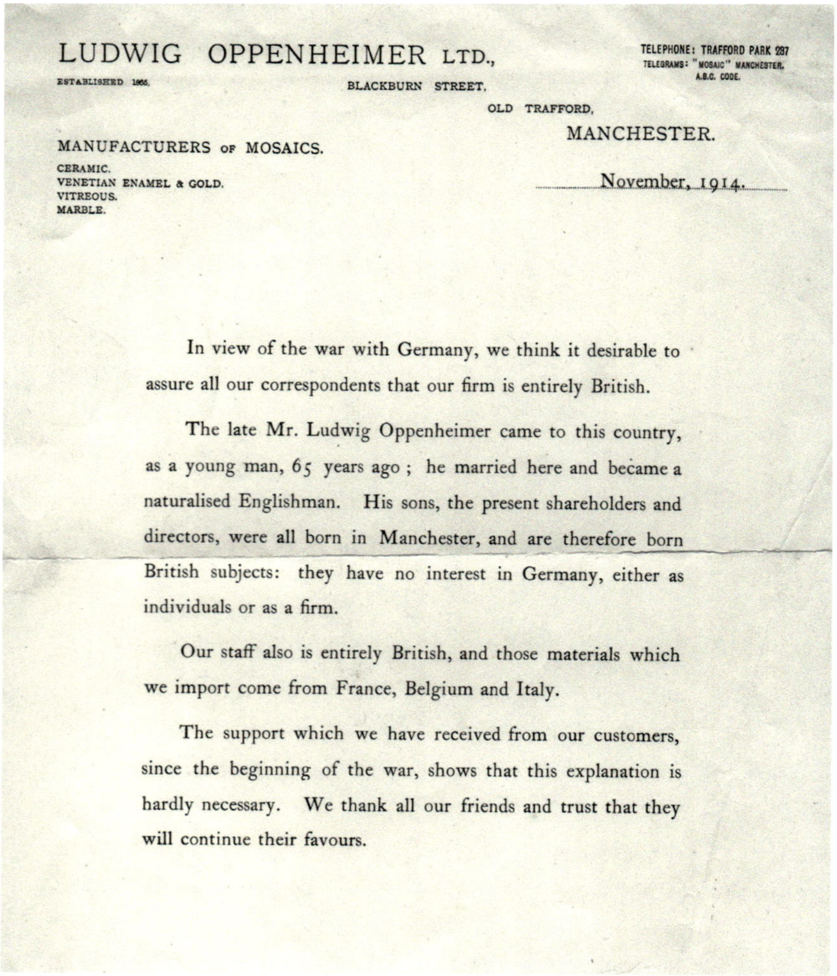

LUDWIG OPPENHEIMER LTD.,

ESTABLISHED 1866.

TELEPHONE: TRAFFORD PARK 297
TELEGRAMS: "MOSAIC" MANCHESTER.
A.B.C. CODE.

BLACKBURN STREET,
OLD TRAFFORD,
MANCHESTER.

MANUFACTURERS OF MOSAICS.
CERAMIC.
VENETIAN ENAMEL & GOLD.
VITREOUS.
MARBLE.

November, 1914.

In view of the war with Germany, we think it desirable to assure all our correspondents that our firm is entirely British.

The late Mr. Ludwig Oppenheimer came to this country, as a young man, 65 years ago; he married here and became a naturalised Englishman. His sons, the present shareholders and directors, were all born in Manchester, and are therefore born British subjects: they have no interest in Germany, either as individuals or as a firm.

Our staff also is entirely British, and those materials which we import come from France, Belgium and Italy.

The support which we have received from our customers, since the beginning of the war, shows that this explanation is hardly necessary. We thank all our friends and trust that they will continue their favours.

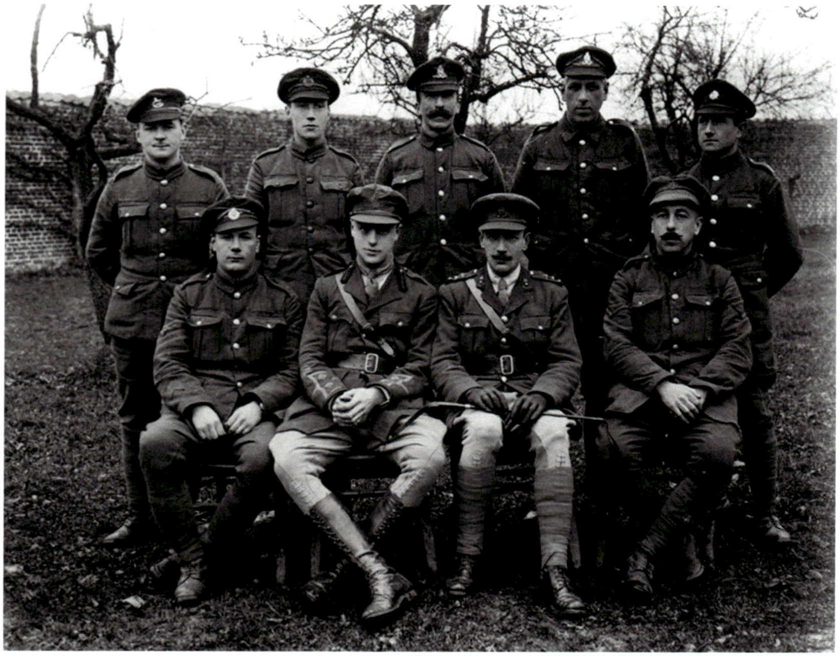

Sir Edward Carson KC, the prominent Unionist and Ulster politician.

Other Oppenheimers suffered.[34] One in particular had his name splashed across the nation's press continuously for eight or more years from 1908. There were coincidences in the lives of Oppenheimer and his namesake Sir Francis Charles Oppenheimer who was also of German-Jewish stock and may even have been a distant relation of the Manchester Oppenheimers.

Sir Francis was the son of Charles Oppenheimer (1836–1900), a Frankfurt am Main merchant and later the British Consul-General in the city. Following his education in Germany and at Oxford, he was articled to Rufus Isaacs MP, later the Marquis of Reading[35], and called to the Bar in 1895. Setting the law aside he moved to Paris in 1896 and for four years took up a painting career. On his father's death in 1900 he assumed the former's unsalaried post of Consul-General for the Prussian provinces of Hesse-Nassau and the Grand Duchy of Hesse. Sir Frances' career actually flourished at first because of his incisive and authoritative commercial reports. Knighted in 1907, Lloyd George drew on his memoranda on German social legislation when framing his own national insurance scheme and called him 'one of the ablest Consuls of the British Empire'.[36] In January 1912 Sir Francis was appointed commercial attaché for north western Europe. It was his memorandum written in 1909, on the unlikely swift efficacy of a naval blockade against Germany in the event of war, which helped to persuade the Asquith government to send the British Expeditionary Force to France in 1914.

However none of this saved Sir Francis. As early as 1908 he had had to defend himself against anti-German sentiment inflamed by international events. In a letter to *The Times* of the 23 October of that year he wrote: 'As I was born in London, took my degrees at Oxford, and am a member of the English bar, it is hardly correct to count me among the foreigners.' And in a sentence that could have been written by or about the Manchester Oppenheimers he continued, 'If my family name does not sound English, I need hardly remind you that I share this disadvantage with a large proportion of the oldest families in England.'

He might have said highest as well. King George V eventually changed his family's name from Saxe-Coburg-Gotha to Windsor on the advice of Asquith's government during the war. Sir Francis was the victim of a Northcliffe Press campaign deriding his views of and actions concerning the blockade of Germany. This saw the Oppenheimer name in large capital letters on *Daily Mail* billboards throughout the nation in August and September 1916.[37]

Family lore suggests that both Oppenheimer and Connie faced anti-German sentiment in Kirkcudbright. It is of course possible but there is

34 Another contemporary, Sir Ernest Oppenheimer (1880–1957) naturalised as a British subject in 1901, moved to Kimberley in South Africa to represent his diamond merchant company. Despite serving as Mayor between 1912 and 1915 and raising the Kimberley regiment, he felt sufficiently threatened to return to London to avoid anti-German sentiment only to re-encounter it.

35 Attorney General (1910–13), Lord Chief Justice (1913–21) and Foreign Secretary 1931

36 *The Times*, 16 October, 1911

37 Sir Francis was sent out of the way to neutral Holland but remained under press attack until recalled to London in September 1918 and sent on extended leave because of prejudice against people 'with German names or of German parentage'. He left the diplomatic service for good in 1920 and spent the remaining forty one years of his life devoted to the arts. He died in London on 25 June 1961, less than three months after Charles Oppenheimer

no surviving evidence for this contention and scant reason to suppose this to have happened in the small and close knit community that had welcomed their arrival only five years beforehand. The couple did indeed return to Manchester in the spring of 1915 but not to get away from abuse. That they personally encountered taunts is entirely possible but it seems more likely to have been in Manchester rather than in their adopted home town.

The Oppenheimers left Kirkcudbright for Connie's family home at 37 Mayfield Road, Whalley Range in March 1915. The *Kirkcudbright Advertiser* reported on 2 April that a letter from Oppenheimer was read to the Town Council. He wrote that for the duration of the War he was to return to Manchester to look after the family business as his brother had joined the army. Oppenheimer would be unable to attend meetings and he thus felt that he had to tender his resignation. He had been proud of his membership of the Council and would always have the happiest of memories of the courtesy and good feeling among his fellow Councillors. The newspaper continued: 'Provost Wallace said that they had all been put to inconvenience on account of the War. Instead of accepting Mr Oppenheimer's resignation they could give him six months' leave of absence. If the War was not finished then they could extend the leave of absence if necessary.' The Provost's motion was greeted with applause.

The brother referred to in Oppenheimer's letter was Lehmann who had volunteered in the spring of 1915 and was commissioned by August 1915. To enlist at the age of forty seven required courage and also doubtless helped to defend the family against anti-German sentiment. Oppenheimer himself now aged 40, followed in his eldest brother's footsteps in the autumn when he 'attested' under the 'Derby scheme'.[38] In December he actually enlisted in the ranks of the Royal Garrison Artillery. Perhaps he had been prompted to join the artillery by a visit to Kirkcudbright made by the RGA just before the War. Oppenheimer had prior military service but at the age of forty to become a private and an ordinary gunner was as courageous a decision as that of his brother.

Conveying the Council's original decision by letter, Kirkcudbright Town Clerk, John Gibson, had written that his colleagues did not wish to lose Oppenheimer's service 'unless it was absolutely necessary'. A further extension of six months was granted by the Council in September 1915 and Town Clerk Gibson's second letter of 30 September expressed the hope that, before the end of that period, peace would be declared and Oppenheimer could return. That hope was of course in vain. A further exchange of correspondence on 25 and 27 April 1916 included the Town Clerk's informing Oppenheimer that the Council would grant yet another extension. 'The Council regret your inability to resume your duties but are pleased to think that in other ways you are doing your duty on behalf of the nation.'

38 The Derby Scheme introduced by the wartime Coalition on 15 October 1915,was named after the 16th Earl of Derby who had been appointed Director General of Recruitment five days earlier. Effectively a half way house between voluntary enlisting and compulsory recruitment, the scheme postponed compulsion so long as enough men attested to ensure plentiful reinforcements for the army if required.

Oppenheimer wrote again on 15 December at the end of that year, not from Mayfield Road but now on YMCA headed paper on active service with the British Expeditionary Force. On this occasion he said that he was actually tendering his resignation as he had now 'had nearly two years' leave of absence' and he felt it desirable 'that my seat may be taken by someone at home who is able to attend to town affairs'. Oppenheimer began his letter which was addressed to Provost Miller by thanking the Provost for his letter of condolence on the death of his brother Lehmann, killed on active service in November 1916.

Lehmann had agonised as to whether he should volunteer and had lied about his age to do so. His son, Eric, had already joined up in 1915. Commissioned as a Second Lieutenant in the Artists' Rifles, 23rd London Regiment, in June 1916, Lehmann Oppenheimer commanded a machine gun unit. Officially, he succumbed to an acute attack of asthma and pneumonia after four months or more in the front line. He was however the victim of a gas attack on allied trenches near Vimy between Lens and Arras that had brought on the fatal symptoms. Poignantly his wife Edith and daughter, Ethel, were able to visit him in his last hours in the hospital in Boulogne to which he had been evacuated. Ethel described the scene vividly in her unpublished biography.

On arrival (in Boulogne) we found the quayside filled with the wounded and the dying ... We made our way to the Cristol Military Hospital where the matron had to search through long lists before she discovered my father's name. The hospitals were almost as bad as the quays – men lay side by side on trestle tables, some dying and a few already dead. We found my father sitting up and gasping for breath. When (he) died, his body was taken to the huge burial ground on the hillside above Boulogne where the sentinel played the Last Post.

Oppenheimer wrote of his brother that he was 'a fine and brave officer' and that the family felt 'his loss terribly but he is only one of so many who have given their lives for their country'. He next replied to a letter from Town Clerk Gibson of 28 December 1916 granting yet another period of leave of absence. His response was hurriedly scribbled in pencil on 30 January on a small sheet of paper measuring about five by three inches of a type much used in or near the front line. He simply thanked the Council in a few words for the further concession.

Oppenheimer's unit was 180 Siege Battery, Royal Garrison Artillery. His younger brother, William Renwick had also enlisted in its ranks. The Battery had been mobilised on 28 September 1916 at Stockcross, Newbury. On 9 October it had left for its port of embarkation, probably Dover, with its four six inch Vickers howitzers and had disembarked in France at 7a.m. on the 13th of the month. Oppenheimer was one of one hundred and thirty other ranks led by six officers.

At 11p.m. on the 16 October the Battery left for the front, some personnel by lorry with the guns and some going by train. At 2.30p.m. two days later, Oppenheimer reached the line to the sound of the artillery to which he and his fellow novice soldiers were soon to become horribly accustomed and to which they themselves were to add. The Battery had arrived at Bethune where its guns were sent to a workshop for overhaul and its personnel were put in billets near to its intended position.

On 21 October, the Battery's war diary records the commencement of the mundane work of digging in, the bane of the ordinary soldier's life in the Great War. Dugouts, ammunition recesses and latrines were soon completed. Two days later the Battery had taken over the forward observation posts from 2nd Siege Battery and they had fired their first eleven rounds in anger at 5.50 a.m. 'D' gun immediately went out of action because of a broken bracket on the quick loading gear. On the 29 better maps had arrived and work continued on more dugouts and camouflage.

For the next nine weeks Oppenheimer took part in the daily routine of the bombardment of selected enemy positions. However on 4 January 1917, the Battery's war diary records that one anonymous Gunner was posted to 1 Corps Intelligence Section. This is the only such record in the war diary and hence is almost certainly a reference to Oppenheimer.[39]

The corridor from Bethune to Lens was bitterly contested in 1917 and 1918. To the north and east of both towns lay strategic railway lines that the Germans used to reinforce their lines. Troop movements both on the railways and nearer the front had to be observed as well as the location of enemy artillery batteries and trenches identified. The skills of an artist in drawing plans and pictures in relief from photographs and marking pictures and photographs were of considerable military use. Oppenheimer's craftsman's skills were employed again. He was also said to have been a motorcycle dispatch rider for a time equipped with flared cavalry style trousers presumably carrying his Section's work to the artillery and front line.

Oppenheimer's niece, Mary Evans, recalled a particularly dangerous way in which his drawing skills were put to use by the Intelligence Section. 'During his wartime service he was several times flown over the war zone to make sketches of the terrain.' These were perilous missions in canvas-covered, wooden framed two seater BE2a bi-planes. Mary Evans continued that Oppenheimer 'was often shot at from below' and that the family believed that he was recommended for bravery awards for this work on three occasions but he was never decorated other than with standard service medals. 'The worry was that his German name counted against him.'

All applications for support aeroplanes were made from frontline

39 There is no other such entry in the Battery's war diaries through to the end of February 1918, the last surviving month in the National Archives. Postings are regularly recorded although not necessarily by name including a later one of 102808 Bombardier W.R. Oppenheimer to Officer Cadet School in England on 24 July 1917. Oppenheimer's younger brother William was later duly commissioned and ended the war as a Second Lieutenant.

officers through the Intelligence Section to No2 Squadron of the Royal Flying Corps based at Hesdigneul les Bethune. 1 Corps' 'Instruction No 16' of 1 February, 1918 records that by then there were three Flights in the squadron. Two Flights did counter-battery work '(Artillery patrols, counter-battery photography and observation of fire on hostile batteries) and the remaining Flight [did] trench work (co-operation with infantry, reconnaissance and photography of the trench system up to about 4,000 yards and observation of fire on to targets in the trench system).'

Usually commissioned officers, or men at least of the rank of sergeant, undertook regular flying missions. Oppenheimer was an exception. He was most likely to have been involved in special tasks such as that at dawn on 23 April 1917 when Royal Flying Corps' planes marked with a black band under their left wings and two streamers from the strut on the left wing took off to observe how far Allied troops had advanced after an attack near Lens. There was no operational ground to air radio at that time and so orders were issued that 'flares will be shown by all advanced troops ... the aeroplane calling for them by Klaxon horn'. Observers like Oppenheimer were required to report on dispositions below or to hang over the edge of the cockpit to work the side mounted cameras whilst pilots avoided ground fire and the attention of enemy aircraft. The results were dropped at 1 Corps Headquarters where, if not aloft, Oppenheimer would have been required to help analyse them. Oppenheimer's duties in 1 Corps Intelligence Section kept him in the vicinity of Lens in north eastern France during the final German offensive in the spring of 1918. He was photographed with his colleagues in either 1917 or 1918. [pl.22] It was in the 1 Corps Intelligence Section that he ended his war when the guns fell silent on the morning of 11 November 1918.

A year later Oppenheimer donated a watercolour to the Imperial War Museum entitled *The Green Crassier, Lens* [pl.20] based on a drawing which he had made in September 1917. The picture is the view from allied trenches showing the canal, crassiers (bings or spoil heaps), and various other features including fires started by shells bursting in Lens behind the German frontline.

Writing in *The Scotsman* in 1961 just after Oppenheimer's death, Wilfred Taylor in *A Scotsman's Log* recalled that 'the grand old man' used to go to the opening of RSA exhibitions in his last years. Mr and Mrs Oppenheimer would make a holiday of this annual event.

> *After attending a musical or theatrical performance he would cross the square to his club to smoke his last pipe. Deep in his chair he would talk in his slow, unruffled monotone, of his experiences in Italy or in the Army in the First World War.*

The War had left an indelible mark.

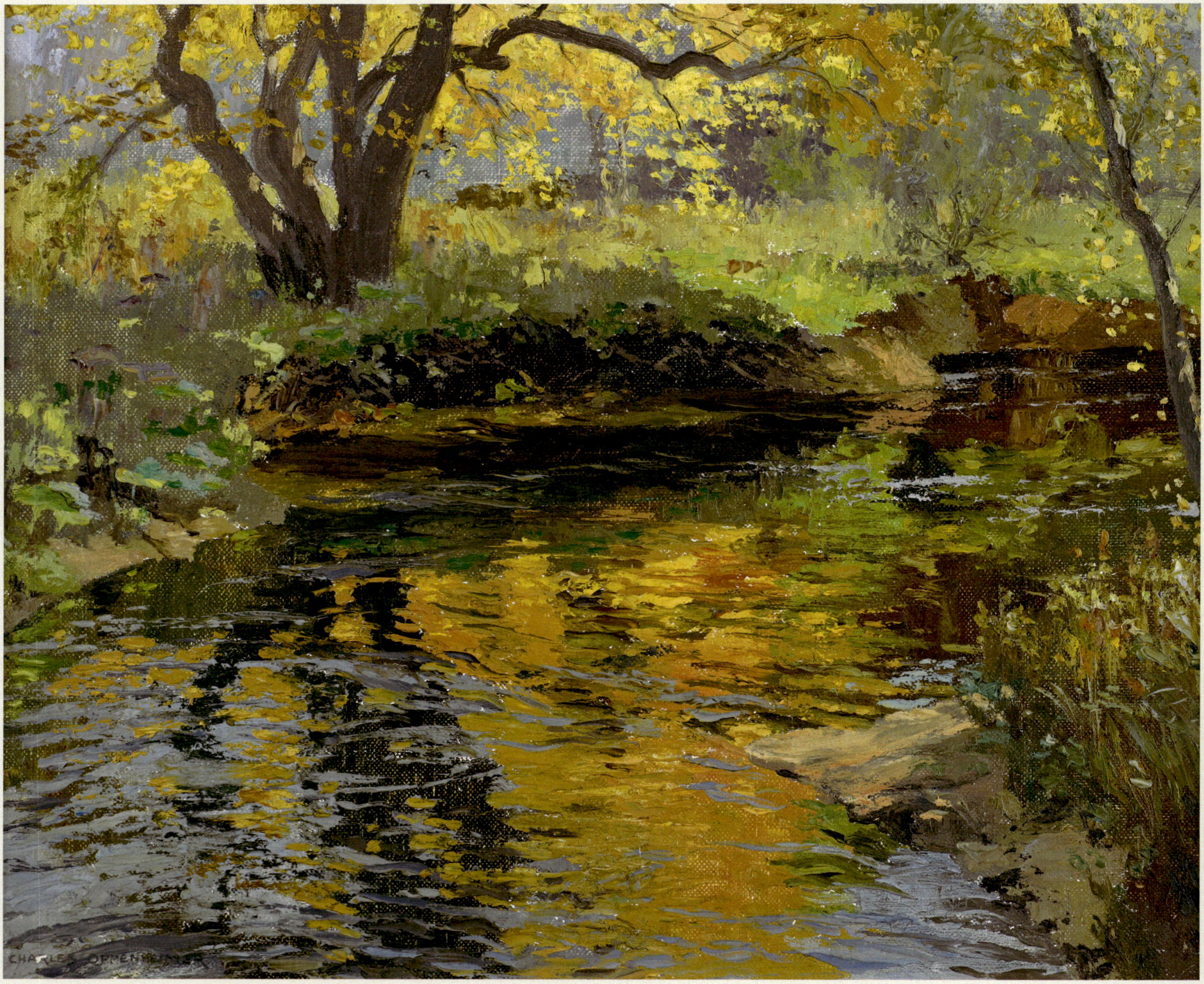

6 BACK HOME

Plate 23 | *Autumn Gold*, 1920, Private Collection, oil on board, 12½ x 15¾ inches

THE OPPENHEIMERS WERE REUNITED in Manchester in time for Christmas in 1918. They returned to Kirkcudbright from Whalley Range in January or February the following year. It was during this period that Oppenheimer finally left the family firm.

The mosaic business had rested in Ludwig Jnr.'s hands during 1917 and 1918. Ludwig Jnr. retired and Albert took over full control with Lehmann's son, Eric, who had also returned from active service on the Western Front. A Lieutenant with the Lancashire Regiment, Eric changed his name to Newton, his mother's maiden name in response to continuing anti-German sentiment, which remained evident in the 1919 General Election and immediate post war period.[40] A description of these changes is contained in the appendix about Ludwig Oppenheimer Ltd.

Oppenheimer's involvement with Kirkcudbright Town Council resumed when he attended his first meeting after just less than four years of absence. Records show that he did not miss a meeting during his remaining tenure of office. Late in March he was appointed to the Council's Committee for Peace Celebrations in the town. In May, his formal motion before the authority saved ash trees on Moatbrae from being chopped down; they were pruned of dead wood instead. In August, he was involved in a site visit about a water scheme and also in promoting the cause of ex-servicemen.

Oppenheimer was a man of conviction. Firmly on the side of free trade, strongly in support of votes for women, he was a determined supporter of the rights of returning soldiers, sailors and airmen. Oppenheimer had become the Chairman of the Kirkcudbright Post of the Comrades of the Great War[41] and on 25 June 1919 he had given notice of a motion for the July meeting 'that the Council strongly recommends that all employers of labour within the Burgh, who have not already done so, should offer to reinstate ex-servicemen in the position they held before joining the forces and that all appointments temporarily made during the War should now be cancelled and the posts permanently filled where practicable by ex-servicemen'.[42] At the meeting on 30 July the Council received a deputation of unemployed ex-servicemen. The discharged

40 Eric (Oppenheimer) Newton 1893–1965, mosaic artist and art critic for the *Sunday Times* from 1947 to 1951 and *The Guardian* 1956–65

41 The Comrades of the Great War became the Royal British Legion in 1921

42 Minutes of Kirkcudbright Town Council, 25 June 1919, Minute Book, Stewartry Museum

soldiers and sailors presented a petition to the Council. After the debate that ensued Oppenheimer's motion was passed.

The issue did not rest there. Oppenheimer wrote formally to the Council in late August drawing attention to one ex-serviceman who had not been reinstated and to certain offices within the Council's prerogative, temporarily filled during the War, that had not been vacated. The Council Minute of the 27 August meeting concluded that the Town Clerk, John Gibson, would write to the employers concerned and that Oppenheimer's letter should lie on the table. It was recorded that after 'some discussion' on the motion the Provost proposed that a Committee be appointed, of which Oppenheimer was not to be a member, 'to consider any such letters hereafter received by the Town Clerk and to decide whether or not they should be brought before the Council.[43]

Clearly there had been a row. Oppenheimer was not going to let the matter lie on or be left on, or brushed under any table. The Council's correspondence book includes a copy of a letter that the Town Clerk sent to Oppenheimer on 21 August referring to a conversation at the Town Hall about the relief of ex-servicemen from Entertainment Tax. Gibson could do nothing as this was a matter for the Inland Revenue in Dumfries, but he did enclose the relevant forms. Oppenheimer was unimpressed by his colleagues' lukewarm responses. Perhaps he had unrealistic expectations. The Entertainment Tax was indeed a national rather than local government matter. Nevertheless he resigned from the Town Council by letter on 13 September. He declared that he had not taken this step 'without careful consideration'. However he found himself 'too completely out of sympathy with the bulk of the Council in their attitude towards unemployed ex-servicemen'.[44]

Ex-servicemen and women did not fare well in many other communities in the 1920s. Oppenheimer's actions were principled but he must have regretted leaving a body that had kept him in touch with home when on war service at the front. Oppenheimer did not stand for election to a public authority again. It was not however to be the last occasion on which he crossed swords with the local authority in Kirkcudbright.

More fortunate than many of his fellow servicemen on their return from the war, Oppenheimer could either resume at Ludwig Oppenheimer Limited or revive self-employment in painting. His intentions were made clear during the five exhibition seasons from 1915 to 1919. With the help of his wife and family when he was at the front, his work was shown thirty six times at the Royal Academy, the Royal Scottish Academy, the Manchester Academy, the Royal Scottish Society of Painters in Watercolours and the Royal Glasgow Institute of Fine Art. The pictures were of both Kirkcudbright and northern Italy.[45] Two Italian watercolours

43 Minutes of Kirkcudbright Town Council, 27 August 1919, Minute Book, Stewartry Museum, Kirkcudbright

44 Charles Oppenheimer to John Gibson, Town Clerk, Kirkcudbright Town Council Correspondence Book, 13 September 1919, Stewartry Museum, Kirkcudbright

45 Some were exhibited more than once. The RSW did not see his work in 1917, 1918 and 1919 and Manchester in 1918 and 1919.

Plate 24 | *The Duck Pond*, 1920, Private Collection, oil on board, 12½ x 15¾ inches

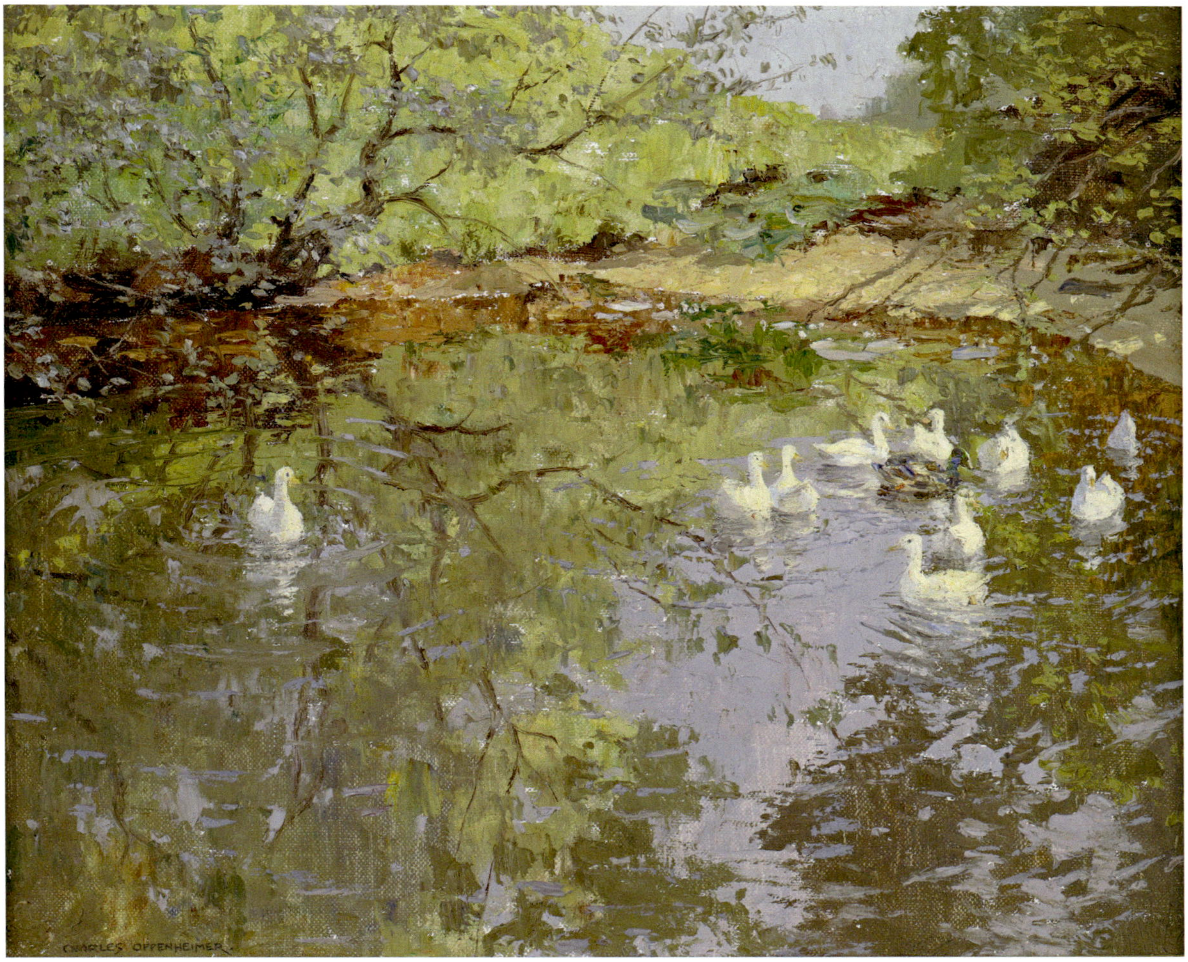

Sunrise Pisa and *Florence* were sold at the RSA in 1917 and 1918 doubtless a welcome supplement to a gunner's pay.

Now he began new work. *Autumn Gold* [pl.23] and *The Duck Pond* [pl.24] were painted in the later part of 1919 and exhibited at Manchester and in Glasgow and Edinburgh the following year.

The Duck Pond is a painterly, impressionist treatment of a shaded farm pond. Unusual in its colours the white of the domestic ducks draws the eye to and fro across the work. *The Scotsman*'s critic declared the painting to be 'a charmingly sensitive rendering' of sunshine on a pond of which 'the feeling is more lyrical and spontaneous and less obviously controlled by a pre-conceived style or preference of expression'. *Autumn Gold* is an early treatment of a repeated theme of later years. A bend in the river reflects the burnished gold of the autumn leaves on the trees that shade the stream. The far bank shelters a salmon or sea trout en route to the spawning redds. A brown trout hovers in the current awaiting an insect trapped in the surface of the water.

Oppenheimer's passion, other than his art, was angling. He took the fisherman's eye to the water's edge. An acute and accurate observer of nature, he was never more proficient in expressing her many moods than in the reflections on the water that he painted of the streams and rivers of Galloway and Speyside. Oppenheimer seldom came home empty handed. A sketch, a painting en plein air or a fish or two in his basket defined his day out in the countryside he loved.

It is a far cry from Manchester to Speyside but Oppenheimer must have discovered the area on one of his many journeys to, and holidays in his mother's home town of Montrose. A Mr and Mrs Oppenheimer are recorded in *The Scotsman* in August and September 1911 as catching a number of trout on Loch Ericht and at Dalwhinnie, on two occasions Mrs Oppenheimer having more in her basket than her husband. In July 1912 a Mr Oppenheimer is said to have caught a 4lb ferox trout on the loch on the last day of the month. In both years the couple were staying at the Truimbank Private Hotel in Newtonmore. If resident for a month they would have shared the hotel's comforts with Prince Sardar Singh Maharajah of Aliwar and his entourage who arrived on the 17 August.[46]

The Calder at Newtonmore appears in Oppenheimer's oeuvre in 1933 and twenty years later. A 1930s watercolour *The Silver Winding Spey* [pl.25] is a striking view of the upper reaches of the river lit by sunlight through clouds on a type of day very familiar to those who know Speyside. Blue tinted hills behind Newtonmore form the backdrop to the scene with an outline instantly recognisable to any traveller on the nearby road to Inverness.

Critical attention was soon drawn to Oppenheimer's work on the resumption of his post war career. The *Manchester Guardian*[47] claimed that he was 'one of the most individual artists in the Academy'. He was 'less successful in his large picture than in much smaller ones as the very attractive *Little Water Mill* at the city's Academy exhibition in 1922. On 8 December of that year, at a meeting in the RSA Galleries in Edinburgh, Oppenheimer was elected by his peers to membership of the Scottish Society of Scottish Artists and *The Scotsman* a day later reported that, among the landscapes, those by 'Charles Oppenheimer and the late John Campbell Mitchell RSA are the most distinctive.'

The *Glasgow Herald* devoted a long piece to a one man show that Oppenheimer held in Taylor and Brown's gallery at 136 St Vincent Street in Glasgow in September 1923.[48] 'Mr Oppenheimer has a keen eye for nature in her most attractive moods, and his landscapes, which are numerous in the present collection, are characterised by a freshness of outlook and true poetic feeling that give them a peculiar charm.'

'He delights in sunny landscapes and radiant skies, but never allows the predilections to degenerate into mannerism.' The article continued

46 The Truimbank Hotel was destroyed by fire on 3 April 1929. Rebuilt thereafter it remained a holiday destination for many years.

47 *Manchester Guardian*, April 1922

48 *Glasgow Herald*, 12 September 1923

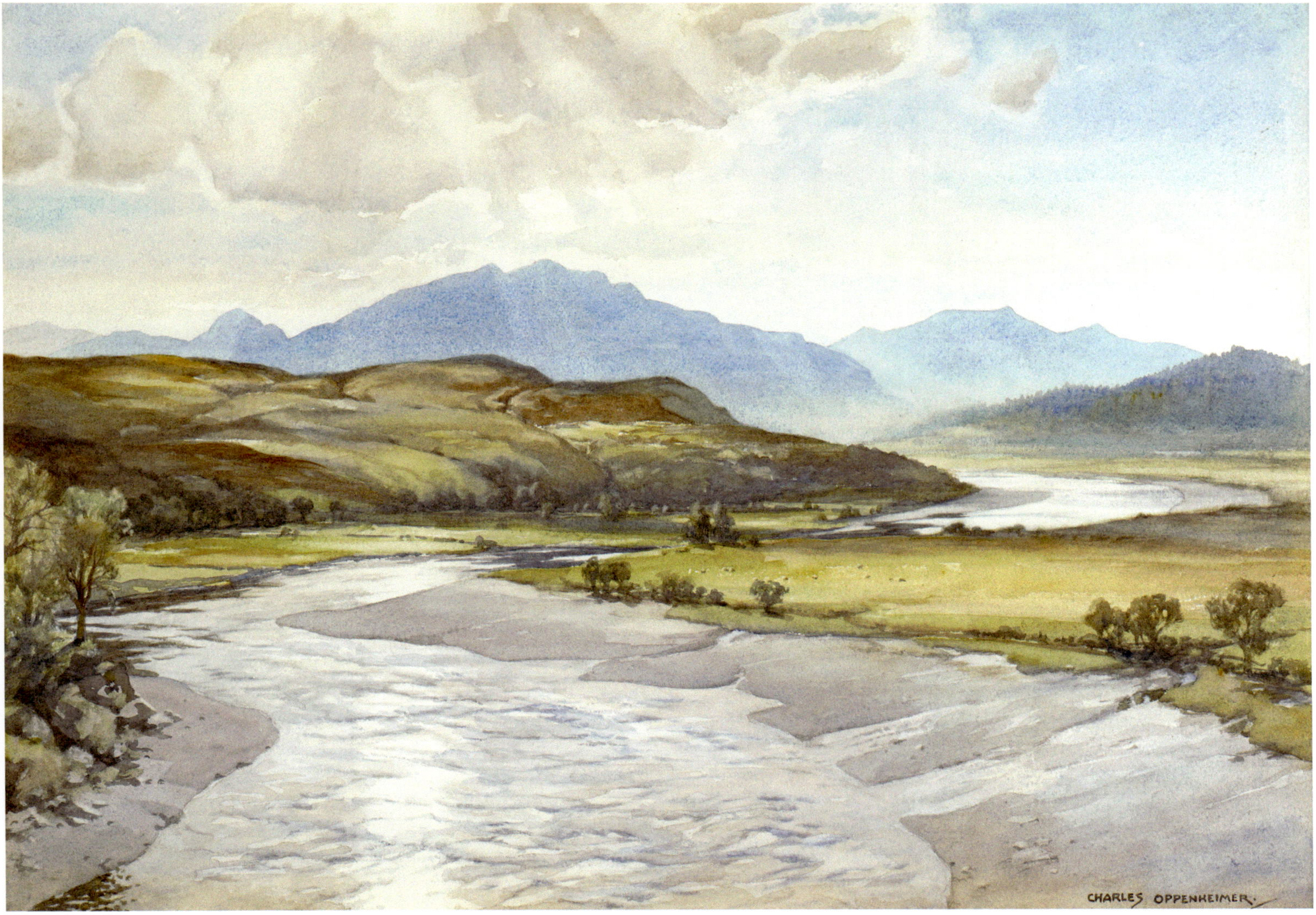

Plate 25 | *The Silver Winding Spey*, c.1935, Private Collection, watercolour, 15½ × 22 inches

that coastal scenes from around Kirkcudbright, moorland views in the Highlands and lowland landscapes strong in human interest formed the subject matter. 'Outstanding in the collection is a drawing entitled *The Farm Pool*, a notable picture which was seen at the last exhibition of the Royal Scottish Watercolours Society (sic) where it was given a prominent position. Very attractive also is *The Village Pool* a work which is poetic in spirit and vigorous in execution.' Other works mentioned for praise included *The Landmark*, a scene in Kirkcudbright Bay, *Clearing after Rain* and *San Miniato, Florence*. All remain as yet untraced.

Reviewing the RSA exhibition in May 1923 *The Scotsman* compared Oppenheimer's work to that of George Houston, a favourite artist among collectors in the west of Scotland. That same year *Evening, Lake Lucerne* [pl.26] was purchased by Manchester City Art Gallery and *Windsor Castle*, a watercolour was sold from the RSA exhibition in 1924. Support for greater prominence for Oppenheimer came when *Pond Lilies* was said to be 'excellently painted, but hanging too high' at the Royal Academy.[49]

In 1924 Oppenheimer gained two further distinctions. He became a member of the Council of the RSW serving for three years until the end of 1926. *Morning Mist – Lake of Lugano* [pl.27] demonstrates his dexterity in the medium. With minimal washes he conveys the morning mist over the lake and hints at the vastnesss and form of the landscape partly in cloud confirmed by the contrast with the figure and small boat in the foreground.

In the same year Oppenheimer was invited by Robert Burns RSA to contribute to the decoration of the Scottish Forestry Hall at the Wembley Exhibition. The Society of Scottish Artists had been approached by the organisers to carry out the work and Burns had been chosen to lead the project. Twenty seven panels were to be produced and it was Burns' inspiration that these should be in the style of the Bayeux Tapestry. Sir Robert Lorimer RSA, A.E. Borthwick and W.C. Crawford[50] were amongst the other contributors and the panels were displayed at Aitken and Dott's gallery in Edinburgh on 8 April for just that day before their journey south.

Oppenheimer undertook a double panel measuring ten feet by five feet, selecting an appealing local subject for the people of his home town *St Cuthbert lands at Kirkcudbright in the Seventh Century*. The *Dumfries Standard* described the work as treated 'with verve and great decorative effect'. Oppenheimer had clearly been 'thoroughly imbued with his subject'.

> *On the right of the double panel, standing on the shore is seen St Cuthbert, wearing a bishop's cope and mitre, and carrying his pastoral staff. Immediately behind him are two acolytes and an attendant monk, the latter bearing the head of St Oswald, the martyr King of Northumbria. In the background is seen an archaic vessel from which the Saint has landed. On board the vessel, with its single mast and yard, are seen the sailors furling the sails. On the left of the panel are seen a group of Picts, who welcome the Saint and kneel to receive his blessing. Mr Oppenheimer's conception of the patron saint of Kirkcudbright is a very fine one, the figure bearing an air of great benignity. Both subject and treatment will no doubt attract attention. The whole is surrounded by an archaic border of grotesques, which helps greatly in the way of carrying out the formal treatment.*[51] [pl.28]

Association with the project did indeed bring Oppenheimer further attention but it also illustrated a certain versatility in his work. Experience in the mosaic business helped with both the conception and execution of the Panel. The influence of Willis and Crane and a Manchester education are evident.

Oppenheimer had no less than seven paintings at Manchester in 1924.

49 *The Scotsman*, 10 May 1924

50 Sir Robert Stoddart Lorimer ARA RSA (1864–1929), brother of John Henry Lorimer RSA RSW RWS ROI (1856–1936); Alfred Edward Borthwick PRSW RBA RSA (1871–1955); William Caldwell Crawford PSSA (1879–1960)

51 *Dumfries Standard*, 9 April 1924

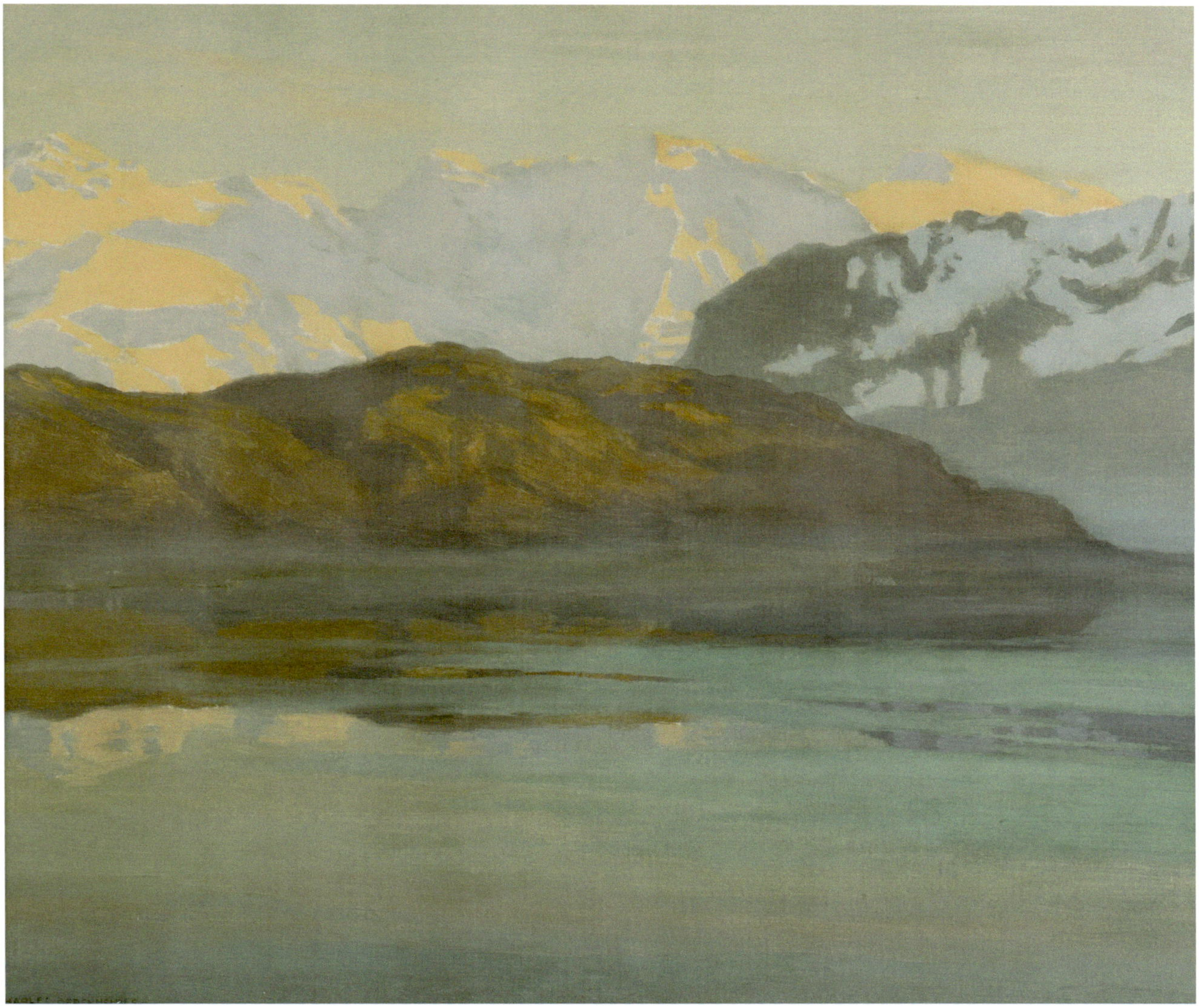

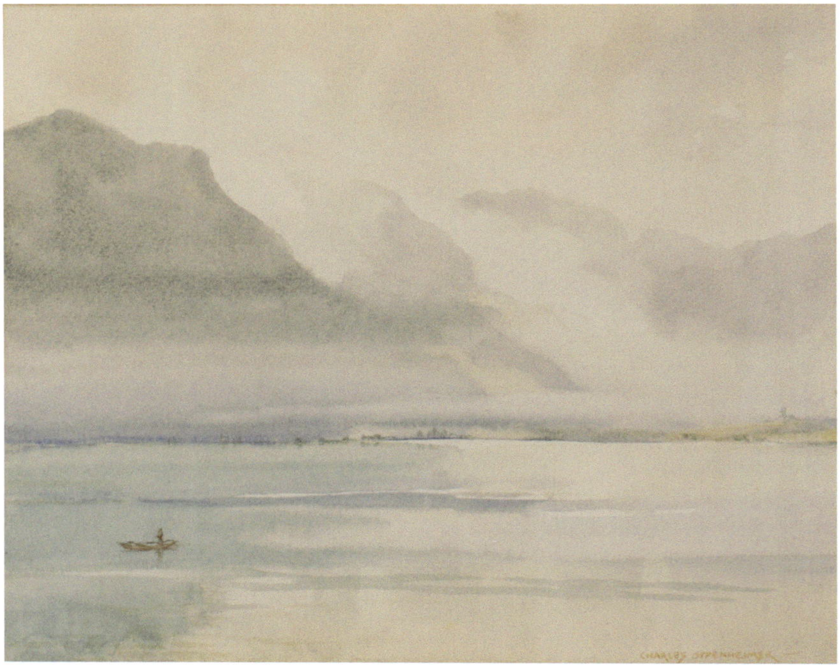

Plate 26 | *Evening, Lake Lucerne*, 1922, Manchester Art Gallery, oil on canvas, 25 x 30 inches

Plate 27 | *Morning Mist – Lake of Lugano* c.1925, Private Collection, watercolour, 11½ x 9 inches

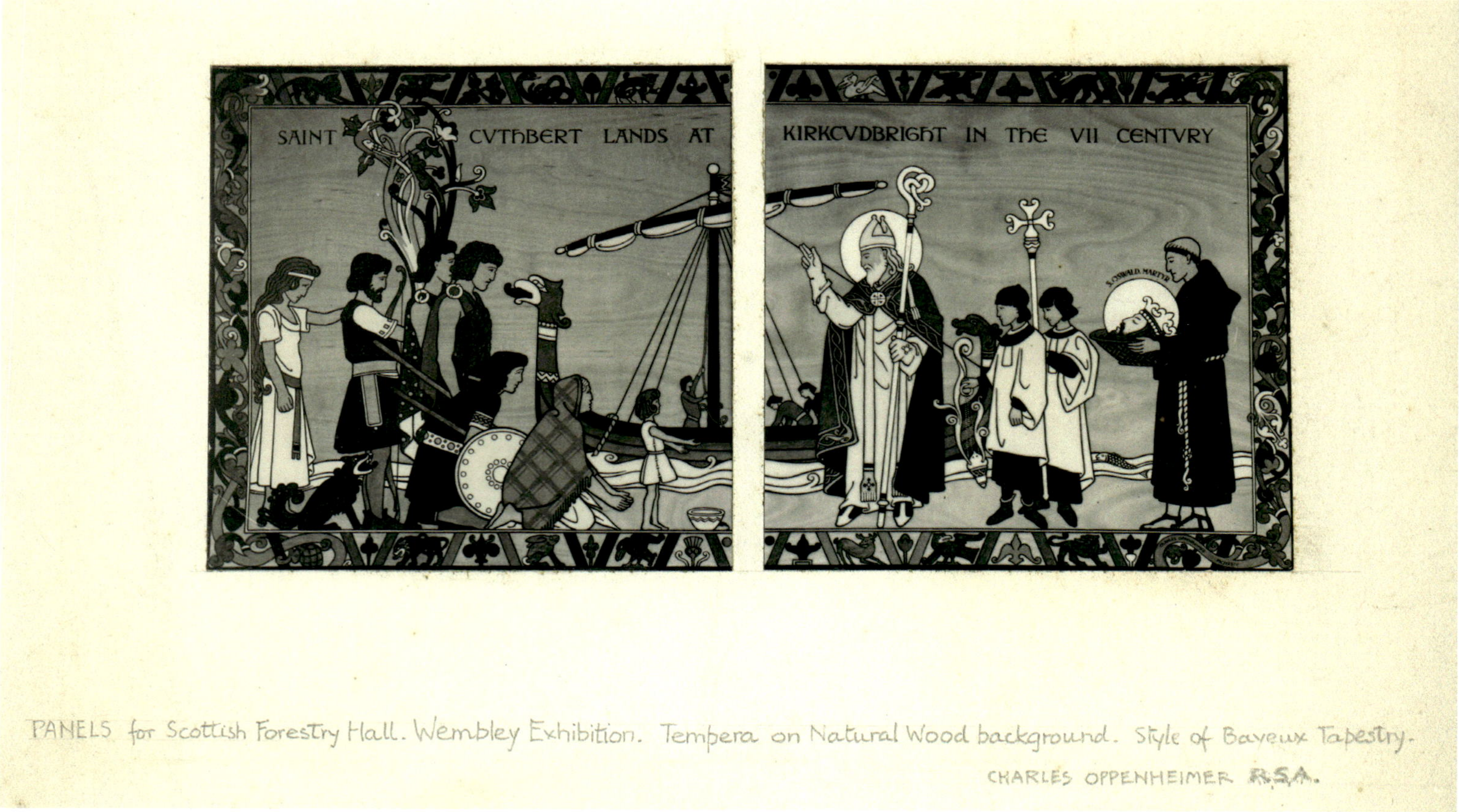

Plate 28 | *St Cuthbert lands at Kirkcudbright in the Seventh Century,* for the Scottish Forestry Hall, Wembley Exhibition, 1924, courtesy of the Stewartry Museum, Kirkcudbright

The *Manchester City News* remarked that the tonal values of *The Last of the Snow* and *At the Gloaming* were produced without loss of colour. The 'mist of evening and luminous sky' was praised as 'the treatment of honest brushwork'. *Kirkcudbright by Moonlight* [pl.29] was painted in 1924. A wonderful rendering of snow covered allotments and the buildings adjacent to the Tolbooth, the scene is bathed in a silvery white light. A single window glows gold with the warmth of a home within. The same device was used in the large canvas, *Kirkcudbright* [pl.16] in the collection of Manchester Art Gallery mentioned on page 43 above. The last rays of the sun bathe the estuary and the old town in yellows and reds. The light from the hearths and lamps offer the promise of warmth and company as night draws in.

By the mid-1920s Charles Oppenheimer's career as an artist was securely re-established. He had work from commissions and his paintings were a focus of critical attention. An example comes from the notes by Roberta Glasgow in the Liverpool Autumn Exhibition catalogue of 1926. She advised the visitor to notice Oppenheimer's *Jungfrau* 'a worthy interpretation of the great mountain'. She then described one of Oppenheimer's fortes, namely his ability to convey sunlight and shadow

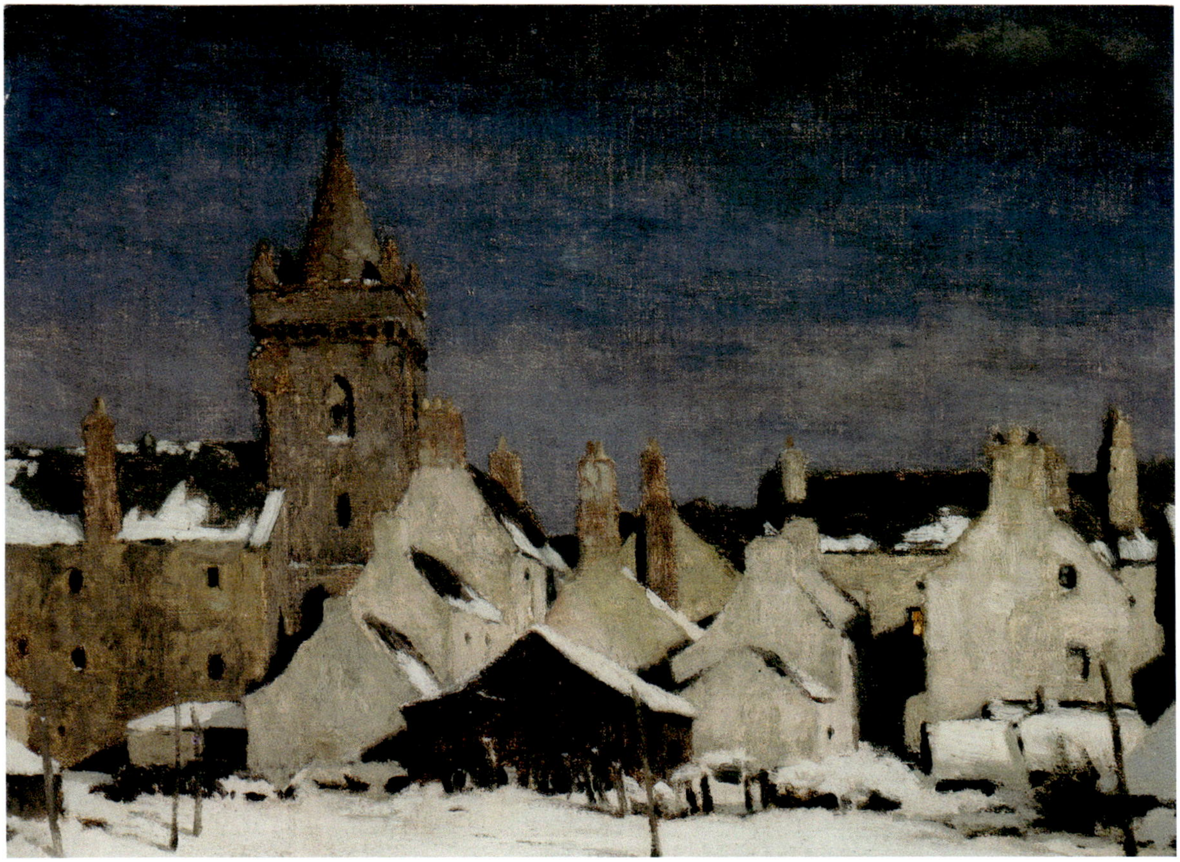

Plate 29 | *Kirkcudbright by Moonlight*, 1924, Bourne Fine Art, oil on canvas, 18 × 24 inches

on snow in paint. 'The afternoon is evidently getting round on to the western face and the well known rock shapes are in warm light. The reflection on the shadow sides of the snow is almost yellow in comparison with the blue of the cast shadows. This facility is seen again in *Snow in the Fields*, a Kirkcudbright scene dating from the late 1920s. Here it is the middle of the day and the winter's day's colours are vivid and the road ahead is inviting as the warmth of the sun makes the walk all the more pleasurable.'

Yet greater recognition and of a substantial kind came to Oppenheimer in March 1927 when he was elected an Associate of the Royal Scottish Academy.

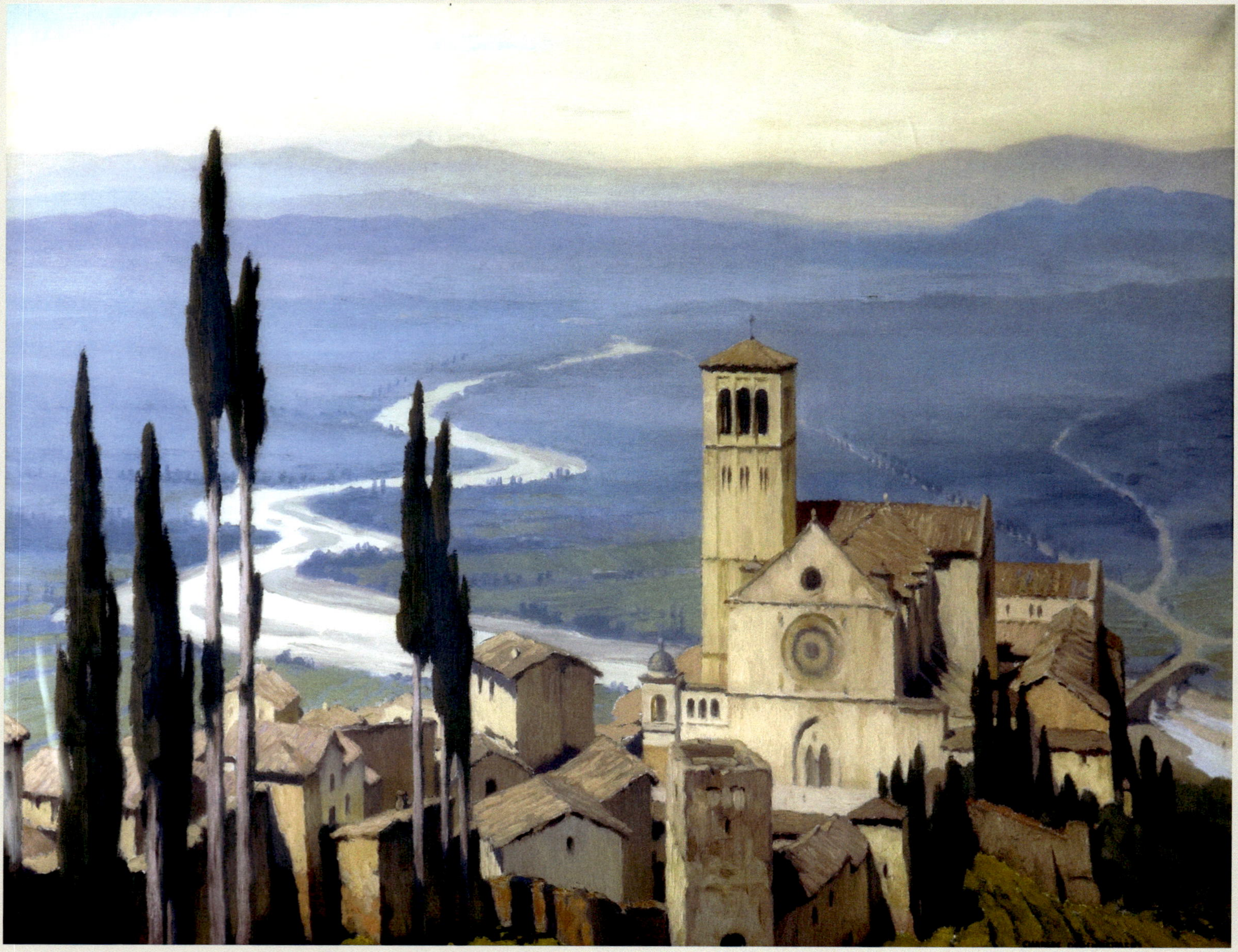

7 THE FUSION OF COLOUR

Plate 30 | *San Francesco, Assisi*, 1930s, by kind permission of the University of Liverpool, Victoria Gallery and Museum, oil on canvas, 22½ x 35½ inches

THE COUNTRYSIDE of Galloway and the town of Kirkcudbright provided Oppenheimer with the inspiration for many of his paintings. A catalogue raisonné of his work would feature many a picture such as *The Tolbooth and Old Town, Kirkcudbright* [pl.31] and *Mill on the Dee* [pl.32]. There were however very different landscapes, both rural and urban, with buildings more venerable and venerated that were of immense significance in Oppenheimer's artistic career and his oeuvre. Italy was as much his muse as Galloway.

The light and colour of Italy, the grace, elegance and substance of her architectural heritage and the warmth of the climate are to be found in paintings which Oppenheimer exhibited throughout the five decades of his professional career from 1910. His association with and affection for Italy began in his youth when, aged twenty one in 1896, he won a cash prize which allowed him to travel to Florence and Venice. He was captivated.

His family were well acquainted with northern Italy. In the 1860s Ludwig, his father, is reputed to have studied mosaic design and manufacture in Venice. The Oppenheimer business may have had Italian clients. It is possible too that there were friends or at least business or professional connections in Venice and the Veneto with whom the young Oppenheimer stayed or by whom he was entertained. His eldest brother, Lehmann, had by family account also travelled in Italy at the age of twenty one in 1890.

Returning for a second visit in 1898, Charles Oppenheimer disembarked at Naples and took time to explore the eastern part of the country passing through Rome before returning again to Florence. Whether Oppenheimer encountered any professional artists on his two trips is not known. Italy was a place of pilgrimage for many but at that time his motivation was to study mosaics.

A close artist friend in later life in Kirkcudbright, William Robson, had had a studio in Florence before moving to the isle of Capri. Robson had returned home to Edinburgh in 1896 with his wife, Carmella, a native of Capri. They eventually settled in Kirkcudbright in 1904 just less than

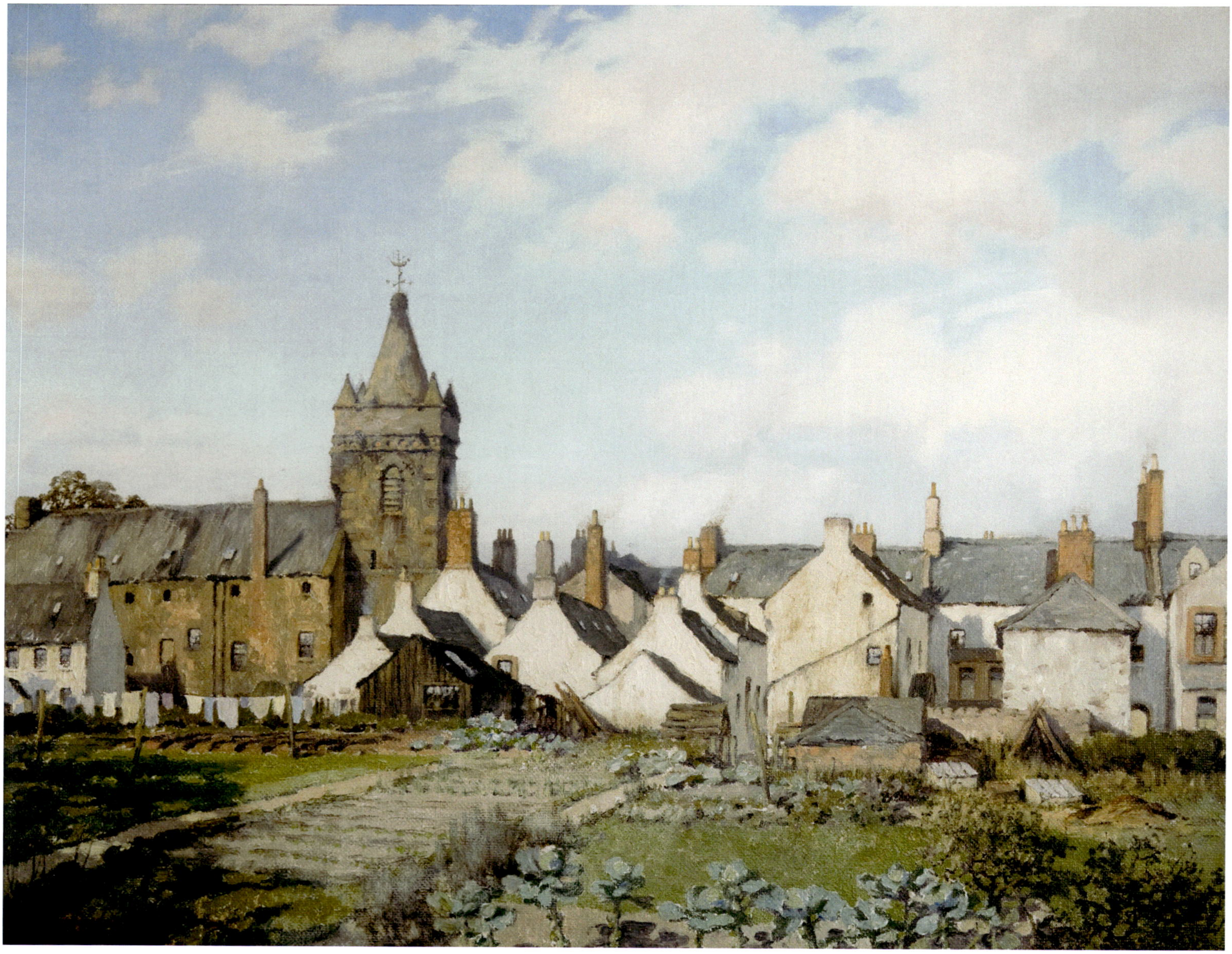

Plate 31 | *The Tolbooth and Old Town, Kirkcudbright* c.1935,
Bourne Fine Art, oil on canvas, 23 × 30 inches

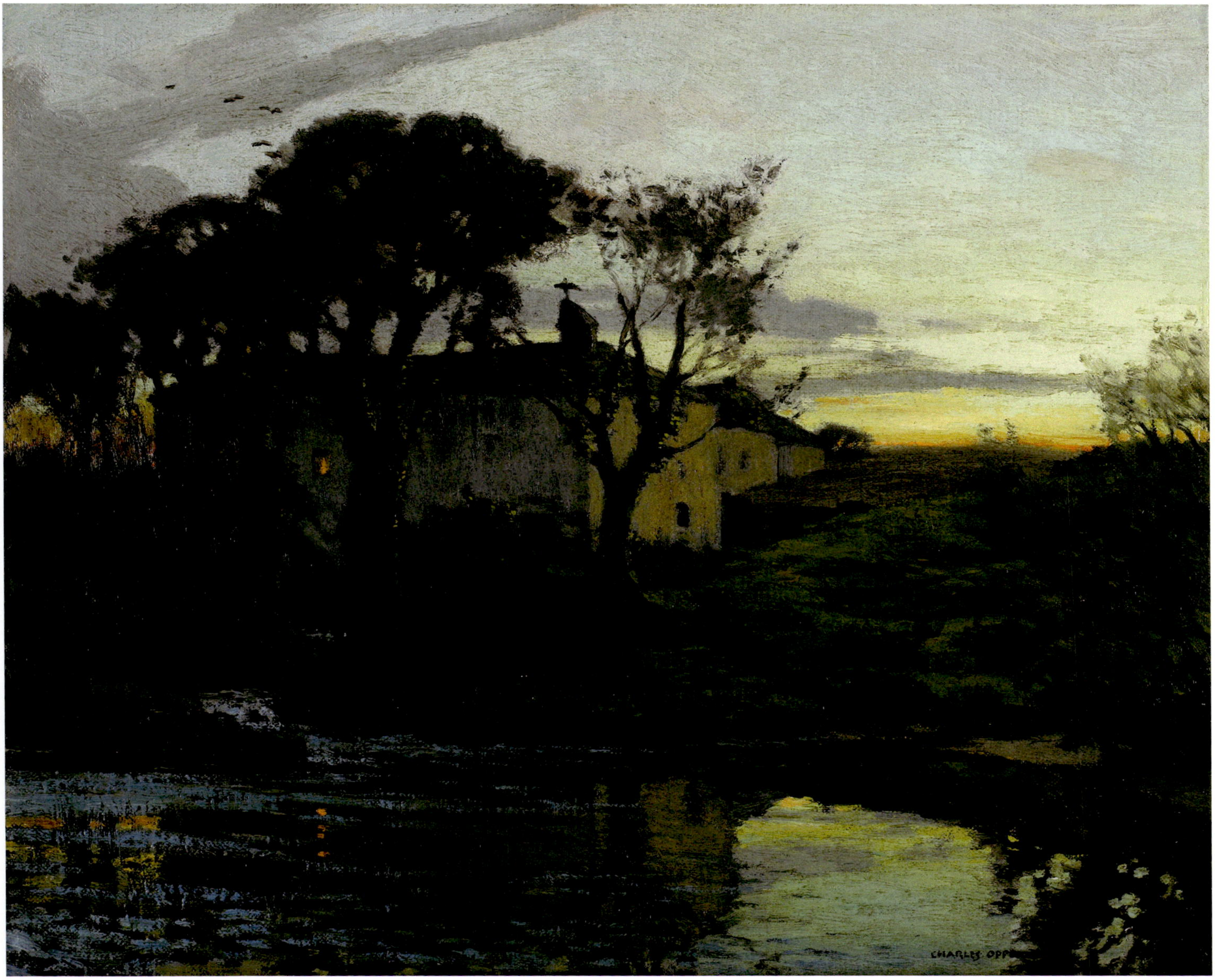

Plate 32 | *Mill on the Dee*, c.1930,
Bourne Fine Art, oil on canvas, 16 × 20 inches

five years before the Oppenheimers. The closeness of their relationship must have been underpinned by shared experience of Italy. Carmella Robson never learned more than a few words of English. Her husband was fluent in Italian and the Oppenheimers, if not fluent, probably had a conversational command of the language.

As mentioned earlier, Oppenheimer exhibited a picture entitled *The Lion of St Mark, Venice* at the Manchester Academy in 1898. It most probably dated from his 1896 travels and must have been an oil painting of a fair size as he asked £31 10/ – for the work, a not insubstantial sum for a student or associate. There is no record as yet uncovered as to whether Oppenheimer returned to Italy in the five years after 1898. Oral family history suggests that he and Connie travelled to Venice after their marriage in 1903. A watercolour of Venice dated 1904 seems to confirm this. They could live cheaply, explore, enjoy the culture and climate and Oppenheimer could draw and paint. It is conceivable that they were both in Italy in 1910 or 1911 as a watercolour *St Marks, Venice – the Baptistry* was exhibited at the RSW exhibition in 1912. The exhibition opened at the end of September in the RSA galleries on the Mound in Edinburgh. Possibly a picture from years before, it would have been a tight deadline to secure its inclusion fresh from the important tour of Italy that Oppenheimer undertook with fellow Gallovidian artist, William Stewart MacGeorge RSA in the summer of 1912.

The diminutive MacGeorge was a native of Castle Douglas. Born in 1861, he had trained in Edinburgh and Antwerp with Hornel and lived for a number of years in Kirkcudbright. MacGeorge shared a studio at Castlemains with Glasgow artist, David Gauld, a regular visitor to the town. MacGeorge clearly influenced Oppenheimer's painting in a critical period of the latter's development. Fourteen years his senior, Oppenheimer found MacGeorge a good travelling companion. Connie Oppenheimer was equally fond of her husband's friend, describing him as 'a lovely little man'. Neat, well presented, even dapper in his early years, MacGeorge's portrait in watercolour [pl.33] was sketched by Oppenheimer in 1913. Presented in 1932 to the Scottish National Portrait Gallery after MacGeorge's death, Oppenheimer replied to Stanley Cursiter, the Gallery Director's letter of thanks from 14 High Street on 23 June:

> *I am very pleased that your Board of Trustees has accepted the drawing of MacGeorge as he was in 1913. He was full of vigour and enthusiasm in those days and I think the best of his work was done about then.*

That vigour and enthusiasm is evident in both artists' paintings from their Italian travels of 1912. They journeyed by train throughout northern Italy. A substantial amount of time seems to have been devoted to Venice and Verona. However, Florence, Pisa, Lucca Nervi near Genoa and

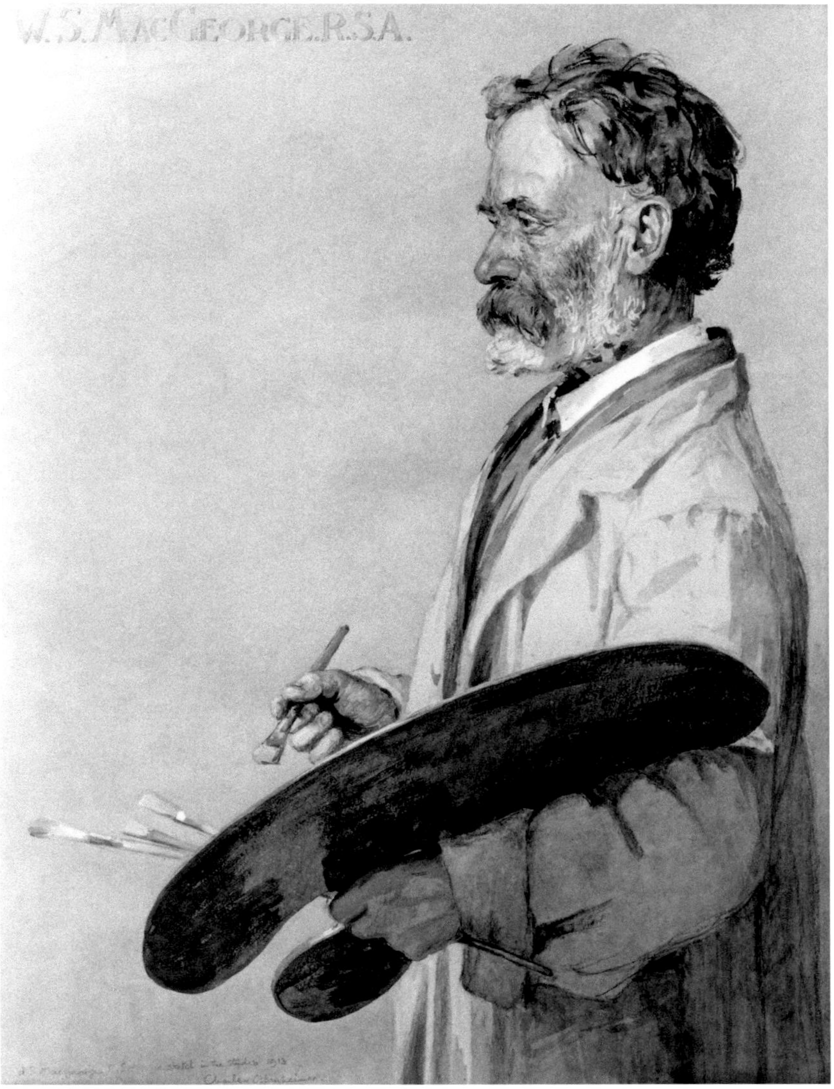

Plate 33 | *William Stewart MacGeorge, 1861–1931*, 1913, Scottish National Portrait Gallery, watercolour, 19¾ x 15¾ inches

Milan were also on the itinerary. In addition the pair explored southern Switzerland staying at Lugano and Zermatt. The exact order is uncertain but in artistic terms Verona and Venice were of primary importance. *On the Guidecca* [pl.36] was painted by Oppenheimer in Venice in 1912 or just possibly 1914. The lagoon waters are calm, reflecting the bright sunlight. It is hot, the middle of the day and siesta time. There are not many sounds except perhaps the occasional creaking of timbers as the barges and boats rise and rub on themselves and the quayside and then fall back gently on the swell of a faint breeze or the ripple from an occasional passing vessel.

MacGeorge and Oppenheimer exhibited the fruits of what one paper described as their pilgrimage to Italy in the 1913 exhibition season. MacGeorge chose Doig, Wilson and Wheatley's gallery at 90 George Street

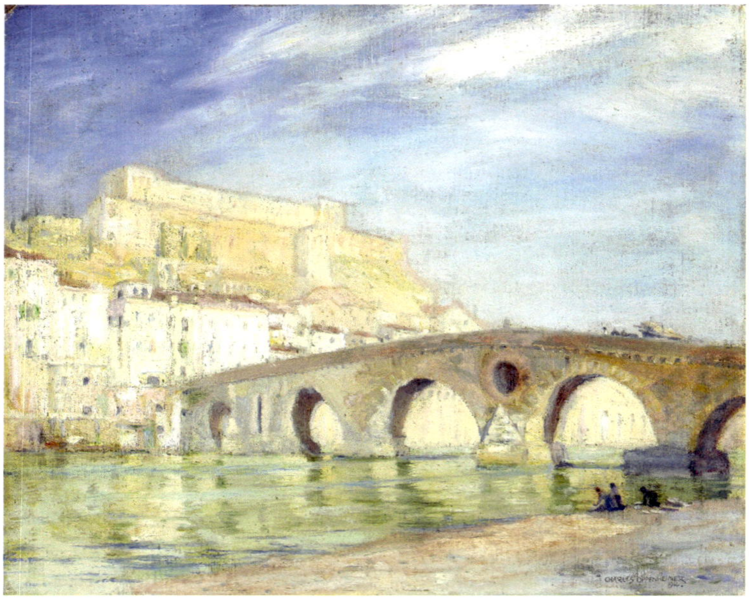

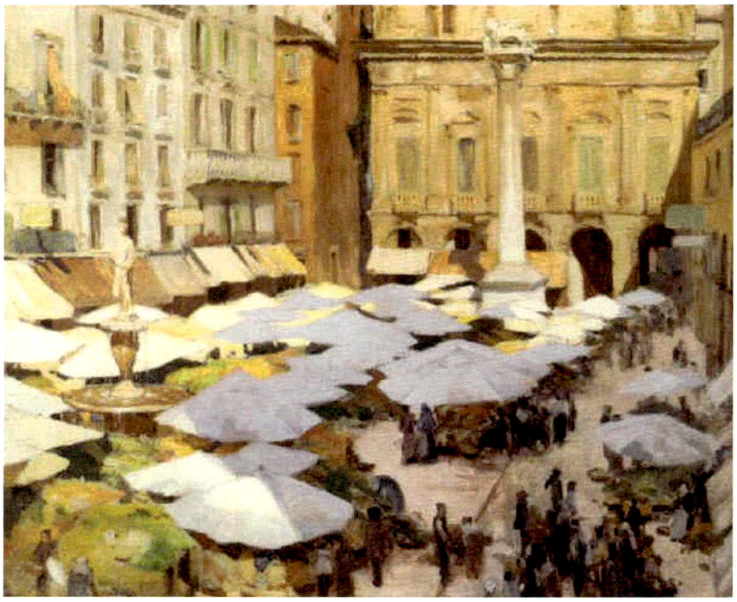

Plate 34 | *Verona*, 1914, Bourne Fine Art, oil on canvas, 16 × 20 inches

Plate 35 | *From a Verona Balcony*, 1912, courtesy of New Orleans Auction Galleries, Inc., oil on canvas, 20 × 24 inches

to show 'Oil Sketches of Venice, Verona and North Italy' coinciding with the RSA's Annual Exhibition. Oppenheimer preceded him in February with a one man show of fifty two paintings in the Sauchiehall Street galleries of George Davidson Limited in Glasgow. The review in the *Glasgow Herald* of 12 February helped to establish Oppenheimer as an artist of considerable note in Scotland and was a landmark of vital importance in his early professional career. The reviewer began by referring to Oppenheimer's 1910 watercolour exhibition in the same gallery. He observed a considerable contrast in subject matter and colour. Here was 'a pictorial pageant' of Venice's palaces, churches, canals and the lagoon.

> *Mr Oppenheimer's work impresses by way of its distinguished draughtsmanship and a refined sense of colour. Every one of these pictures possesses exhilarating sparkle and there is subtle restraint in colouring: there are none of those lurid splashes which give some pictures of Italy the effect of mere garishness.*

The critic was especially taken by an interior of St Mark's calling it 'an exceptionally fine rendering'. Oppenheimer was particularly praised because the 'marbles and precious mosaics are suggested with real skill and never obtrusively and the soft yet luminous golden colour filling the vaulted roof contributes to make a fascinating harmony'. Oppenheimer's mastery of colour is discussed. 'No colour is more elusive or more difficult to control; a touch too many may transform the yellow into dingy muddy alloy. It is a tribute to Mr Oppenheimer's colour judgement that he knew the crucial stage when the brush must be arrested and the glamour secured.'

Turning to other pictures, the critic continued 'skies and waters are full of tenderness and radiant with light and atmosphere, suggestive of that drowsy felicity which belongs to life in these pleasant places'. … Oppenheimer] 'uses all his colours effectively and his harmonies of blue and white, as in *The Mischabel* are delicious'.

Not everyone is privileged to bask in the sunshine of Italy, the article concluded:

> *But it is something to be able to step out of the strenuous streets of this city of grey skies and spell winds into these cosy galleries and feast the eye on the lovely scenes Mr Oppenheimer so vividly depicts. With the aid of a decent amount of imagination a spectator may even persuade himself that he catches the salt breeze of the lagoon, and before these shining palaces, picturesque canals and the Alps under shimmering skies he may forget, at least for a little while, the bleak streets of St Mungo.*

In the many articles on art in the Edwardian and Georgian Glasgow press there can have been few that were so full of praise. No record survives as to how many of the pictures sold but the one man show was most likely a commercial success given its prominence in the press.

The 1914 exhibition of the Royal Scottish Society of Painters in Watercolour was held jointly with the Glasgow Art Club in the McLellan Galleries from February to April. Of the three Oppenheimers present, two were of Kirkcudbright and one of Verona. *On the Dee, Kirkcudbright* priced at £80 was an ambitious catalogue price for a watercolour even for an RSW member. The three pictures at the RSA and the sole Royal Academy entry were all Italian scenes. *From a Verona Balcony* [pl.35] and *St Mark's Venice* travelled north to Edinburgh from Manchester unsold. The *Manchester City News* declared that *From a Verona Balcony* 'has light and space and air and we like it better than his more important and ambitious contribution, *St Mark's Venice*. We like him better still when he is treating homely rural subjects in the J.F. Millet vein'. The Scottish critics were more enthusiastic. 'An important architectural subject, carried out on a large scale alike with industry and talent, by Mr Charles Oppenheimer, Edinburgh [sic], is the interior of St Mark's Venice. The stately pile has been impressively rendered. The draughtsmanship is accomplished and the subdued lighting exceedingly pictorial.'

The *Kirkcudbright Advertiser* said that *St Mark's, Venice* 'is the best work we have seen from [Oppenheimer's] hand. This is one of the paintings which lend so much dignity and character to the Royal Scottish Academy exhibition'.[52]

Oppenheimer returned to Italy in 1914 where he painted *Verona* [pl.34] a vibrant near impressionist study of the town in full sunshine. He was back regularly after the Great War and exhibited both watercolours and oils especially of the north of the country through to the 1950s.

52 *Kirkcudbright Advertiser*, 15 May 1914

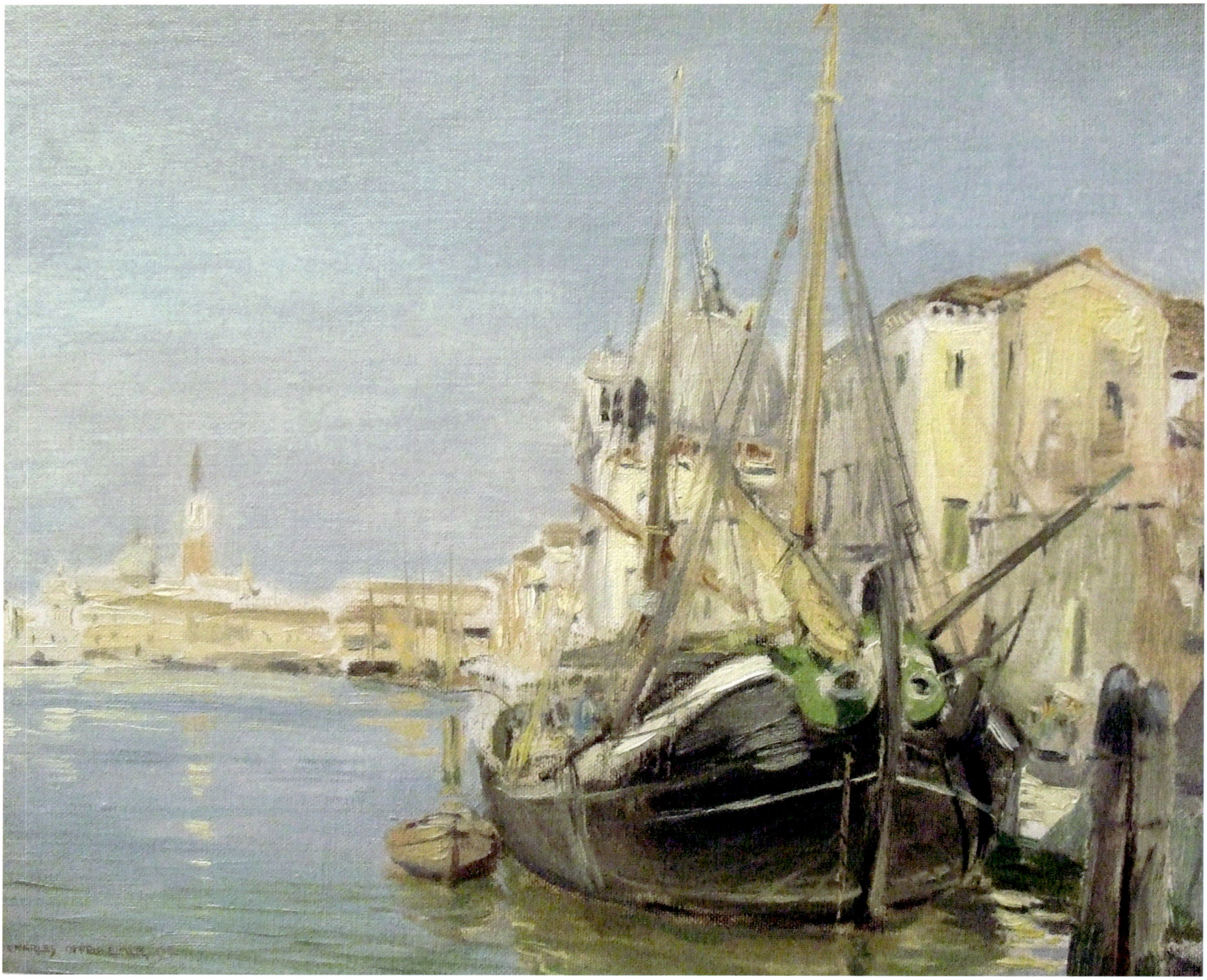

Plate 36 | *On the Guidecca*, c.1912, Private Collection, oil on canvas, 12 × 15½ inches

Oppenheimer's method was to draw and to sketch his subject en plein air. He would either paint in the open and complete the picture in the studio or work on a blank canvas indoors from outdoor sketches annotated with observations about colour. All paintings were meticulously finished before being framed and made ready to fulfil commissions, for major exhibitions or to await a visitor to the studio.

Two 1912 oil paintings, *Piazza Erbe, Verona* [pl.37] and *From a Verona Balcony* feature prominently in his Academy and Institute entries in 1913 and 1914. *Piazza Erbe, Verona* was first in the Royal Scottish Academy in 1913 and then at the RGI a year later. A black and white image of this large and currently untraced work remained among Oppenheimer's possessions throughout his lifetime. The painting was in a Broughton House retrospective exhibition in 1981 and was snapped on a relative's an instamatic camera but the colour photo was slightly out of focus. *The Crowned Madonna*, an adapted Roman sculpture, stands on top of the Consignor fountain dating from 1368. The splashing water helps to emphasise the cool of the shade in the piazza. Bright sunshine floods the pale browns, fawns, golds and yellows that make up the walls of the houses and apartments that overlook the market. Washing hangs from black balcony railings and the painted shutters are like musical notes on a stave. Below, under white umbrellas, the traders prepare their stalls. It is early morning before people arrive in numbers for the day's business. The greens, reds, yellows and pinks of the produce make a sumptuous carpet of colour for the eye. Detail intrigues. What is the subject of the conversation between the man and woman to the left in the foreground? How scented are the lilies? Are the birds drinking or bathing in the fountain? Did Oppenheimer and MacGeorge rent a room overlooking this market scene little changed for decades and even longer?

Some sense of the colour and the painterly style of *Piazza Erbe* can be seen in *From a Verona Balcony*. A smaller work, it is less intimate, although still a particularly striking celebration of the piazza. The market is under way but it is later in the day. The Palazzo Mafia, Verona's only Baroque building dating from 1668, forms the backdrop. The sun is higher in the sky above the umbrellas and there is more of a throng in the timeless scene.

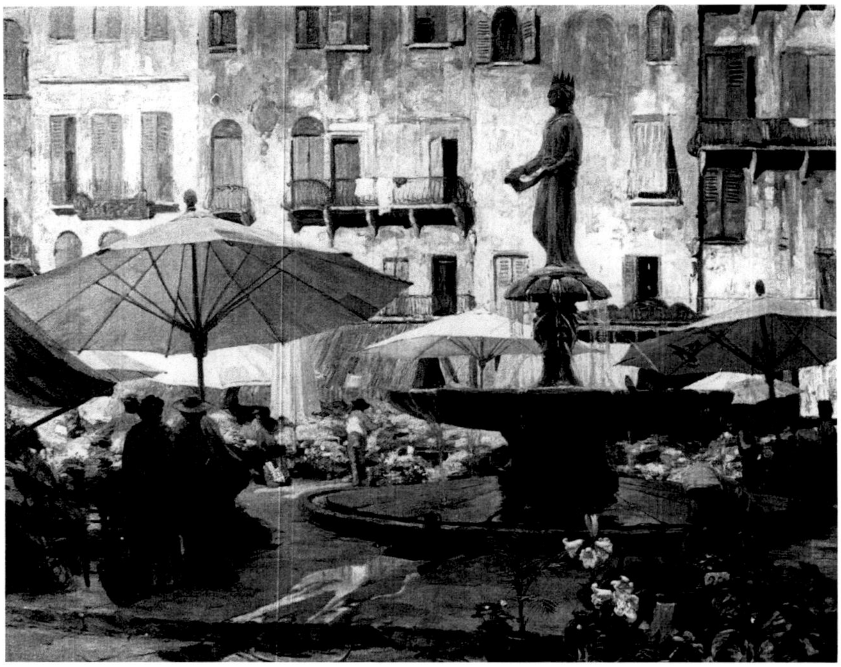

Plate 37 | *Piazza Erbe, Verona*, 1912, courtesy of the Stewartry Museum, Kirkcudbright

These two works together with *On the Guidecca* and *Verona* are key examples of Oppenheimer's earliest Italian style in oils. He captures the subtle blending of colours to transport the viewer to the warmth, the light and the grandeur of Italy. His painting is less linear and more expressive than in later years. In *Verona* it verges on the ambiguous in passages and he seems more concerned with light than form.

The war interrupted Oppenheimer's expeditions to Italy and to southern Switzerland. It would of course still have been possible to visit as Italy was an allied power and Switzerland neutral, but business and then active service intervened. Paintings from these foreign fields nevertheless populated Academy exhibitions, six out of ten Oppenheimers at the Manchester Academy in 1916 and 1917 for example. Two watercolours were sold at the RSA exhibitions of 1917 and 1918 at 18 guineas apiece to a Mrs Grahame of Woodbrae in Dunkeld, doubtless helping to sustain hearth and home in addition to military pay.

The Oppenheimers were back in Italy and southern Switzerland quite often during the 1920s and 1930s. The exact number of their visits is unrecorded but clearly there were many. In 1923, for example, new Italian subjects began to appear at exhibitions. *A Song of Venice*, untraced, was illustrated in the 1923 RGI catalogue. A collection of gondolas lit by lanterns float together of an evening, the gondoliers and their passengers listening to a recital by a chanteuse delivered from the prow of one of the boats.

Mary Evans recalled her uncle's advice when she and a friend planned an educational holiday in Venice and the Veneto. 'He said to stay on the Guidecca, or at least in that area, as it was inexpensive but well placed for visiting most parts of the city. Also he gave me a guide written in his own hand of everything to see in Venice: it was very comprehensive and must have taken many visits to compile'.[53]

If motivation was ever needed for another trip, there was stimulation enough in Kirkcudbright. William Robson's household in Twynholm and then at 51 High Street would bring ready reminders of the sights, smells and sounds of Italy. Robson and the Oppenheimers were often to be found together. It was open house in High Street if the lights were on and the curtains drawn back. Many a winter's night must have been warmed at the respective firesides and with the memories of Mediterranean climes, the Oppenheimers perhaps practising their Italian with the native speakers in the company. The cooking at 51 High Street was Italian, the ingredients coming from the Italian Warehouse store in Kirkcudbright at the time. Chianti bottles were seemingly recycled in Robson's garden as fern containers. *An Artist's Garden* [pl.38] was painted by Oppenheimer in the 1930s and includes Carmella Robson or

53 In conversation with Mary Evans, 19 February 2005

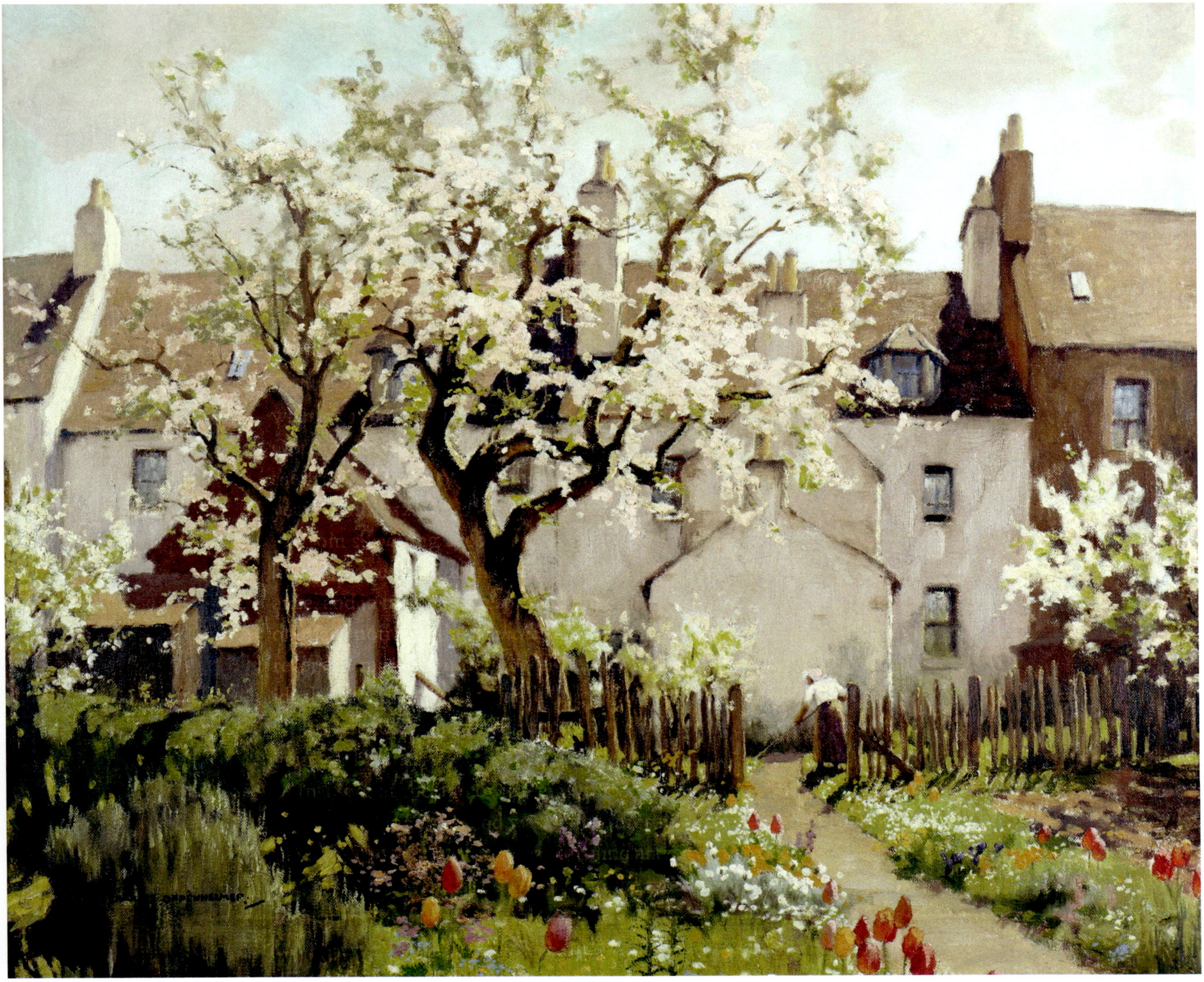

Plate 38 | *An Artist's Garden*, c.1927, The Ellis-Campbell Collection, oil on canvas, 22½ x 29¼ inches

possibly her sister, tending the kitchen garden at the back of the house.

On his trips to Italy, Oppenheimer liked to draw classical and Renaissance structures, monuments and buildings. He obviously had some trouble with the pace of contemporary Italian bureaucracy when seeking access to government controlled historic sites. He needed permits from the Ministry of Instruction to allow entry. In March 1928 wearied by experience, he asked James Paterson, President of the RSW and also a Royal Scottish Academician and its then Secretary, for proof of his credentials. 'My experience is that the more they can be impressed the quicker one gets the necessary permits'. Therefore could the President please 'use the paper with the Royal Arms or put the stamped seal of the Academy on it 'as that 'might save me time over there?'

Oppenheimer also asked Paterson to sign as an Academician and 'as the letters mean nothing to them, the titles of the Societies might be given in full'. Paterson duly obliged, the document was then endorsed by the Italian Consul and accompanied the artist to the continent.

The type of sketches that Oppenheimer made on such trips can be seen in *Palazzo Desdemona, Venice* [pl.39] and *Olive Garden, S. Domenico, Orvieto* [pl.40]. The former appears to have been carried out as preparation for a larger work of the same title. The latter is a charcoal drawing heightened by watercolour done en plein air.

Plate 39 | *Palazzo Desdemona, Venice*, c.1928, Private Collection, watercolour, 9½ × 10¼ inches

Plate 40 | *Olive Garden, S. Domenico, Orvieto*, c.1930, Bourne Fine Art, watercolour and pencil, 9 × 11½ inches

The fruits of Oppenheimer's labour were evident in a 1930 show at The Fine Art Society in Bond Street, London in October of that year. Eighty four pictures were on display, forty six of which were of Italian and southern Swiss scenes. The exhibition was not a great commercial success, only five paintings finding buyers at the time.[54] There appears to have been a reason if the London art critic of *The Scotsman* is to be believed. Commenting that this was Oppenheimer's first one man show in the capital, he described it as 'a most attractive collection'. His canvasses included 'characteristically sincere and charming views' of Kirkcudbright.

> *Mr Oppenheimer is always a careful designer and his landscapes are composed with a breadth and simplicity which is entirely satisfying. The mere manipulation of paint seems to afford him great satisfaction and the quality of his surfaces is always varied and delightful.*

The Italian landscapes were interesting and capably painted but the critic felt that Oppenheimer had not caught the spirit of the place as readily as he did in Kirkcudbright and Galloway. Oppenheimer had succumbed a little to the 'sugary picturesqueness of Italy'.

> *Even in some of his Scottish landscapes, the artist has allowed the force of his colour to be subdued by a too great dependence upon certain shades of cloying sweetness. Of these, one is a honeyed yellow such as one sees on haystacks when they are bathed in the warm light of the setting sun, another a cold virginal light seen in the shadows that objects cast upon the snow. These and like shades have a fatal tendency to find their way into Mr Oppenheimer's landscapes. Even the most starkly patterned and solid paintings would be weakened by the intrusion of colours like these, and they give a sentimental note to the landscapes of this gifted Scottish artist.*[55]

Examples of the yellows and yellow ochre colour that offended are to be seen in *Tesserete, near Lugano* [pl.41] probably number 23 at the Fine

54 One of the five was sold to a niece at a discount!

55 *The Scotsman*, 2 October 1930

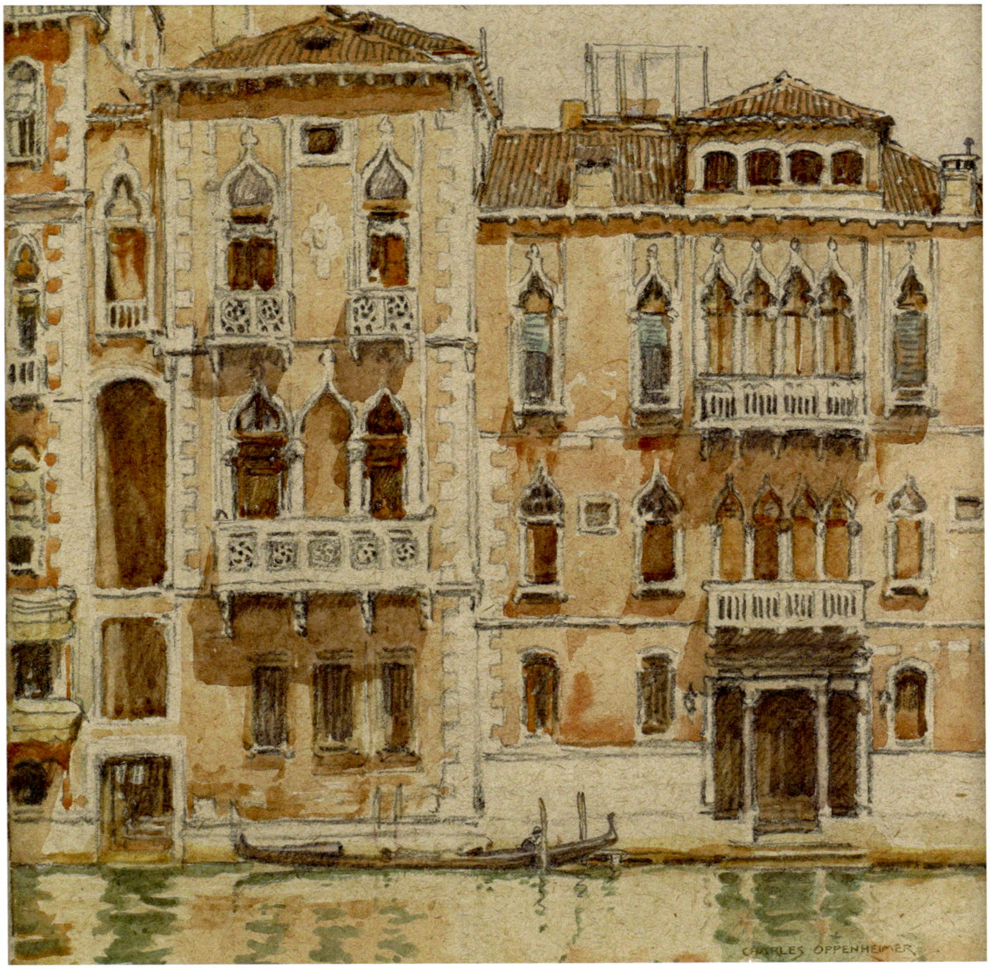
CHARLES OPPENHEIMER

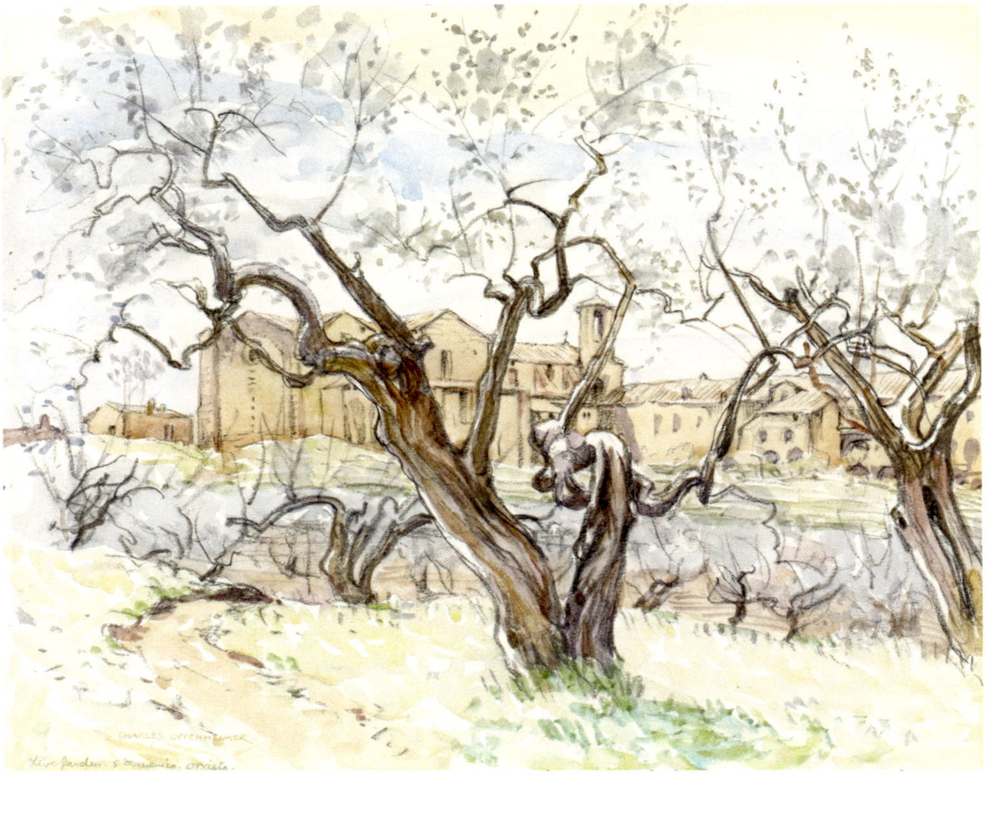
CHARLES OPPENHEIMER
Olive Garden. S. Domenico. Orvieto.

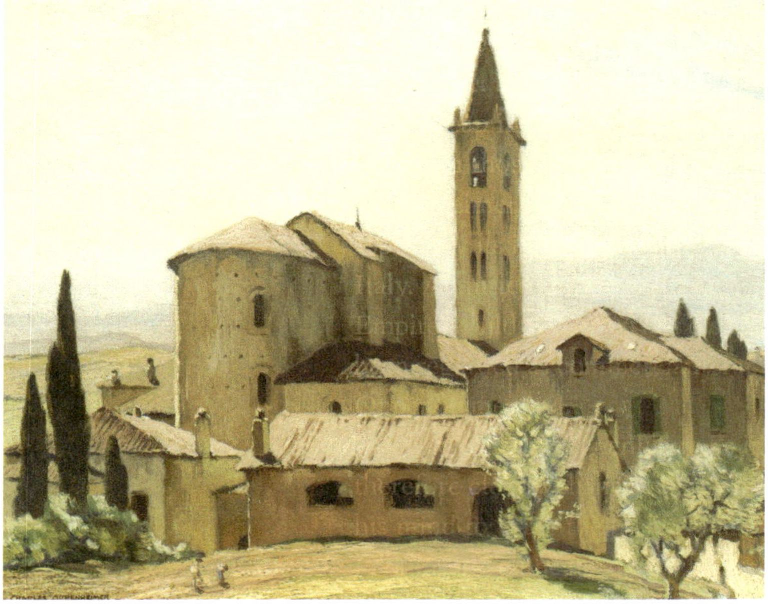

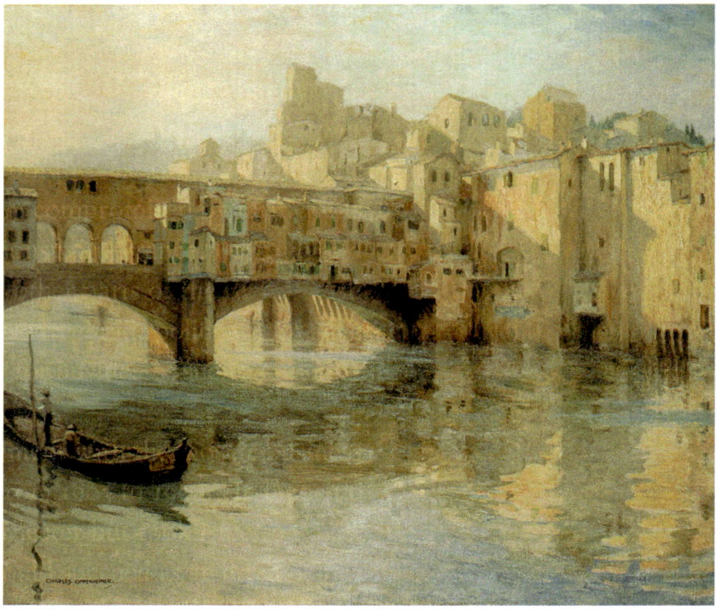

Plate 41 | *Tesserete, near Lugano*, c.1928, Bourne Fine Art, oil on canvas, 16 × 20 inches

Plate 42 | *Florence – Early Morning* c. 1930, Bourne Fine Art, oil on canvas, 25 × 30 inches

Art Society Show and [pl.42] *Florence – Early Morning* possibly number 60 in the catalogue. In both pictures Oppenheimer produces solid form from the careful blending of a restricted range of colours on the palette. The church buildings and bell tower at Lugano stand foursquare against the distant hills dimly seen in the heat haze and are defined in shades of yellows and browns. The same is true of the Ponte Vecchio and other Florentine structures in the latter painting. The counter point of the boat on the river Arno is in black and brown with minimal use of blue in the sky and water. Punctuation in green on two doorways completes the range of colours used.

A similarly restricted palette was employed for *Piazzetta at Dusk* which was featured in the *Country Life* magazine in March 1993.[56] Oppenheimer creates an extraordinary picture of night falling over the very familiar scene in Venice again by the exquisite use of a small range of browns, yellows, greys and blacks, with occasional pink hues and splashes of red on the gondoliers' garments. *The Piazzetta* [pl.43] is a day time rendering of exceptional quality of the same scene. Even more intense and of high tone is *Ponte di Cannareggio* [pl.48], a well-known Venetian scene.

The critic's distemper was likely caused by unfamiliarity with Oppenheimer's work and there being too many similar pictures in the exhibition. This was as the critic conceded, the artist's first London show and his audience south of Liverpool and Manchester had been limited hitherto to one or two pictures annually at the Royal Academy. These paintings separately or side by side are a delight. To put more than a few together could well have overwhelmed the senses which appears to have been *The Scotsman*'s critic's experience

56 *Country Life*, 4 March 1993, page 64

57 In conversation with Joe Campbell, 13 June 2007

A watercolour from this period *Siena at Dusk* [pl.44] was a particular family favourite and stayed in the Oppenheimers' possession throughout their lives. Oppenheimer in later years said that he could no longer produce a work of such intensity and refinement. It was a highpoint to him among his watercolours. Simultaneously, Connie used to delight in telling the picture's admirers that the couple had been able to walk all the way from the bottom of the hill to the top of the tower 'but not now'.[57] *Cathedral Interior* [pl.45] is a watercolour showing the marble banded decoration around the columns in the nave of Siena Cathedral and conveys admirably the form and height in the building's structure. It dates from before 1914 and it is just possible that Connie is the figure in the foreground.

Despite any setback occasioned by the Fine Art Society show,

Plate 43 | *The Piazetta*, Sotheby's, 1931, oil on canvas, 22 x 30 inches

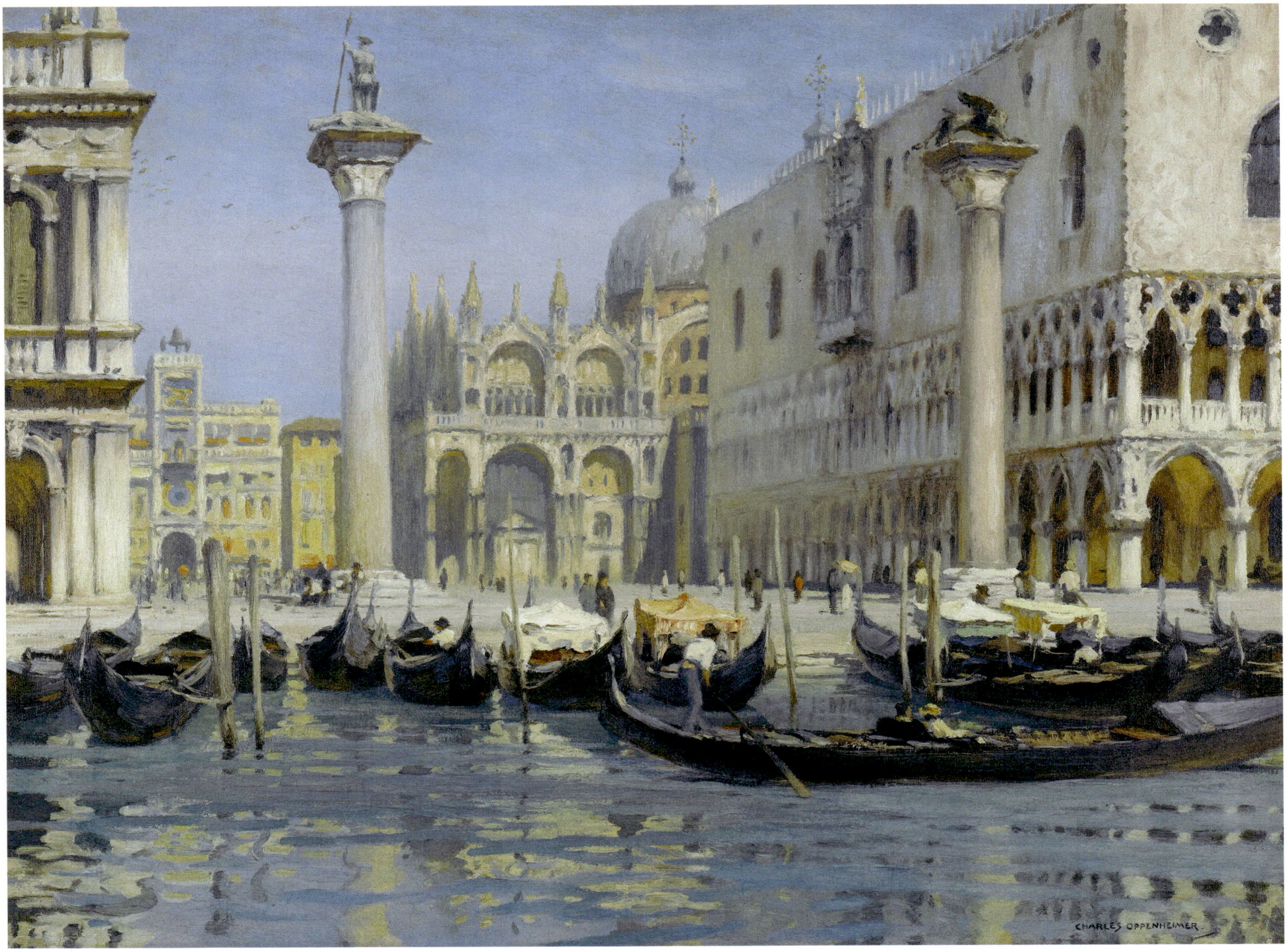

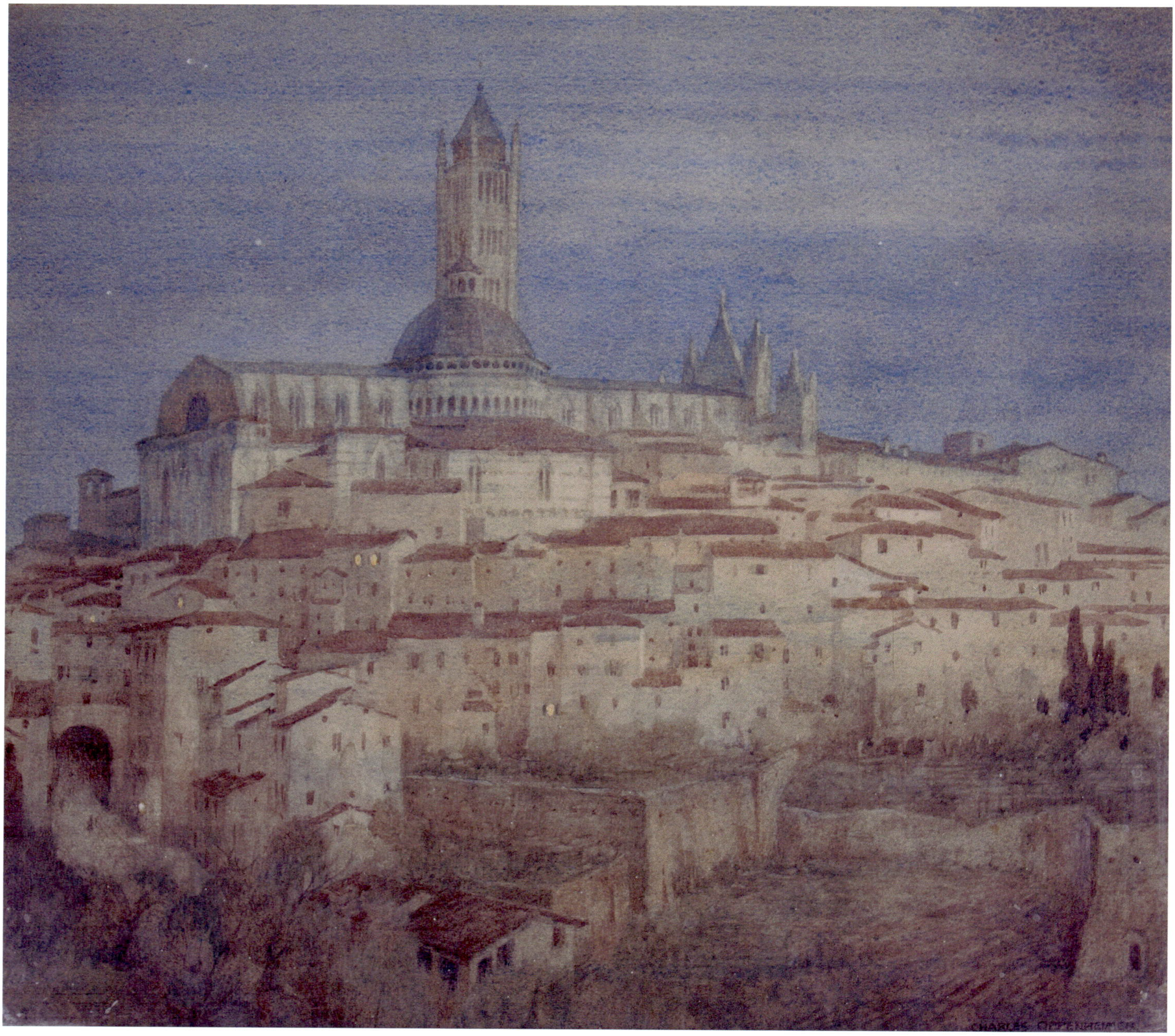

Plate 44 | *Siena at Dusk*, c.1929,
Private Collection, watercolour, 18½ × 21½ inches

Plate 45 | *Cathedral Interior*, c.1908,
Private Collection, watercolour, 21½ × 15 inches

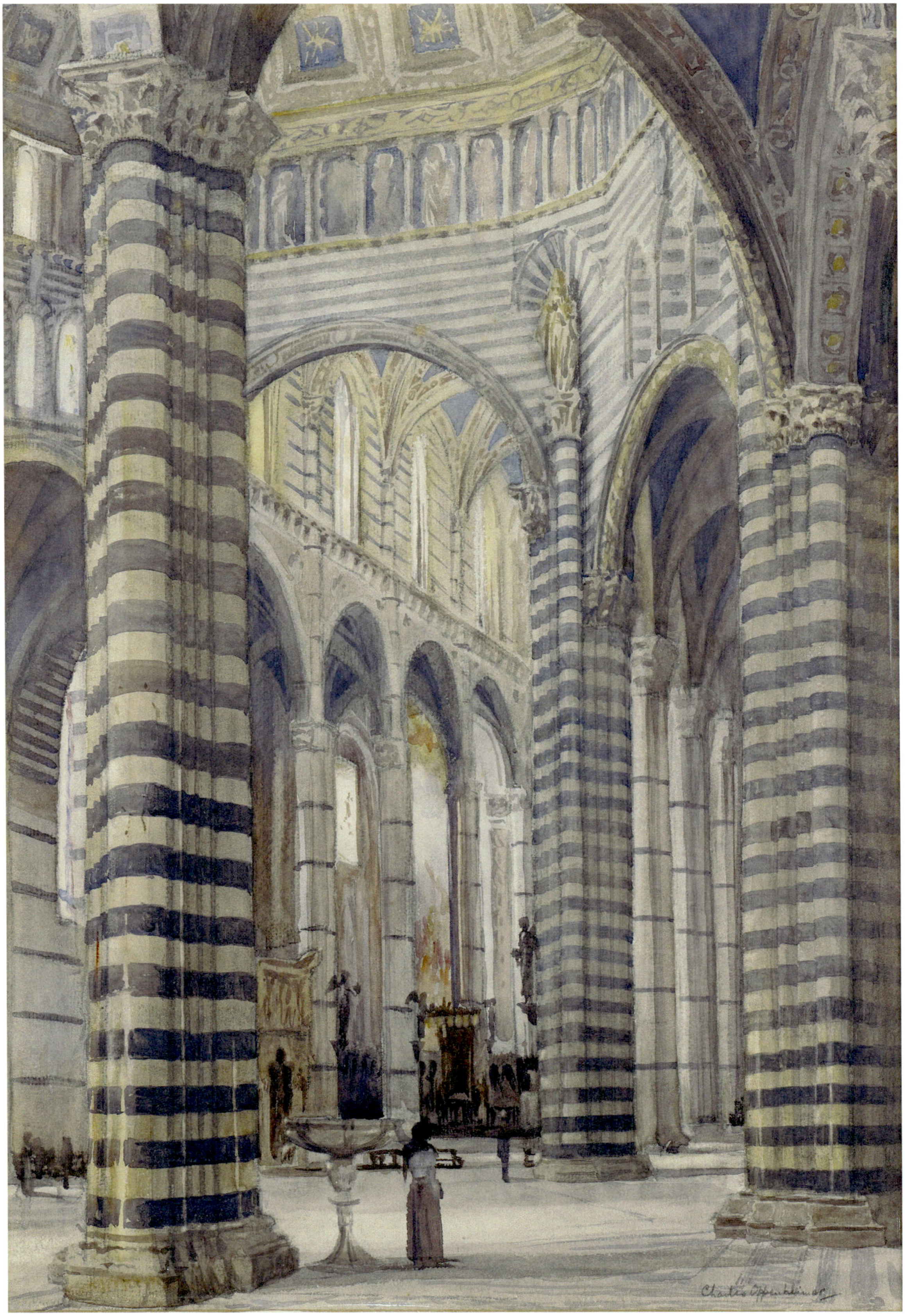
Charles Oppenheimer

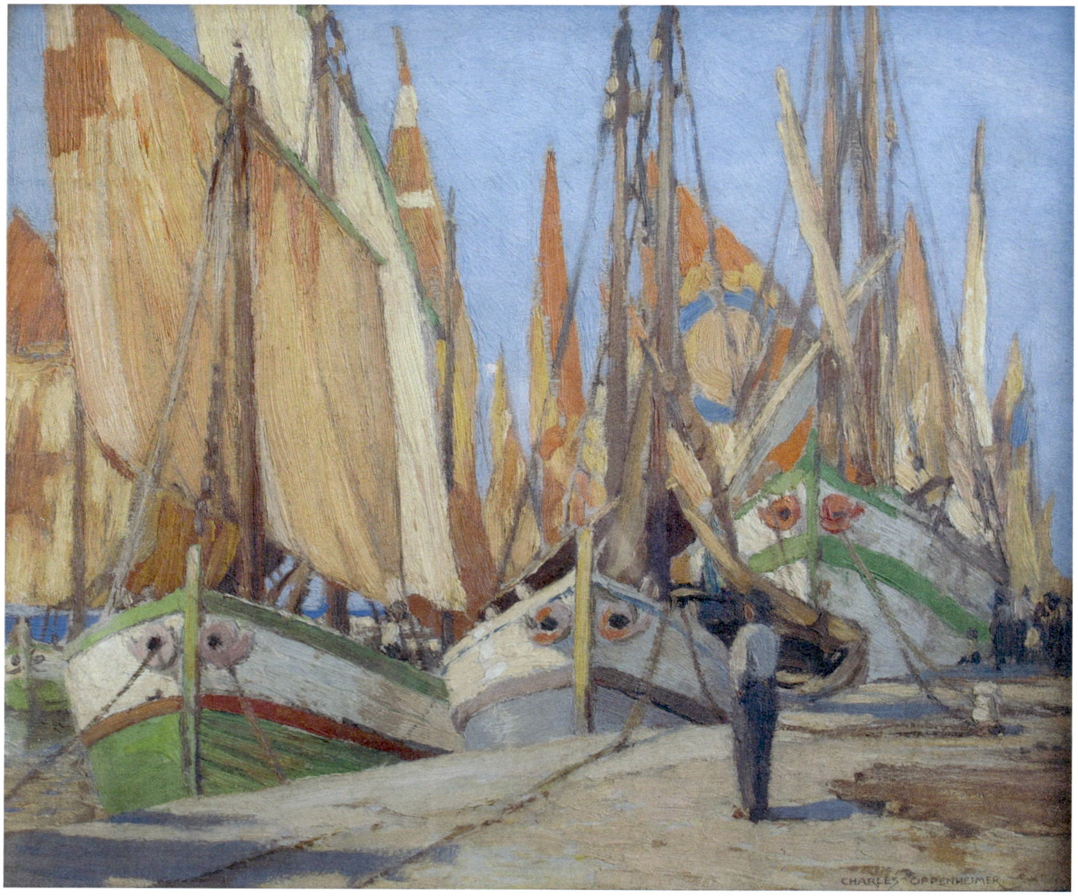

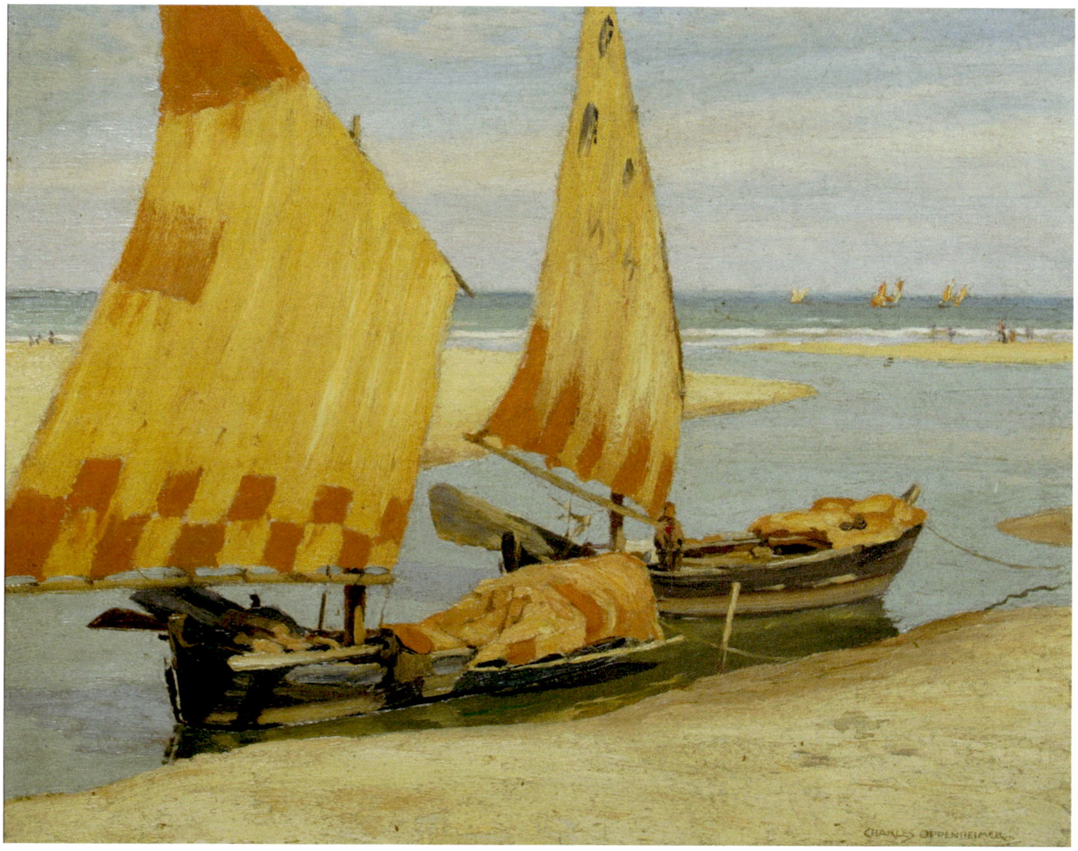

Plate 46 | *Painted Sails, Rimini*, c.1928, Private Collection, oil on board, 13¼ × 17 inches

Plate 47 | *The Beach at Rimini*, 1928 Private Collection, oil on canvas, 13¼ × 17¼ inches

Oppenheimer continued to visit Italy and to paint its splendours. *Venetian Barges* [pl.1] is a superb rendering of the subject matter with subtle use of colour laid down to create the atmosphere of the quayside. A family friend recalled an earlier occasion at Rimini. Oppenheimer carefully took out his paints and brushes and organised himself ready to paint local fishing boats. They were nowhere to be seen. He waited. A couple of hours or more passed; nothing, just an empty harbour. Perhaps another day might be better and so carefully, the brushes, paints,

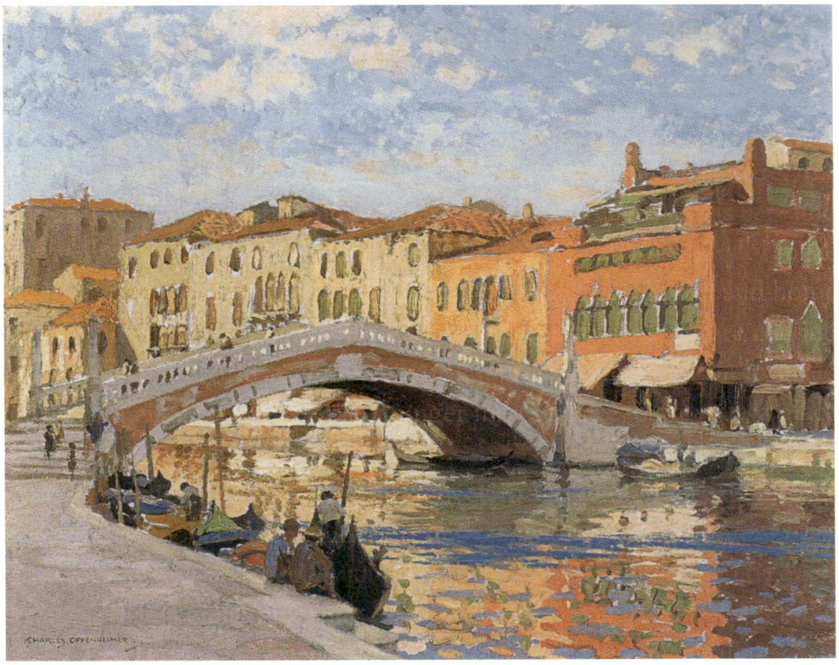

Plate 48 | *Ponte di Cannareggio*, 1928, Bourne Fine Art, oil on board, 14 × 18 inches

canvasses and everything else was meticulously packed up. He walked away but took a last look back. Suddenly, silently they were there, carried home by the on shore breeze. Hurriedly all was unpacked and *Painted Sails, Rimini* [pl.46] was created. Such fishing vessels appear in a number of Oppenheimer's Italian pictures. *The Beach at Rimini* [pl.47] is another fine example of the theme.

Italy was in many ways as important to Oppenheimer as Kirkcudbright. The light and the subject matter were different and refreshed his palette and canvasses at key intervals in his career as can be seen in *San Francesco, Assisi* [pl.30] in the University of Liverpool's collection. Italy was especially significant in maintaining his abilities as a consummate draughtsman. It was however in the experience of its vivid colours that Italy most influenced Oppenheimer's art. He was profoundly concerned to convey that experience. As he said once to Joe Campbell, so far as he was concerned the essence of art was the fusion of colour.

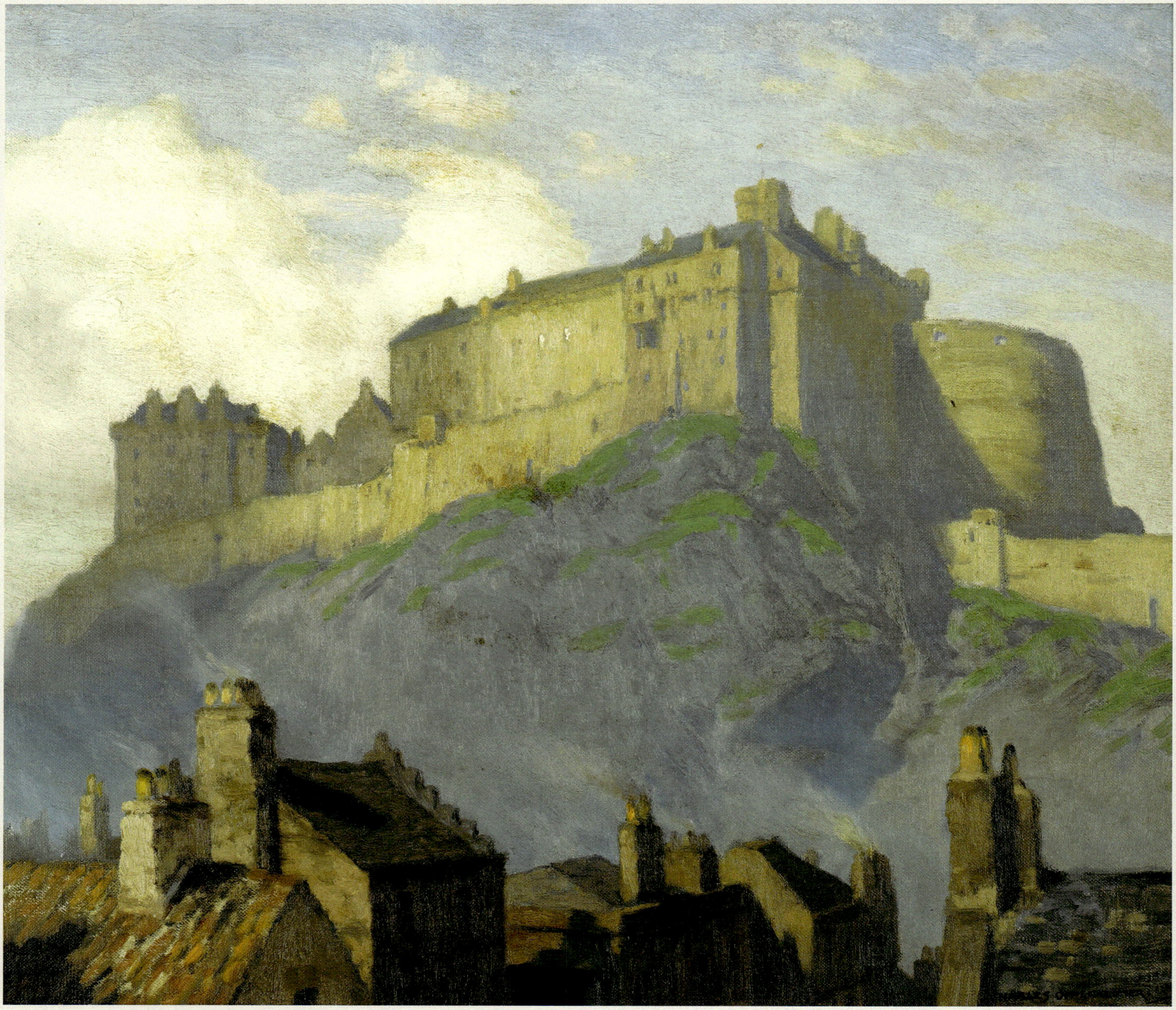

8 'A STUDENT IN ART'

Plate 49 | *Edinburgh Castle*, c.1938, Sotheby's, oil on canvas, 20 x 23¾ inches

CHARLES AND CONNIE OPPENHEIMER were generous hosts. Their home at 14 High Street was the scene of many convivial evenings, Sunday lunches, overnight visits and longer stays from artists and other friends, and a holiday destination for Mancunian relatives. Mary Evans, their niece, recalled going with her brother in the 1920s and 1930s to wonderful New Year parties where they joined Oppenheimer's fellow artists, the Provost, the Town Clerk and numerous friends from Kirkcudbright and further afield:

> *In one room upstairs a billiard competition was held, in another room there was a very busy gaming table! We ate down in the large basement which had been transformed, one year into a ship's interior, another year into Japan. The whitewashed stone walls were painted with Japanese landscapes and the ceiling hung with Japanese lanterns and handmade cherry blossom branches.*

14 High Street was (and indeed remains) a fair sized property with a number of passages and stairs. It was sub-let in 1917 and 1918 and the advert of October 1916 gives an idea of the facilities available.[58] 'Artist on active service wishes to let furnished house; drawing, dining and billiard rooms, 3 bedrooms, all conveniences'. There was a garden of a size befitting such a property, having a focal point of a circular pond containing goldfish,water lilies and reeds. Oppenheimer's studio was not in the building but in another part of the town. He walked to and from it every working day.

For a time in the 1920s and early 1930s the crime writer and novelist, Dorothy L. Sayers, rented 14A High Street during the summer months. Her well known novel *Five Red Herrings* set in and around Kirkcudbright tells the story of the murder of a member of a fictional artists' colony. Sayers used members of the town's actual artists' colony, or elements of painters' lives or physical surroundings, to populate her book and bring her characters to life. One evening on the trail of clues to solve the crime, Lord Peter Wimsey, Sayer's amateur detective, strides down High Street past the house of one of the artists under suspicion. No lights are on within. Despite the hour, perhaps the

58 *The Scotsman*, 11 October 1916

suspect is still in his studio, a converted small barn up a turning off the Tongland Road.

Off goes Wimsey to look for his man 'past the Castle, up the little flight of steps and over the green by the harbour', Wimsey's fictional footsteps following Oppenheimer's daily walk to work:

> *The tide was dropping, and the long mudflats of the estuary glimmered faintly in the pale midsummer night. The yacht that had come in that morning still lay close against the harbour wall, her spars and rigging making a bold foreground of interlaced verticals and horizontals against the galumphing curves of the ugly concrete bridge.*[59]

The masts of a sailing ship docked at the harbour loom over High Street in *Kirkcudbright High Street at Night* [pl.50] This masterful portrayal of light and shade under the lamps in High Street was painted by Oppenheimer a year or two before Sayers used the same scene in her plot.

Sayers makes Wimsey cross 'the open space where the buses congregate by day' and then plunge 'down the little alley by the gas works and (come) out past the station on to the Tongland Road'. 'Crossing the street, he turned off again to the right and found himself in a happy backwater, with an ancient over-shot watermill, a few cottages and a wide open space, grassy and forlorn, surrounded by sheds and derelict out-buildings.' The Millburn studio 'was approached by a little winding path among overgrown bushes and lush grass'.[60] For Wimsey the door was locked but Oppenheimer always had a key.

Oppenheimer's friends and relatives recall that inside his studio all was orderly. It was often cold. The coke stove was hard to light and would go out frequently. Such was the artist's concentration that he would forget to stoke it. Oppenheimer kept to his routine. He worked as if he was still in business in Manchester with his father looming over his shoulder. His training and self-discipline never left him. He was, as has been said of him by a number of commentators, the antithesis of the bohemian artist.

Mary Evans, described him as 'fastidious'. In the studio or at the sketching ground everything had its place. An artist friend and fellow Lancastrian Academician, William Maxwell Reekie, the Manchester born son of a Fife family, used to stay in Kirkcudbright and visited Oppenheimer when on painting expeditions to Scotland. He would always look in on Oppenheimer's large and orderly studio. 'This concern for order was a lesson not lost on Reekie. He was aware that the strength of a picture was built upon solid, compositional foundations – a product of solid structure and harmonious spacing of principal forms undertaken early in the picture's development.' Oppenheimer was equally so aware.[61]

In Sayers' novel one of her fictitious artists describes Oppenheimer's methodical approach to painting. 'I could lay my hand on any of my

59 *Five Red Herrings* by Dorothy L. Sayers, 1893–1957, first published in Great Britain in 1931 by Victor Gollancz Ltd, chapter five

60 Ibid

61 *A Northern School, Lancashire artists of the twentieth century* by Peter Davies, Redcliffe, Bristol, 1989, page 72.

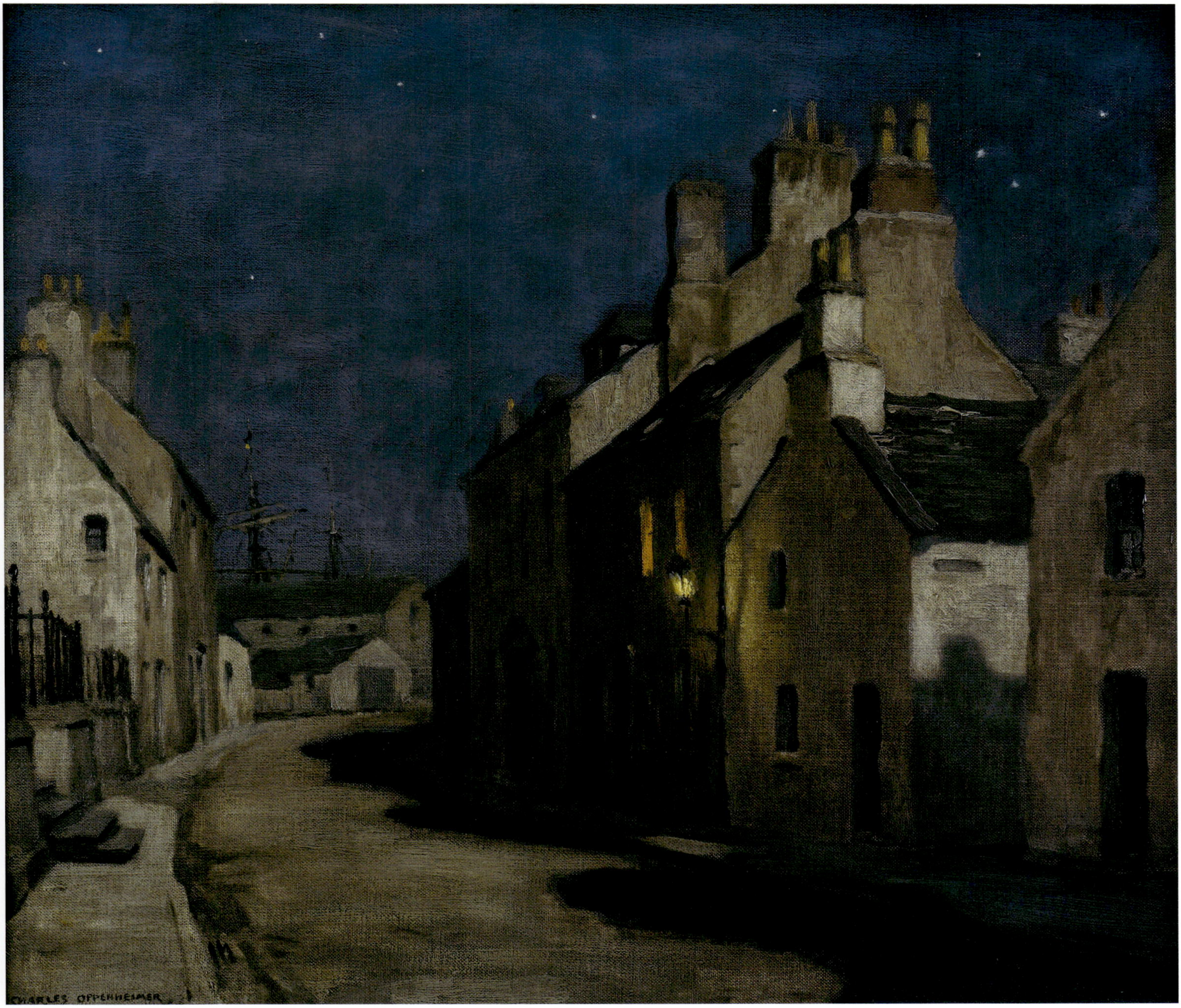

Plate 50 | *Kirkcudbright High Street at Night*, c.1925
Private Collection, oil on canvas, 20 × 24 inches

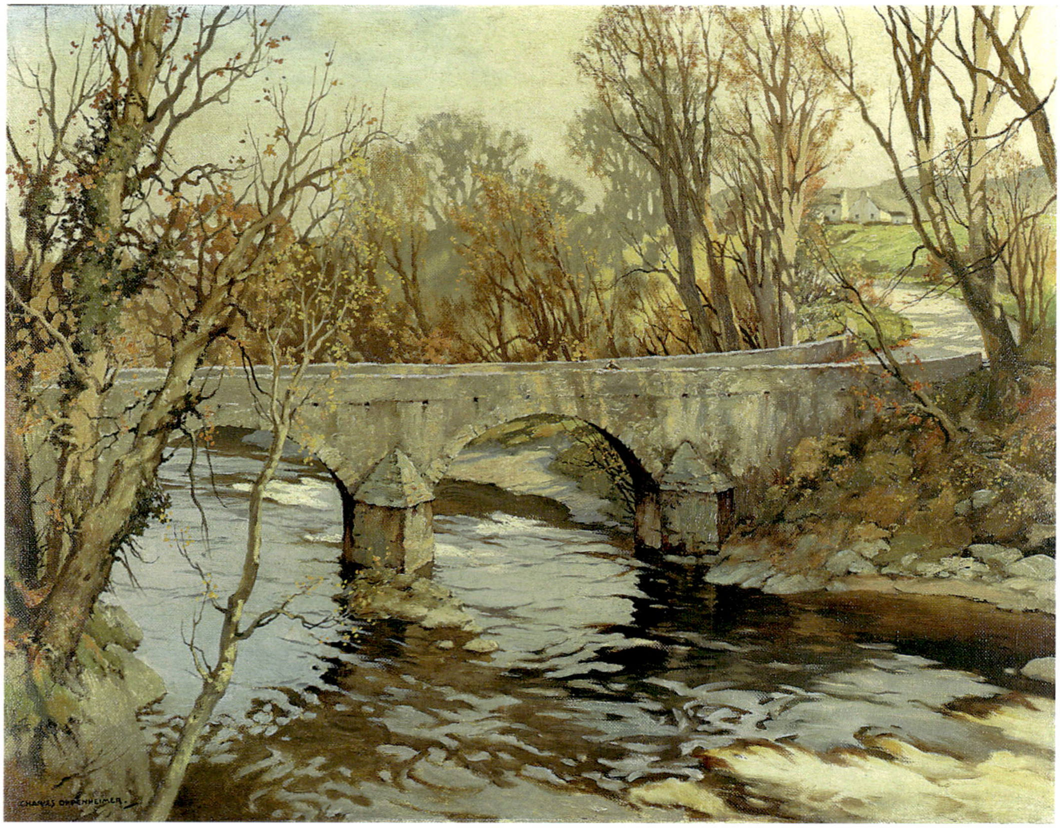

Plate 51 | *Kirkcudbright An Old Bridge in Galloway*, c.1935, Private Collection, photo © Christie's Images, The Bridgeman Art Library, oil on canvas, 28 × 36 inches

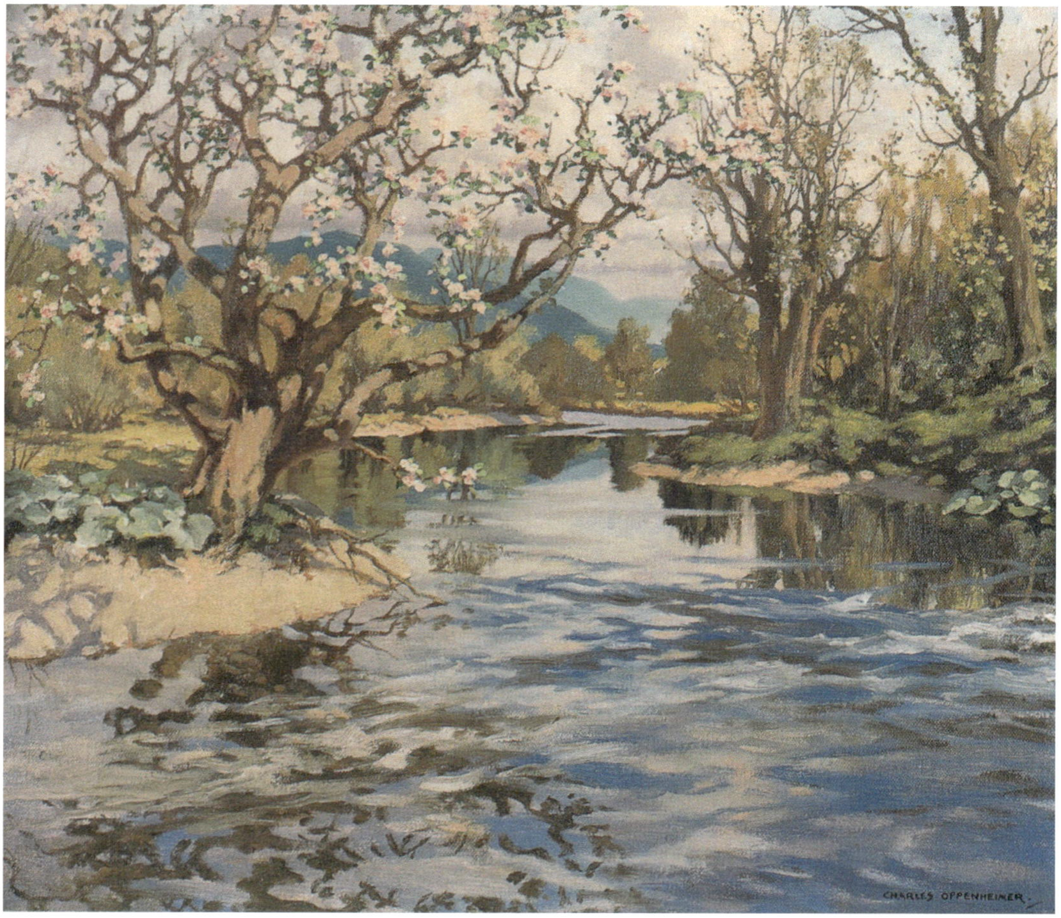

Plate 52 | *Blossom, Buckland Burn*, c.1940, Bourne Fine Art, oil on canvas, 20 × 24 inches

tools in the dark. Some people seem to like muddle, and all their stuff chucked into a satchel anyhow. I lay everything out before I begin – tubes of colour in the same order on my tray, dipper just here, spare brushes hung on there – even my palette is always made up in the same order, though not always with the same colours, of course. But roughly speaking, it follows the order of the spectrum.'[62] These may well have been Oppenheimer's own words.

Oppenheimer's friendship with Sayers spanned many years. It is said

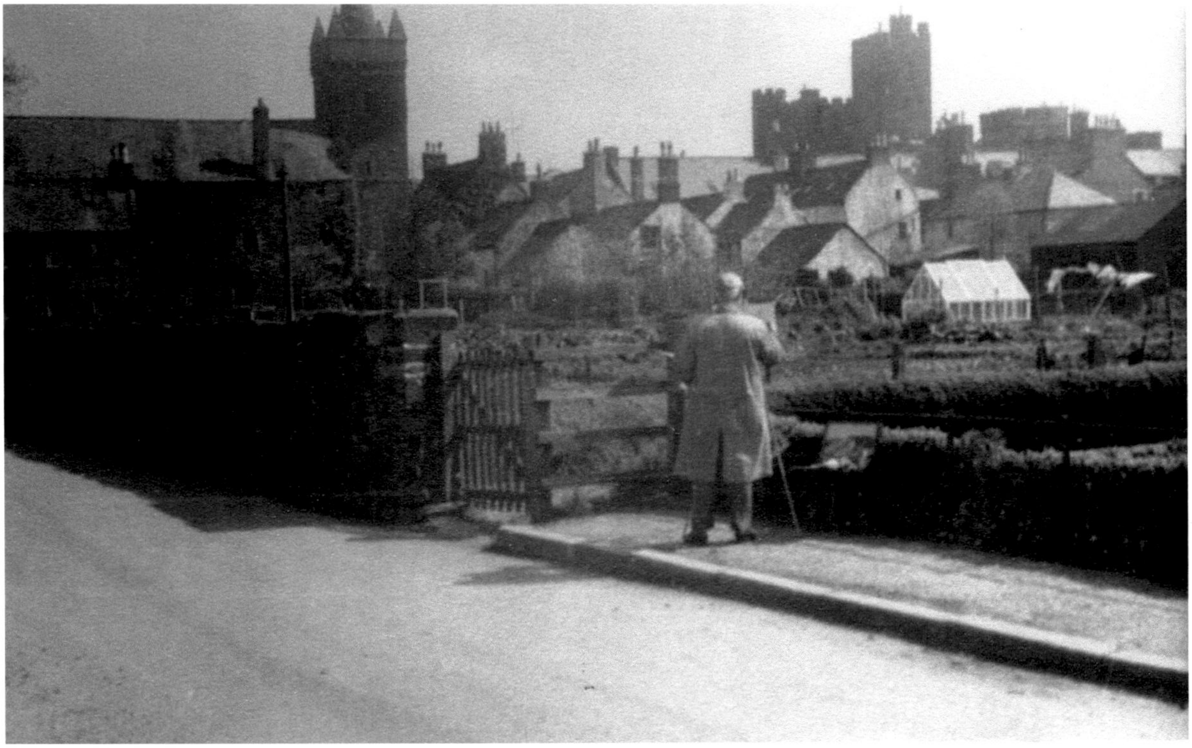

Plate 53 | Oppenheimer 'hard at it', The Crofts, Kirkcudbright, courtesy of the Stewartry Museum, Kirkcudbright

that Oppenheimer gave Sayers the idea for one of her finest novels *The Nine Tailors* when he loaned her a copy of a book called *The Nebuly Coat* by John Meade Falkner.[63] Published in 1903, *The Nebuly Coat* is a novel which tells of the experiences of a young architect sent to the fictional Dorset town of Cullerne to supervise restoration work on the Minster. *Edinburgh Castle* [pl.49] was among Sayers possession when she died.

Oppenheimer's training in mosaic work and design imbued his approach to painting. He was systematic. He was painstaking. He was deliberate and intense. A frequently repeated story about Oppenheimer comes from his later years. By then he had moved house to Woodlea near the edge of the town. It stood at the top of the Puir Hoose Brae. He would remark to friends that the Hoose's proximity would make his next move quite easy! Connie would place a lunch tray outside the studio

62 *Five Red Herrings* by Dorothy L Sayers, Victor Gollancz Ltd, 1931, Chapter 16

63 John Meade Falkner (1858–1932) English novelist, poet and businessman. Chairman of Armstrong Whitworth arms manufacturers from 1915 to 1921, he then became Honorary Reader in Paleography at the University of Durham, as well as Honorary Librarian to the Dean and Chapter Library of Durham Cathedral

in Woodlea on a small table, call to him within that it was there, only to return hours later to find everything completely untouched.

Although he would allow ready access to his studio, Oppenheimer would permit very few people to watch him painting. Jessie King is said to have taken the young Bill Baillie[64] a future President of the RSA to watch the artist hard at it close by the harbour one day. The pair was abruptly told to go away. In a rare photograph of the artist at work in the Crofts in Kirkcudbright [pl.53] the photographer was, quite possibly, as close as anyone might safely have approached.

Oppenheimer's attitude was beyond reticence. Whilst there is no known record as to why he was unapproachable, there is at least a passing sense that he may not have been entirely at ease with his technique or at least he may have worried about his peers' reaction to its disclosure. Oppenheimer after all came to be a professional artist later in life. Was he a craftsman or an artist? Was he troubled by this question? Drawing had been a fundamental part of his career in business until his thirties. Drawing was an essential skill for a mosaic designer. However mosaic designs required templates of geometrical precision to permit their transfer from paper to walls, ceilings or floors. Oppenheimer seems to have carried the technique across to his watercolours which were painted over a grid system. The paper, carefully drawn into equal sized rectangular boxes was apparently painted in rectangle by rectangle. Perhaps he was unsure that this was how an artist ought to paint.

Oppenheimer's career as an artist might have been short lived because of the Great War. He had had some success as a painter particularly in 1912 and 1913 but back in Manchester in 1915 in the family business and an attested volunteer for active service, he could have been forgiven for wondering if and how he would ever return to his peacetime career. His brother's death was followed by two years in France. He might then have had to have stayed in the family business after the war. It was a tribute to his dedication that he returned to painting. Recognition did not come quickly. He was fifty two when he became an Associate of the Royal Scottish Academy in 1927. The critics were not always generous. Oppenheimer lived well away from his native city. He was not a Scot or from the mainstream of the Scottish artistic community. He had not trained in Scotland. This is not to say that he was not welcomed and accepted. In his later years he became an important Academician and was regarded by public and critics alike as a Scottish artist. But his ascent was not rapid by any reckoning.

Perhaps it was a reflection of his natural modesty. Oppenheimer was never flamboyant or a self-publicist. As Mories said in his article in *The Artist*, he was 'devoid of ostentation.' He may have had some of his

64 In conversation with Bill Smith

65 Quoted from *Leonardo da Vinci* by Charles Nichol, Penguin Books, 2004 referring to the Ashburnham Folio 20/38 27v formerly part of Folio 1490–1492, Institute de France, Paris (MS 21/85)

66 In conversation with Joe Campbell in the Scottish Parliament, 6 September 2005

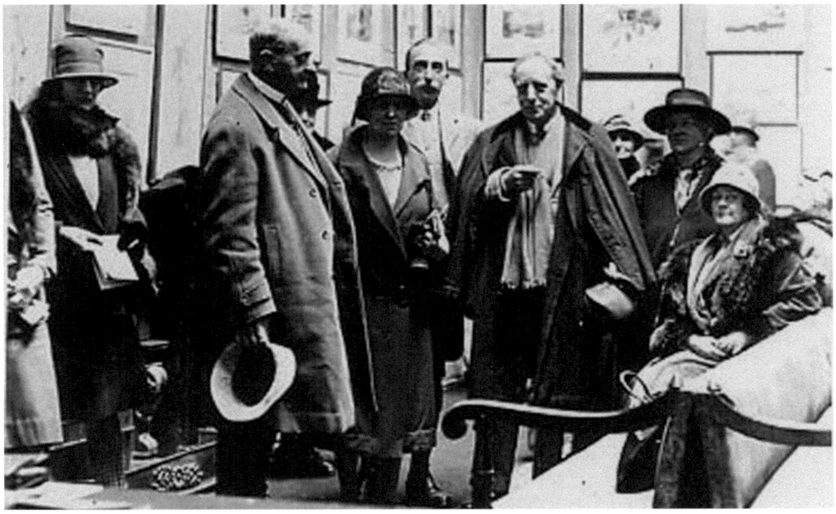

Plate 54 | Dumfries and Galloway Fine Art Society opening of an annual exhibition, c.1932, courtesy of the Stewartry Museum, Kirkcudbright

natural inclinations reinforced by his experiences of anti-German sentiment in the war years. There is no-one now to tell us. Without doubt though, he would not suffer any intrusion when he was working. Total concentration was required and maintained.

Charles Oppenheimer was very well read. He travelled widely in Italy, drew and painted in many locations throughout the country over the years. A favourite region was Leonardo da Vinci's Tuscany. Perhaps Oppenheimer's solitary behaviour was because he knew of and subscribed to Leonardo's advice to the painter. 'While you are alone you are entirely on your own: and if you have but one companion you are but half your own'. The painter should 'withdraw apart, the better to study the forms of natural objects'. He should 'remain solitary, especially when he is intent on studying and considering those things which continually appear before his eyes, and which furnish material to be carefully stored up in the memory'.[65]

Oppenheimer's concentration needed to be fixed to make the most of the precious moments when inspiration came. A favourite adage repeated to several friends was that an artist should always use the best of materials because you never know where or when you will do your best work. Best work was always what he strove to do, always his aim and most often his accomplishment. He had to have tranquillity to get there.

Oppenheimer never taught. He gave occasional help and advice to interested young people. Joe Campbell once asked for an opinion about a small oil that he had completed. 'Full marks for endeavour but don't try to paint reeds singly', whereupon Oppenheimer added an extra with two strokes of the brush 'transforming the picture'. Campbell then told Oppenheimer that one of his own works on display was perfection to which came the reply, 'I'm only a student in art'.[66]

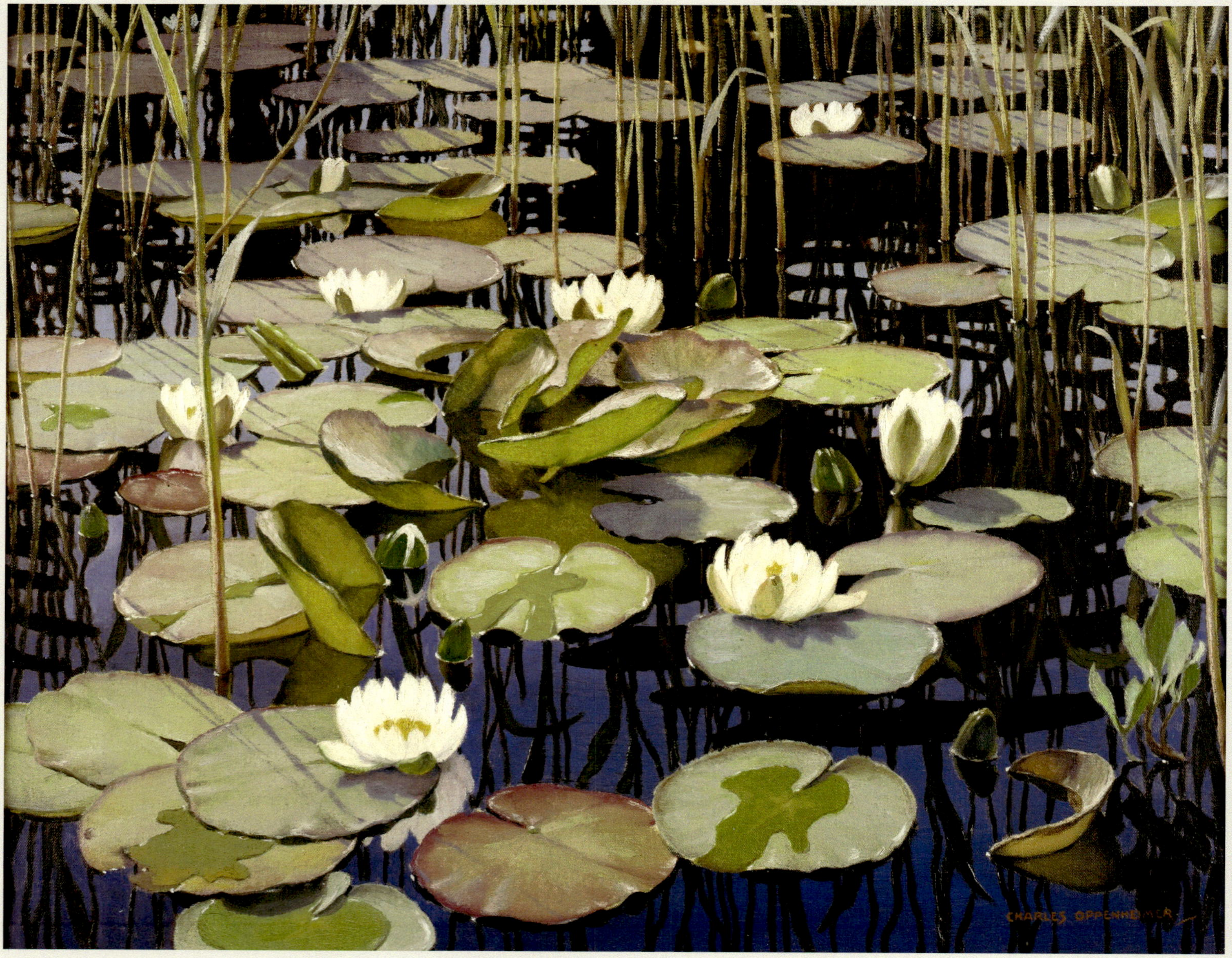
CHARLES OPPENHEIMER

9 'A GENTLE PAINTER'

Plate 55 | *Among the Reeds*, c.1938, The Ellis-Campbell Collection, oil on canvas, 25 x 30 inches

Charles Oppenheimer's prodigious talent reached its full maturity in the decade after he was elected as an associate member of the Royal Scottish Academy in March 1927. *The Scotsman*, reporting his election, opined that his work was characterised 'by a sensitive feeling for natural effects'. Oppenheimer had recently exhibited a number of snow scenes at which he was particularly adept and the article continued that he was 'an exponent also of the subtle charm and mystery of low toned effect'.[67]

Although he painted many commissions, Oppenheimer's favoured method of selling his work was at public exhibitions. His pictures were shown at a number of venues other than the major outlets of the Royal Academy, Royal Scottish Academy, the Royal Glasgow Institute of Fine Arts and the Manchester Academy. He exhibited at the Society of Scottish Artists from 1922 to 1935. For some reason he discontinued his membership some time after the closure of the 1935 show on 30 November. The Society passed through experimental and conservative phases and, as Edwin Muir said in his essay for the 1944 Jubilee catalogue, 'what was new then has since been accepted'.

Oppenheimer could not be said to be a modern artist by the 1930s. His style was now well established and would remain unaltered henceforth. He was not in sympathy with new developments.

As his reputation grew so his work was to be found further and further afield. The *Exposición de Artes e Industrias Británicas* was held in Buenos Aires from 14 March to 27 April 1931 under the auspices of the Royal British Colonial Society of Artists. The fine art catalogue includes an illustration of *Winter Sunshine* by Oppenheimer, a view across the snow covered crofts to the Tolbooth with the shadows of the branches of trees spreading like wizened fingers across the frozen land. Two pictures *Edinburgh Castle* and *On the Grand Canal, Venice*, the latter published as a postcard in Paris, were shown at the Paris Salon and, according to Mories, he was also by invitation asked to show his work in Prague, New Zealand, the United States and Canada.

Oppenheimer found constant inspiration in and around Kirkcudbright

67 *The Scotsman*, 17 March, 1927

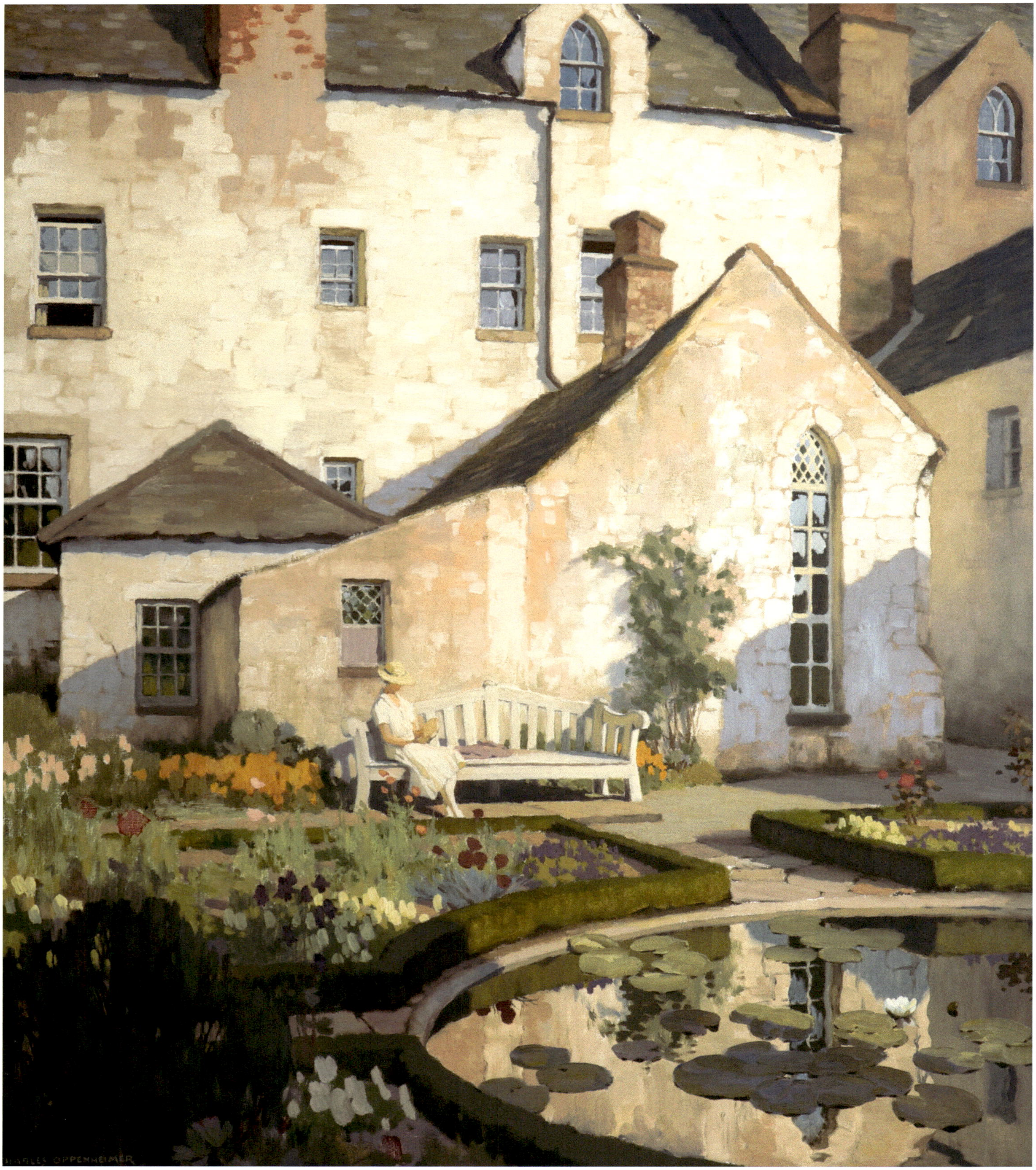
OPPENHEIMER

Plate 56 | *The Artist's Garden*, 1927, Gallery Oldham, oil on canvas, 44 x 40 inches

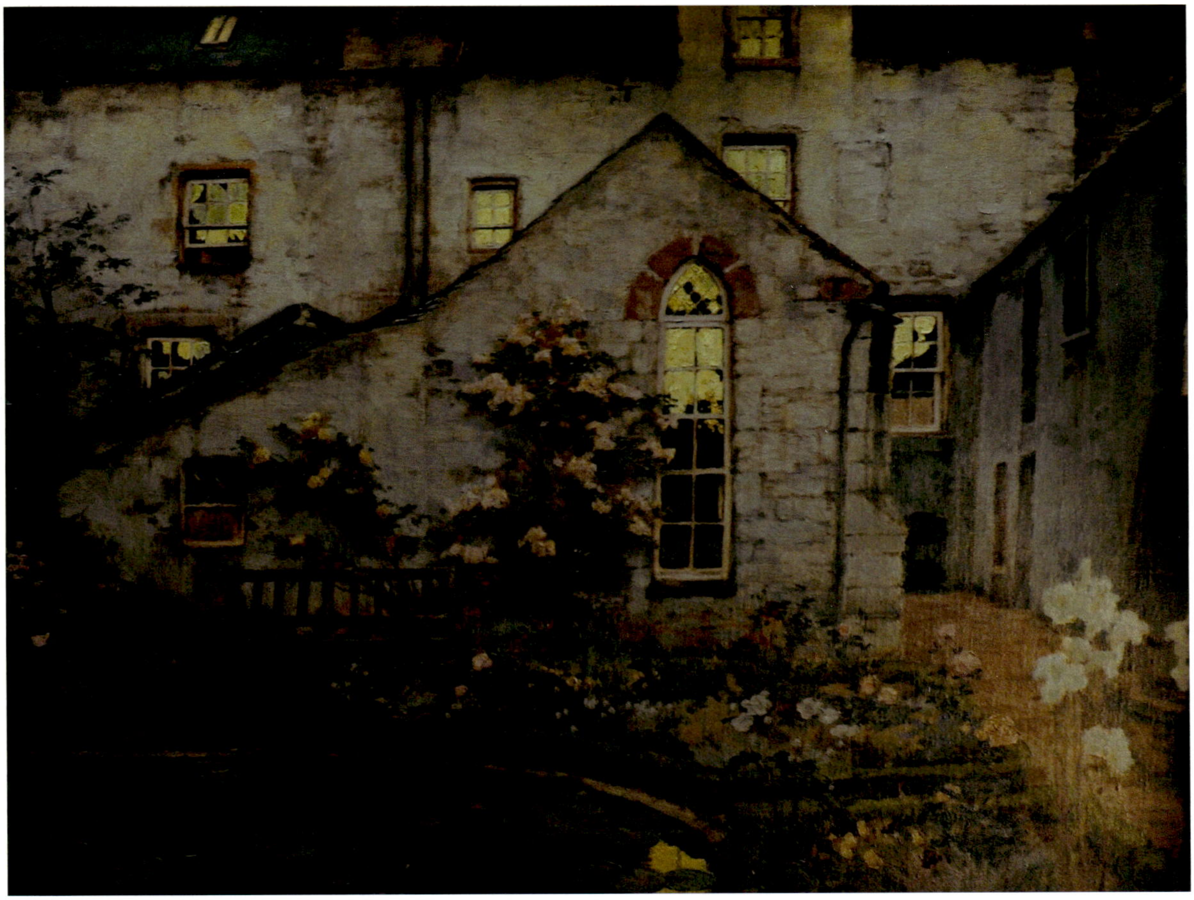

for the paintings that he sent to exhibitions throughout the country and abroad. Indeed a series of works involved his home at 14 High Street. *In my Garden, Twilight* was at the Royal Academy, Manchester and Liverpool in 1926. A year later he painted his garden in afternoon sunshine. *The Artist's Garden* [pl.56] shows the rear of 14 High Street and most of the garden bathed in bright light. Connie Oppenheimer is reading seated on the bench. In the foreground is the lily pond, the still surface reflecting the walls and windows of the house interspersed by lily pads and other plants.

Plate 57 | *My Garden at Twilight*, 1937, National Trust for Scotland, oil on canvas, 36 x 44 inches

Oppenheimer painted the same scene again ten years later in the summer of 1937. *My Garden at Twilight* [pl.57][68] catches the last of the day's light in the house windows. The flowers are a counterpoint to the mellow tones of the stone of the building and the lilies float on the pond's still surface giving cover and shelter to the fish that occasionally dart to and fro looking for a last crumb or insect before night descends. 'If your bedroom were [*sic*] big enough', said one commentator, 'you would never tire of Mr Charles Oppenheimer RSA's delicious picture of his Garden at Twilight'.[69]

68 The painting is now in the National Trust for Scotland's permanent collection at Broughton House, Kirkcudbright.

69 *The Scotsman*, 23 April 1937

Records in the Royal Scottish Academy show that this picture was widely exhibited. After making its debut at the RSA annual exhibition in June 1937, Oppenheimer wrote in March 1938 to a correspondent that the painting had 'been exhibited by invitation at the National Exhibition at Toronto, and at the Walker Gallery, Liverpool. Just before receiving your letter the picture was invited to the '*Exhibition of eminent living artists*' at the Russell-Cotes Gallery at Bournemouth where it will be shown till 11 June.' After these travels the painting was shown at the RGI exhibition in 1939 and illustrated in that year's catalogue.

The garden pond provided the subject matter for an important group of pictures of water lilies. The first reference to any such work is in 1911 when an oil entitled *The Lily Pool* was exhibited at Manchester. Either a smaller oil or more likely a water colour *Water Lilies* was in the Royal and Manchester Academies in 1916. In 1920 *Lily Pool*, another but larger oil than 1911, was on display again at both venues and *Water Lilies*, a more expensive oil, was in London in 1921 and in Glasgow the following year. *Pond Lilies* in 1924, *Lily Pool* 1929 and *Study of Water Lilies* 1932 completed the Glasgow sequence. Manchester saw *Lily Pool* in 1930, probably the same picture as at Glasgow the year before but then another entitled *A Lily Pool* was on show in 1935. That painting had previously been on show at the Society of Scottish Artists' exhibition in Edinburgh from November 1934 to January 1935. Its 'cool beauty' said one critic 'must have appealed to many visitors as a restful note among a galaxy of colour during the currency of the exhibition'.[70] The Royal Academy had *Pond Lilies* in 1924 but nothing thereafter in the same vein. Curiously, the Royal Scottish Academy saw no Oppenheimer lilies until *Madonna Lilies* in 1937. It is unclear whether these were in the pond at High Street. Thereafter *A Lily Pool* in 1942 and *Water-Lilies* in 1956 were shown in Edinburgh.

This sequence serves to illustrate Oppenheimer's custom of returning to some subjects on a regular basis. Furthermore some paintings were put away and re-titled and re-exhibited. Disentangling which picture was painted when can be difficult and certainly frustrating as of course they are very seldom dated. Joe Campbell recalls that Oppenheimer would not date paintings as if he did so it would be harder to try them at exhibition again years later if they did not initially sell.[71]

This seems to be confirmed by the RSA lilies' paintings. They were unlikely to have been painted in the 1940s as Oppenheimer moved from 14 High Street in 1938 leaving his beloved pond behind. He may just of course have completed new paintings from old sketches but this was not his method. Dating works can also be difficult as his style altered only marginally from the mid 1920s and to complicate matters there were

70 *The Scotsman*, 9 January 1935

71 In conversation with Joe Campbell, 13 June 2007

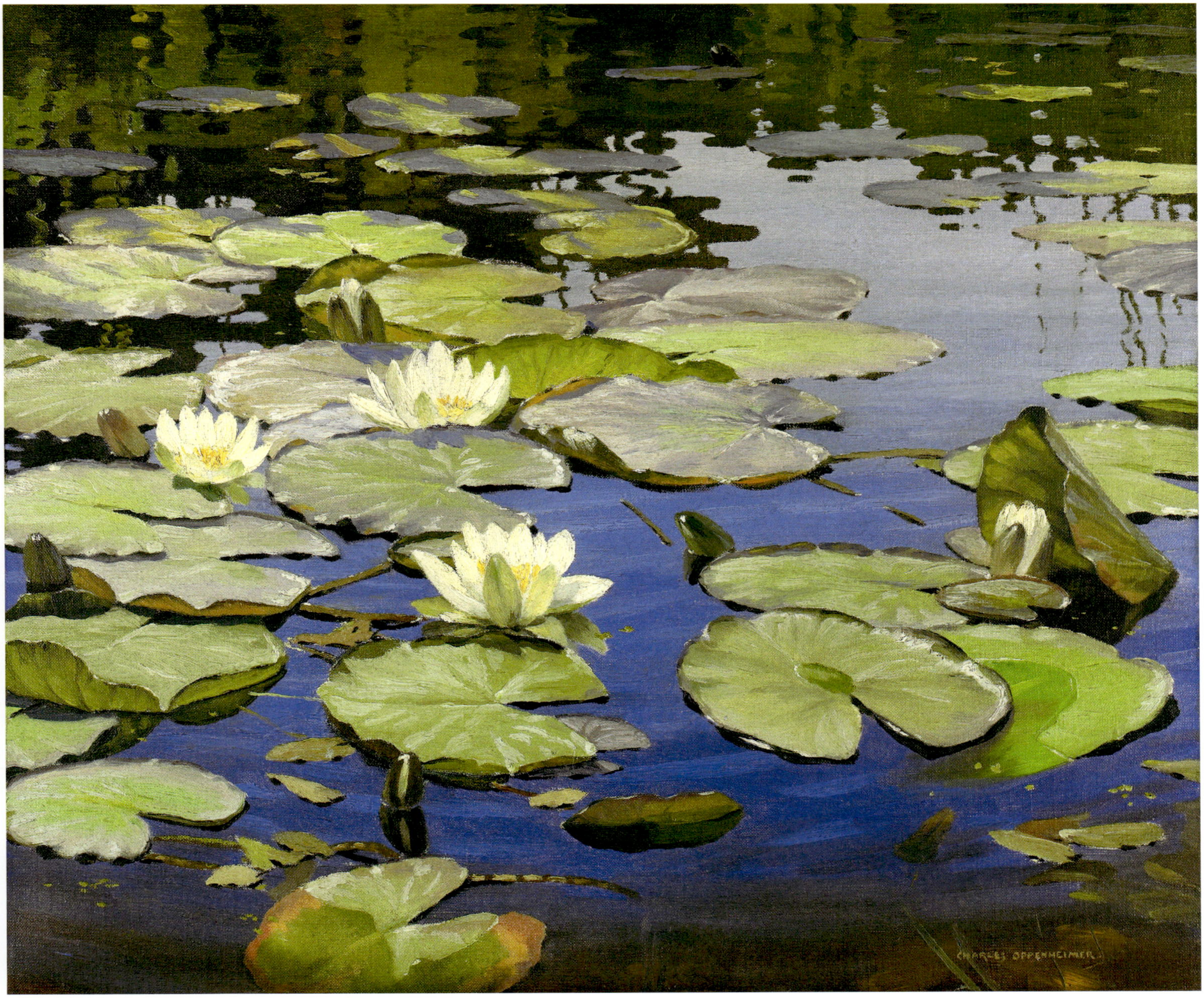

Plate 58 | *Pond Lilies*, 1924, Bourne Fine Art, oil on canvas, 25 × 30 inches

commissioned works and gifts such as a lilies' watercolour in a niece's possession that were never exhibited. However, *Pond Lilies* [pl.58] could be the painting of the same name exhibited in Glasgow in 1924 but is not *Lily Pool* illustrated in the RGI catalogue in 1929. We can be fairly certain that *A Lily Pool*, reproduced in *The Scotsman* on 1 December 1934, was the painting of the same name at the RGI a few weeks later in 1935. The painting *Among the Reeds* [pl.55] is yet another version of the theme and was painted between 1934 and 1938 the later date being the more likely.

Oppenheimer delighted in Kirkcudbright harbour and the estuary

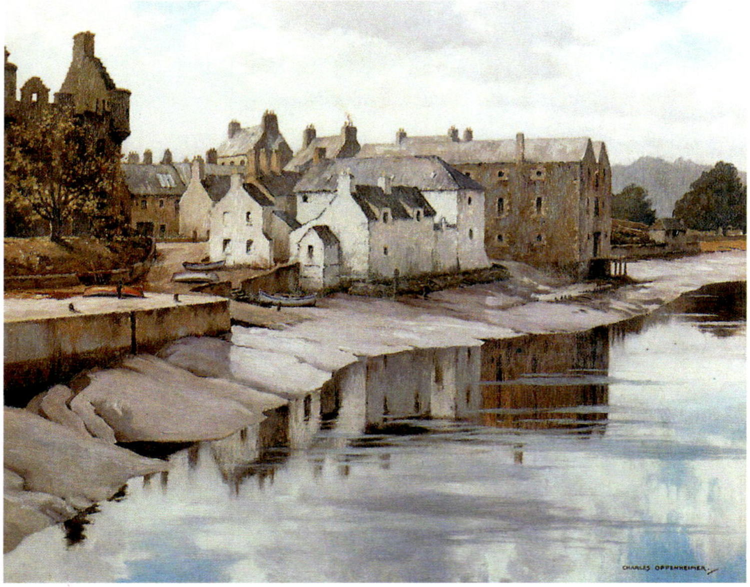

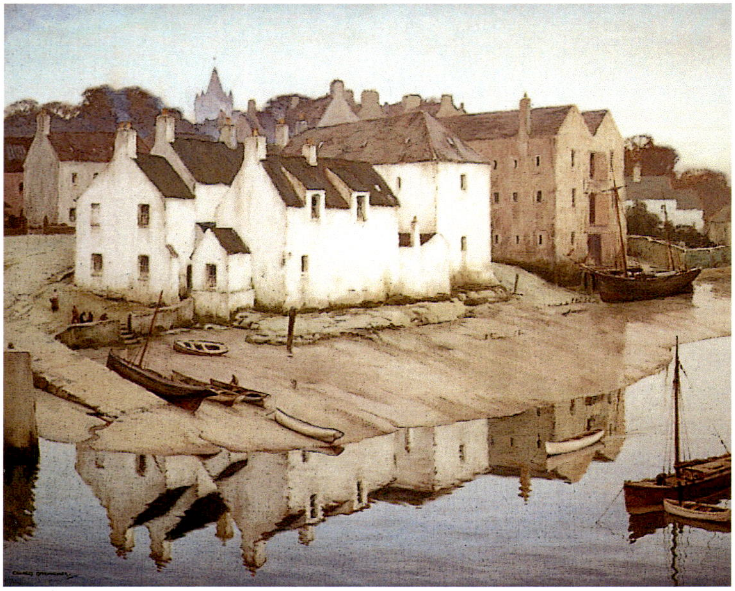

Plate 59 | *Waterside Kirkcudbright*, c.1935, Bourne Fine Art, oil on canvas, 23 × 30 inches

Plate 60 | *Early Morning, a Solway Port*, 1937, Worthing Museum and Art Gallery, oil on canvas, 38¼ × 48 inches

of Dee. Reflections of light on water were a constant fascination for him. The solid forms of the old waterfront buildings with Kirkcudbright Castle behind were perfect subject material that demonstrated his dexterity. The tide is in and small boats fully afloat in *Water-side, Kirkcudbright* illustrated in *The Scotsman* of 21 April 1933. The town is covered in snow and the boats are riding at anchor on a full tide and one is in full sail in *Winter Morning, Kirkcudbright* illustrated in the same paper on 26 April two years later. *Kirkcudbright* painted from a position on the quayside and *Waterside, Kirkcudbright* [pl.59] from a more distant vantage point prove Oppenheimer's sensitivity to colour. The subtleties in the smallest changes in hue and tone produce an effect of strength and solidity in the harbour buildings and yet convey the softest, fleeting breath of a breeze enough only to disturb the mirrored surface of the water in small patches. The tide is out in *Early Morning, Solway Port* [pl.60] and now the mud banks are fully exposed but still truncated reflections are mirrored in the water below the stranded boats. *Low Tide, Kirkcudbright* in the collection of the Botanic Gardens Museum, Southport is a very similar view. Another painting entitled *Kirkcudbright Harbour* in a private collection [pl.61] includes small boats and a yacht which may be a depiction of the *Zulu*, a visitor to the harbour on many occasions in the 1930s. The *Zulu* apparently had two masts. Oppenheimer depicted it with a single mast in a watercolour presented as a wedding gift and now in the recipients' daughter's possession. It would have upset 'the balance of the picture' to have included the second he was reputed to have said.

Ebb Tide, Kirkcudbright [pl.62] purchased by the Dumfries Education Trust in July 1943 is a view of the town and harbour from a distant

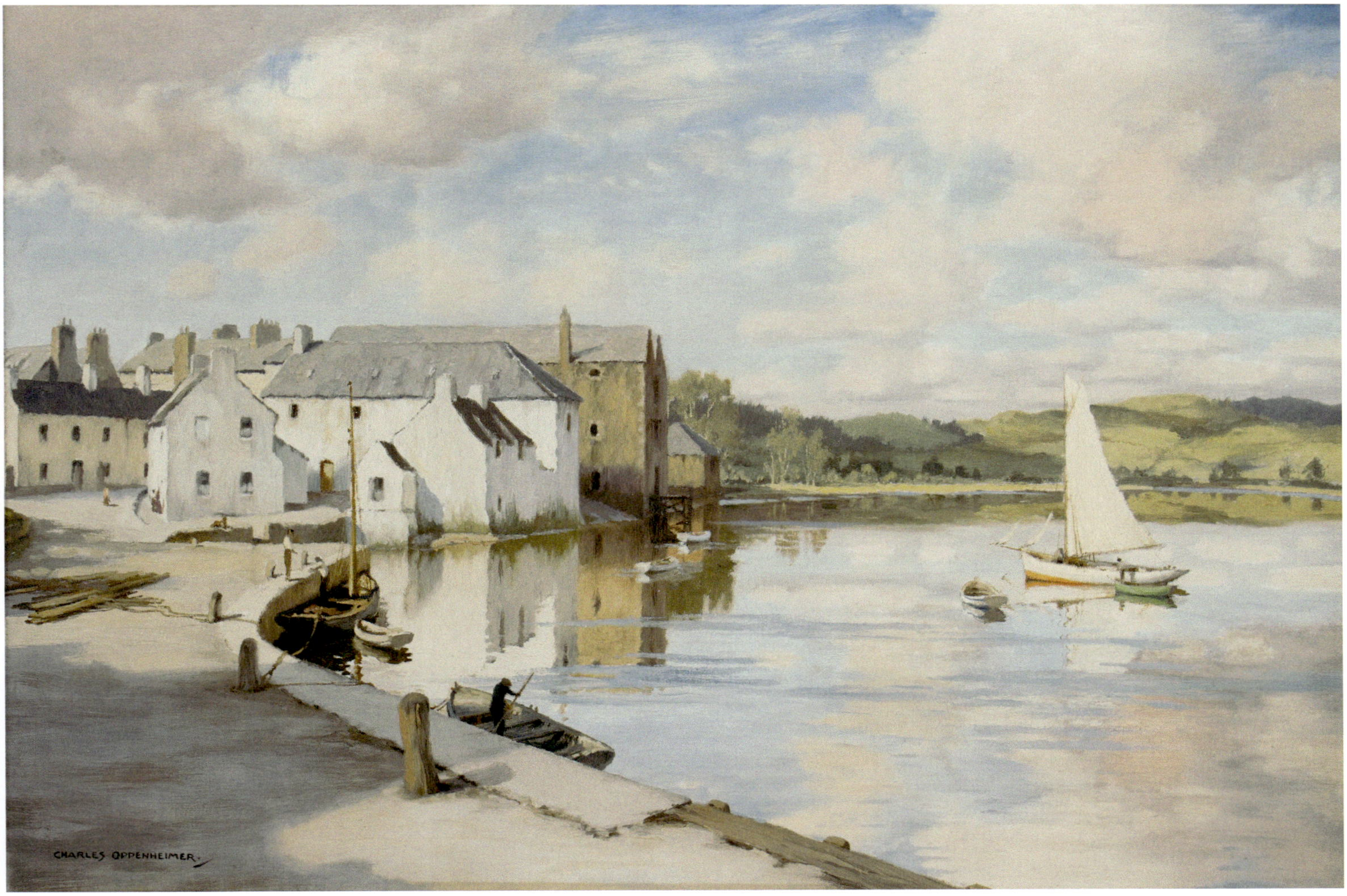

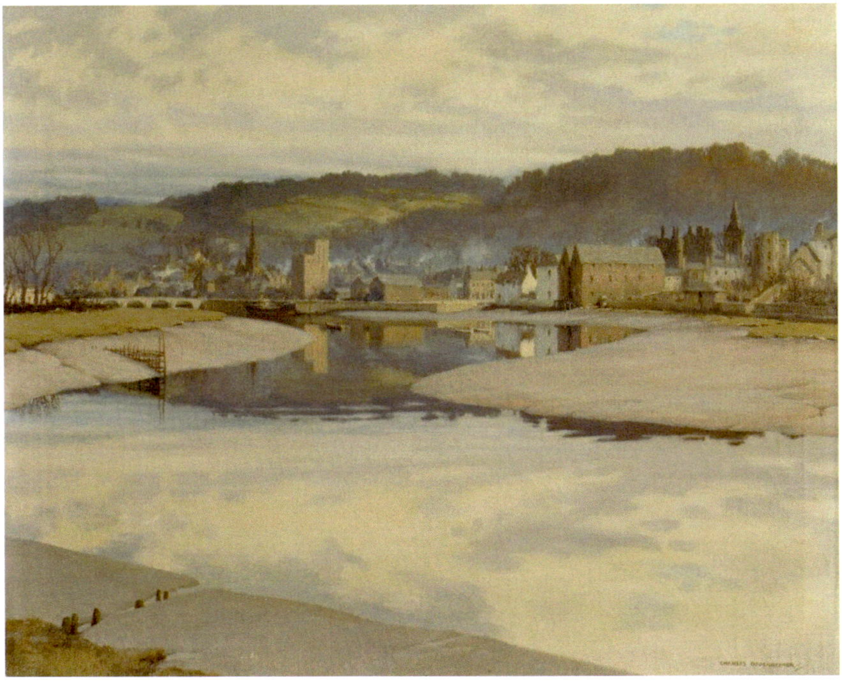

Plate 61 | *Kirkcudbright Harbour*, c.1935, Private Collection, oil on canvas, 19¾ × 30 inches

Plate 62 | *Ebb Tide, Kirkcudbright*, 1942, Dumfrieshire Education Trust, Gracefield Art Centre, Dumfries, oil on canvas, 27 × 35 inches

perspective on the opposite shore of the estuary. Exhibited the previous October at the Royal Glasgow Institute, it provoked an enigmatic review in the columns of *The Scotsman*:

Perhaps ... it is the ebb that is most important in the picture's imaginative appeal. We have the impression of a small country town retiring in a kind of self-effacing way – a psychological deduction of which may not perhaps have been entirely intended.[72]

E. A. Taylor wrote in *The Studio* in April 1927 that Galloway had 'supplied' Oppenheimer 'with the inspiration for many of his most notable pictures'. Exhibition catalogues record the depiction of Gallovidian hills, rivers, fields and woodlands in all the four seasons. *Old Tongland Bridge* [pl.63] is a fine example from the late 1920s or early 1930s of the type of painting that Taylor had in mind. Seldom from 1927 is Oppenheimer not mentioned in reviews and commentary on the main annual Academy and Institute shows. It was thus not a surprise that he was elected a full Royal Scottish Academician on 14 February 1934. His diploma work *Kirkcudbright under Snow* [pl.64] attracted much favourable attention. 'Characteristically bold in design and crisp and clear cut in execution' was one example.[73]

New Academicians were expected to participate in committee work and the mid 1930s were especially busy in that regard for Oppenheimer. In the *Round the Studios* column in July 1934 edition of *The Artist*, Oppenheimer, 'one of Scotland's finest landscape artists,' told the correspondent that 'he had not touched a brush for five weeks' because of all the visits he had had to make on being in London for the Royal Academy. 'He was obviously itching to get back to work and laughingly

Plate 63 | *Old Tongland Bridge*, 1940s, Private Collection, watercolour, 15¾ x 22¼ inches

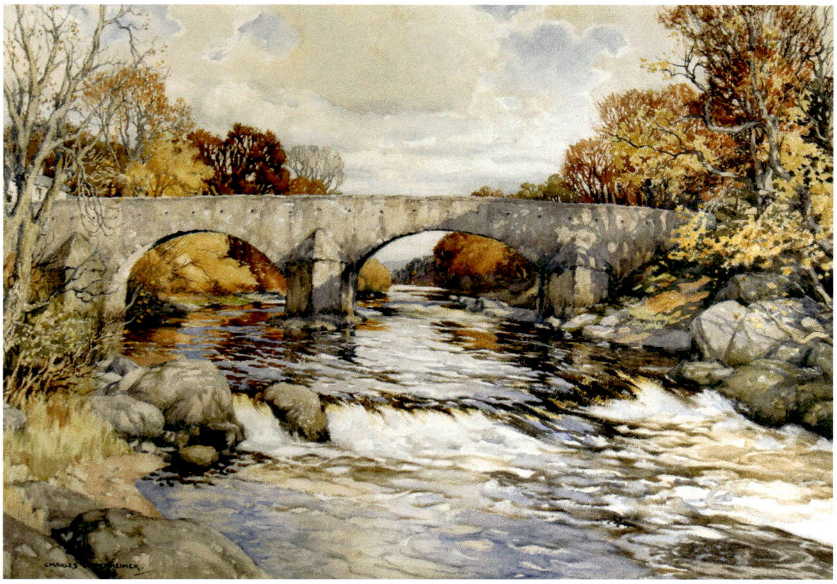

72 *The Scotsman*, 3 October 1942

73 *The Scotsman*, 26 September 1936

74 *The Artist*, July 1934, page 150

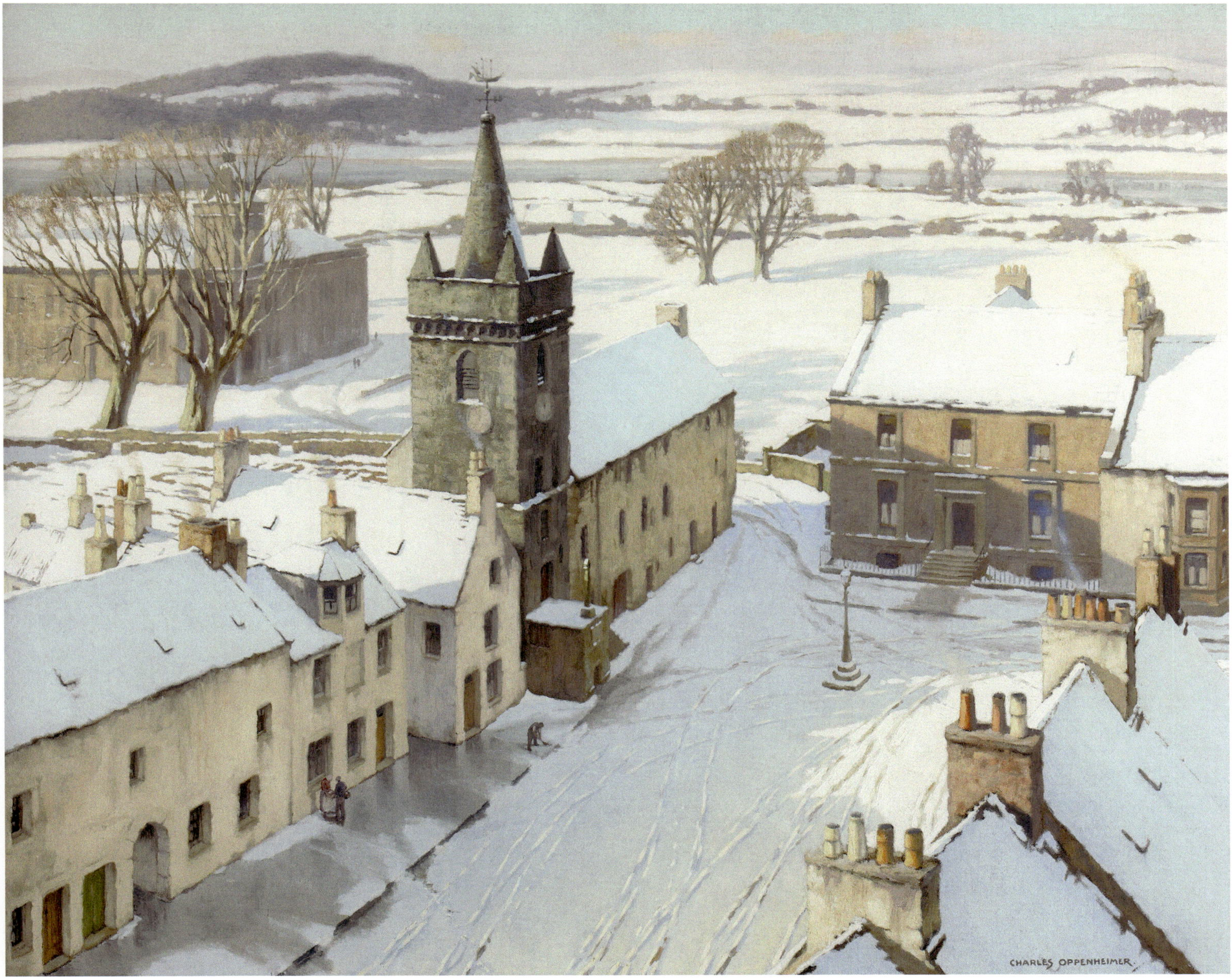

Plate 64 | *Kirkcudbright under Snow*, 1934, Royal Scottish Academy (Diploma Collection), oil on canvas, 38 × 48 inches

informed me that, if he did not do so soon, he would have to learn to paint all over again.'[74]

That was not to be necessary. Oppenheimer next produced a series of paintings of high quality depicting the various stages of construction of the Tongland dam for the Galloway Hydro-Electric Scheme. The project cost a total of £3 million and was constructed in 1934 and 1935. Tunnels were dug from Clatteringshaws Loch or reservoir to Loch Ken and from Loch Doon to feed the River Deugh which was dammed and thence to Loch Ken. The hub of the scheme was and still is Glenlea power station at Loch Ken. For spectacle however, the Tongland dam holding back

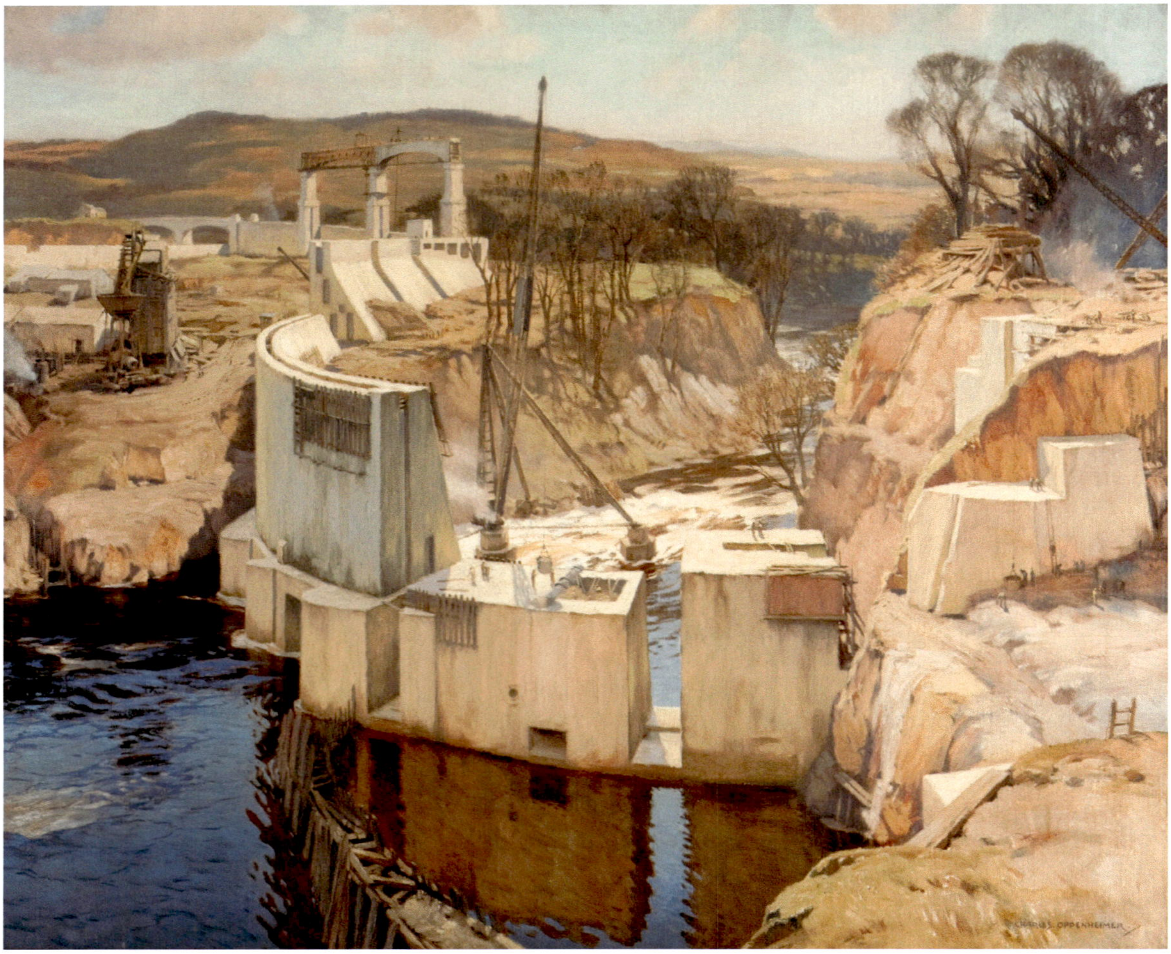

Plate 65 | *Harnessing the Dee*, 1934, Culture and Sport Glasgow (Museums), oil on canvas, 48 × 60 inches

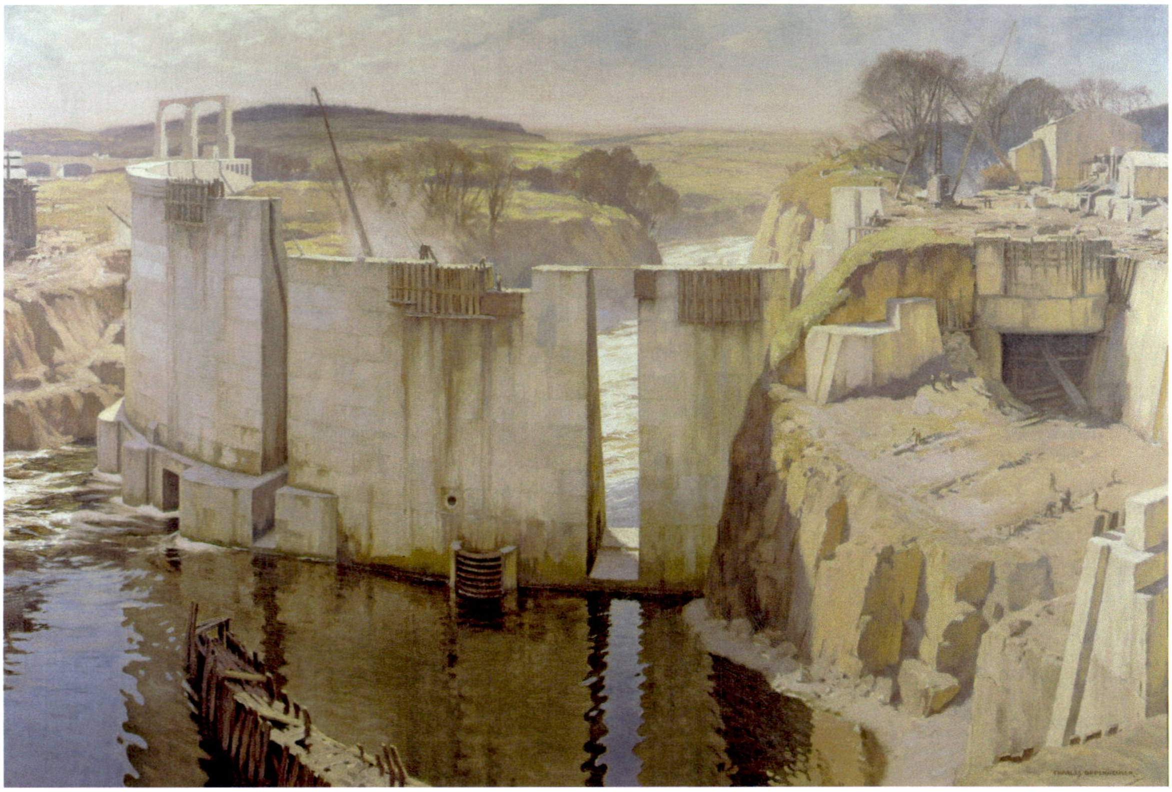

Plate 66 | *The Galloway Dam nearing completion*, 1935, The Fleming-Wyfold Art Foundation, oil on canvas, 48 × 72 inches

the Dee just before its escape to the sea and the associated electricity generation hall, is the most compelling.

Harnessing the Dee [pl.65] was at the RGI in 1934 and then loaned by Glasgow Corporation to the RSA in 1935. *The Galloway Dam nearing completion* [pl.66] was shown at the RSA in 1936. *Engineering in Concrete* the third in the series of industrial paintings was exhibited the following year. Contemporary critics were of mixed opinions. *Harnessing the Dee* inevitably caused the more pronounced views. It was better received at the Royal Academy than *The Galloway Dam – nearing completion.* Some liked neither; others marvelled that concrete should be treated as an art form.

All are tours de force. Standing in front of these large canvases their impact is self-evident. They are perhaps the supreme example of Oppenheimer's contention that great buildings and feats of engineering grow organically out of the landscape in which they are positioned. He conveys not only the strength and substance of the structure but its eventual harmony with its surroundings. Man is almost a mere prop in the final form. This is perhaps why in several pictures careful observation reveals that human figures are technically too small in scale. This was not a flaw of technique but rather a deliberate device in his middle and later career to emphasise the greater significance of buildings and their relative longevity compared to the human span in his paintings. Oppenheimer told admirers that a great landscape painting can have people in it, but should not rely upon figures to give the painting meaning or hold the viewer's interest. People should be subordinate to the landscape. He said as much in discussion with his interviewer F.G. Mories in *The Artist* in 1947.

> *... landscapes being pictures, wherein the figure of man and the form of beast are subordinated to the contours of fields, trees, rivers and the great surge and sweep of the sky. Pictures of* [Oppenheimer's] *in which architecture predominates show us architecture as influenced by the air in which it lives and by the sky whose blues and greys it reflects. He paints as one who feels that where trees are planted round a church these trees 'become soon dear as the temple's self.' The buildings in his pictures seem to have grown naturally out of the ground; the trees by long propinquity appear to have taken on the personality of the masonry; wind, rain and sun have played their part in unifying the whole, and it is that unity that gives his pictures their distinction.*[75]

In *A Bit of Old Edinburgh* [pl.67], Oppenheimer's very last entry at the RGI in 1958,[76] the beautifully observed and drawn figures in the foreground are smaller than would seem to be life size in comparison to doorways and windows. They nevertheless do not detract from the impact of the image. Nor do the figures in *The Tolbooth, Kirkcudbright*

75 *The Artist*, August 1947, page 132

76 Entered in 1958 and painted after 1938, the painting most likely dates from the 1940s

illustrated in *Kirkcudbright: 100 years of an Artists Colony* in which some in the middle ground are clearly undersize even if they were only local children. Meanwhile the woman stooping to hoist the washing line with a clothes' pole in *Winter time – Kirkcudbright* [pl.68] is nearer but not perhaps quite life size. This picture first exhibited in 1944 is perhaps the pinnacle of Oppenheimer's Kirkcudbright painting.

Oppenheimer's use of figures compares interestingly with that of other artists and, in particular, his fellow Royal Scottish Academician, George Houston. Houston used figures sparingly in his landscapes until 1916; thereafter they were very rarely employed. The two men knew each other well, but did not influence one another directly. As Douglas Percy Bliss said in May 1939, 'Charles Oppenheimer and George Houston again have obvious affinities. Each has a penchant for large scale and sweet and harmonious colour. Each is a 'gentle' painter, though neither lacks grasp of design or certainty of handling.'[77]

However a year previously the same critic had compared Houston and Oppenheimer's contributions to the RSA and had been disappointed.

Plate 67 | *A Bit of Old Edinburgh*, 1940s, Private Collection, oil on board, 13¾ x 17¾ inches

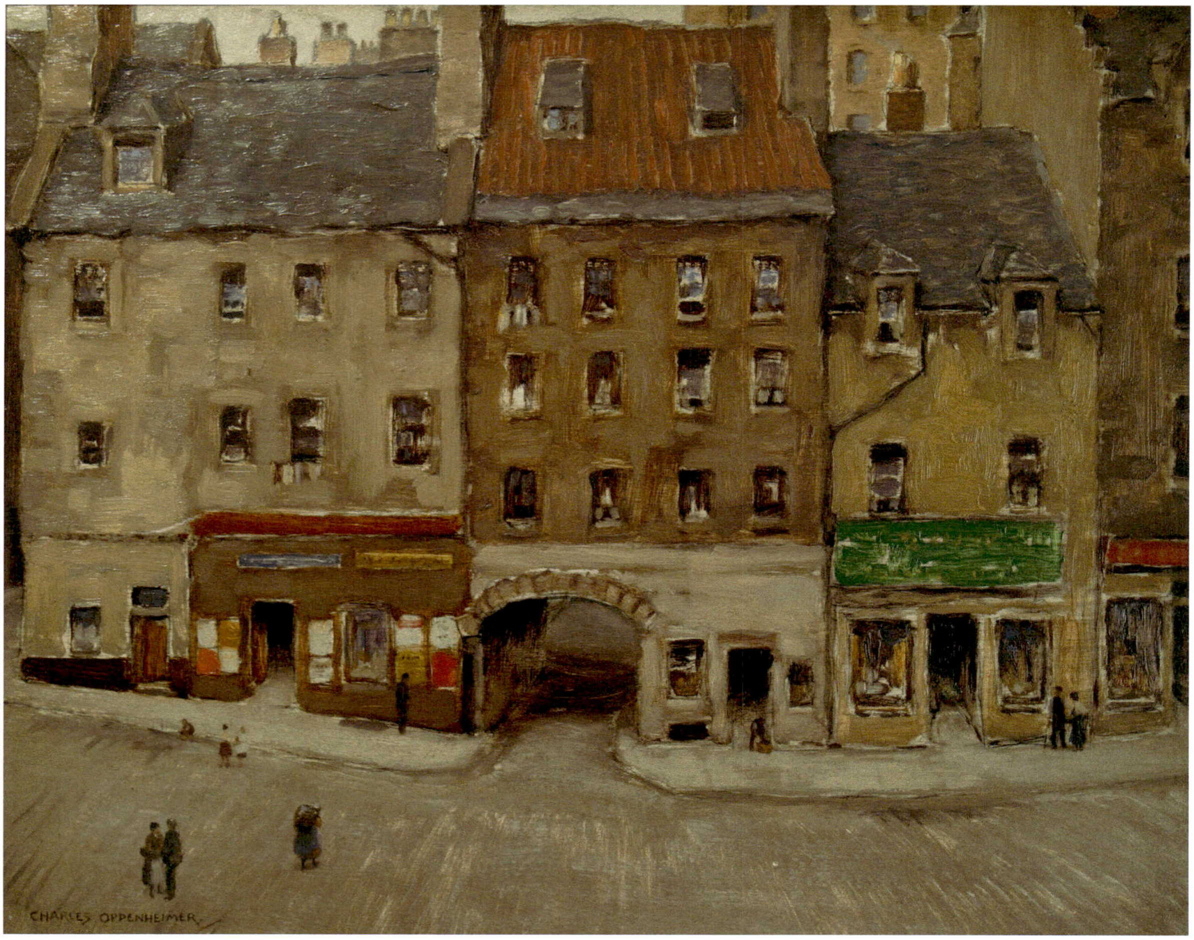

77 *The Scotsman*, 15 May, 1939

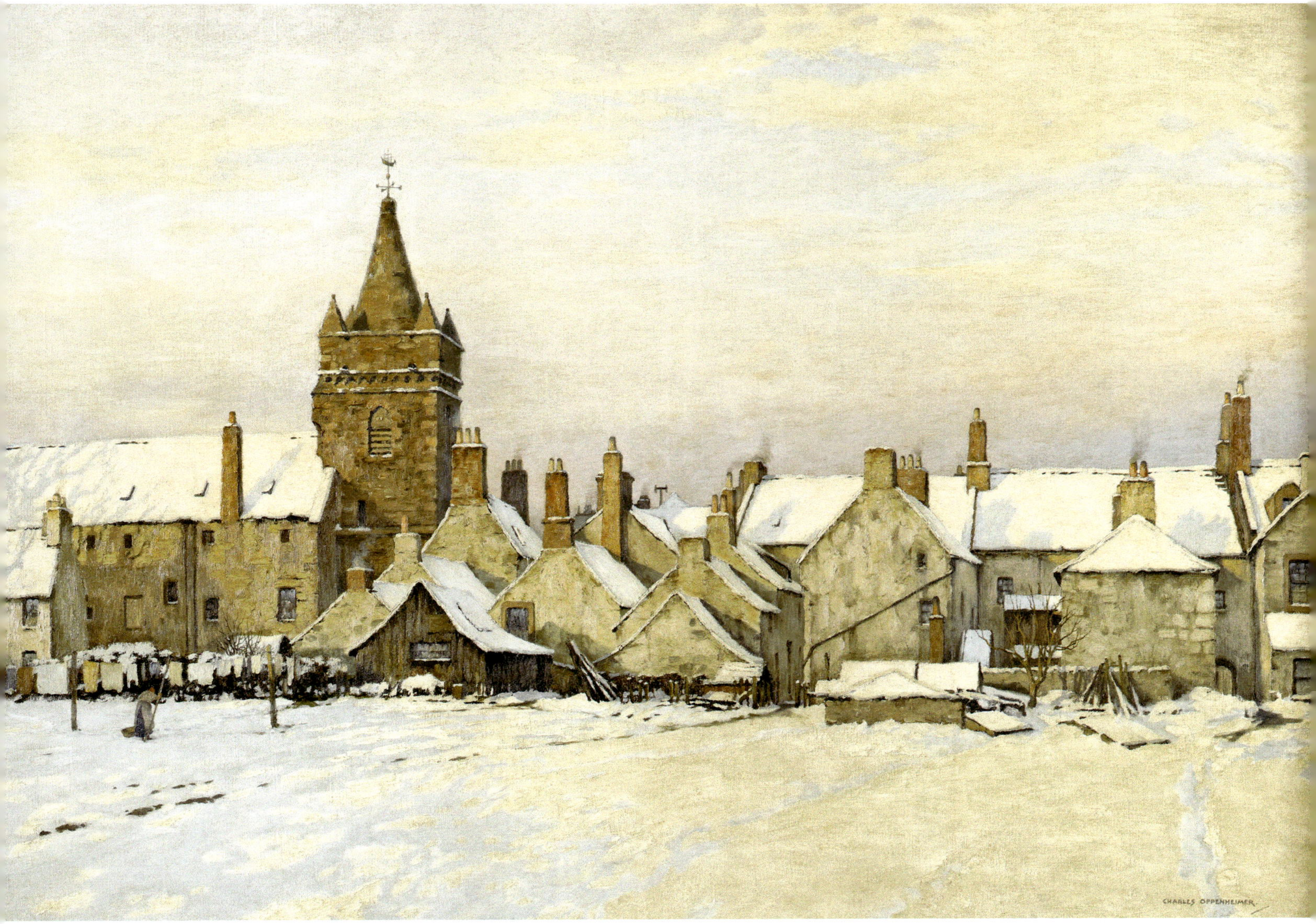

Plate 68 | *Winter time – Kirkcudbright*, 1944, Bourne Fine Art, oil on canvas, 48 × 68 inches

Houston's smaller pictures were not his best and Oppenheimer had chosen his subject unwisely. Bliss thought that *The Red Roofs of Whitby* was 'certain to be popular' although it was 'too much a view of the type from Holiday Hand-books'. Ironically the painting was later to form the main image in a 1950s railway poster [pl.65] tending to confirm the critic's complaint. What was too familiar to Bliss and his contemporaries is much less so now with changes in the vacation habits of millions brought about by relatively inexpensive foreign travel. Bliss also pondered why artists did not consider 'new forms' brought about by industrialists and engineers but this thought provoked a concession. 'And now it occurs to me that I have not been entirely just to Charles Oppenheimer for has he not given us of recent years two fine pictures of the new Galloway dam.'

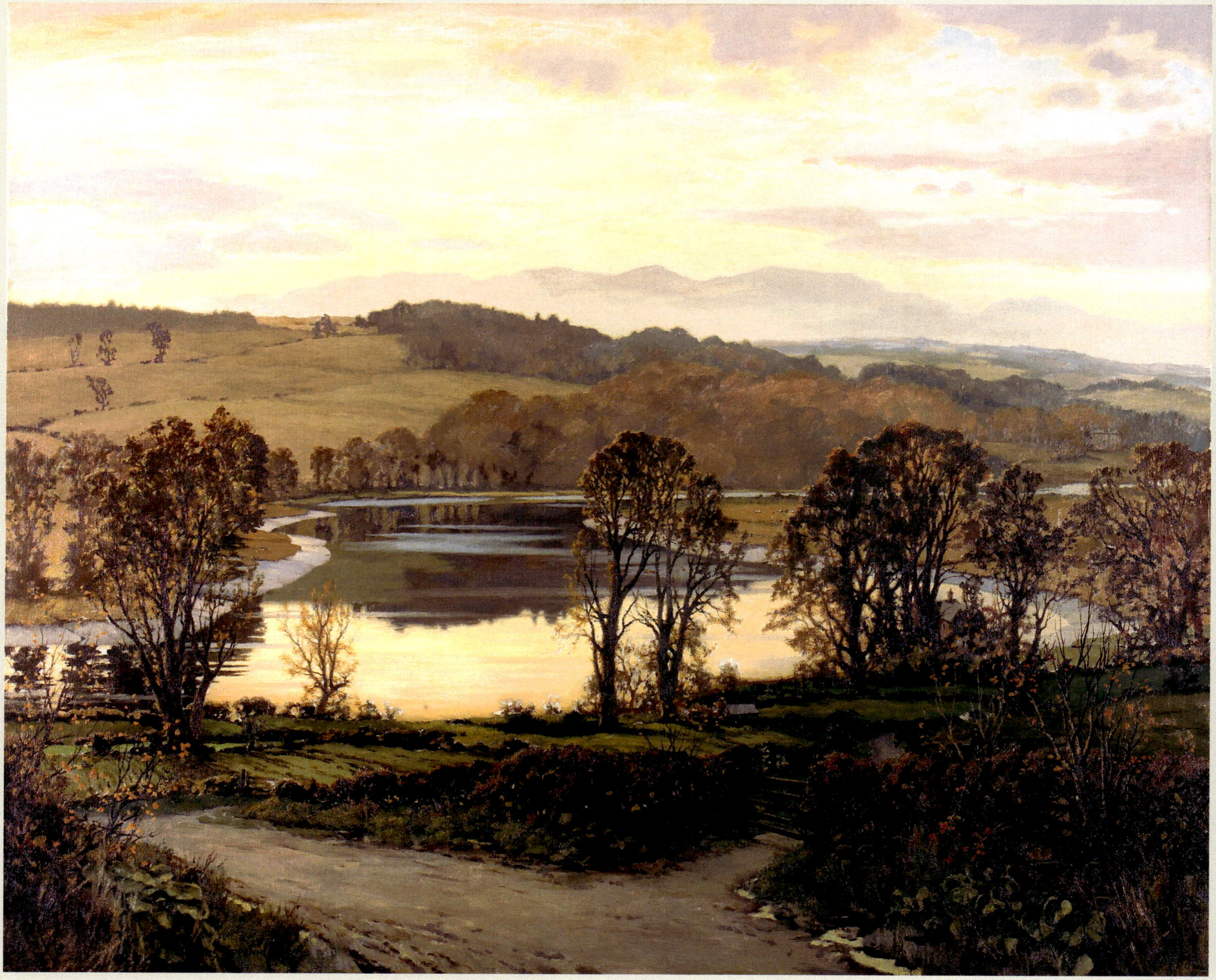

10 'ONCE THERE WERE GREAT MEN ...'

> *As you will see from the heading we have moved from the High Street (after almost 30 years there) to a smaller, but much more convenient house ... It is a pleasant change for we are out in the country, just on the edge of the golf course and high up with fine views. The house was built by William Mouncey in the '90s and when his widow died last autumn we were able to buy it.*[78]

Plate 69 | *The Dee from Woodlea*, 1940s, Bourne Fine Art, oil on canvas, 48 × 60 inches

The Robson family had been Mrs Mouncey's tenants at Woodlea before moving to Twynholm and afterwards to High Street. Oppenheimer continued:

> *It has a studio as part of the house and I am giving up my old one and will try to sell it. I am now working in the new one and am bringing my things over. My wife finds the smaller place much more easy to work as it is on two floors instead of the many stairs of the rambling old house in High Street.*

The old studio in Millburn passed to Tom Lochhead, the potter whose ceramic works and teaching in this branch of the arts achieved considerable distinction in post war years. It was transformed 'with little more than a hammer and saw 'into a home in which Lochhead and his wife brought up five children.[79]

To the new studio Oppenheimer added a large Pilkington's plate glass window in 1942, sourced through a relative's connections with the firm. The spectacular view over the Dee estuary through the window to the hills beyond became the subject of works over the next twenty years depicting the changing colours and moods of that landscape. *The Dee from Woodlea* [pl.69] is a particularly fine example.

At Woodlea Oppenheimer retained his disciplined, business style approach to work. He would enter his studio promptly in the morning after breakfast and emerge in the early evening. Visitors to Woodlea recall its dark wood interior and dark wallpapers, some of deep mauve. The background helped to display his pictures and those of other artists – especially Fred Jackson – which Oppenheimer had acquired over the years. 'My pictures are my windows on the world' he would explain to visitors, artists amongst whom he would ask to sign

78 Oppenheimer to J.E. McGill Duncan Esq, 5 May 1939

79 *Tales of Kirkcudbright Artists* by Haig Gordon, Galloway Publishing, 2006, pages 120–122

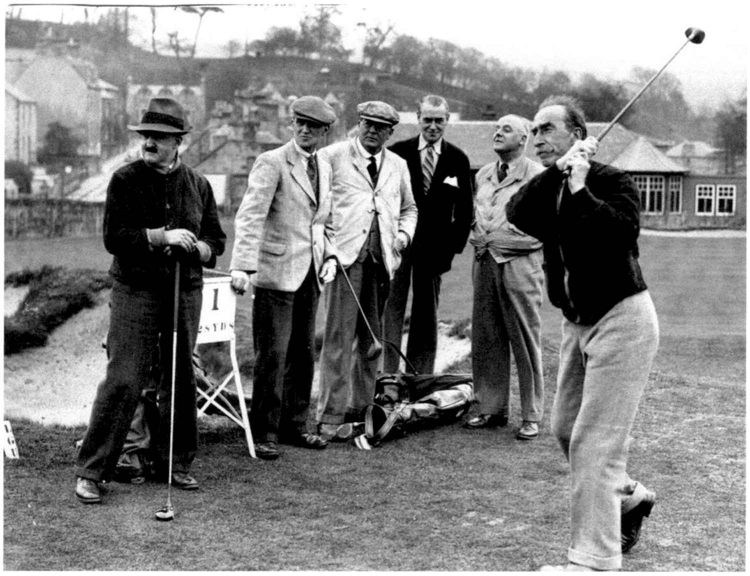

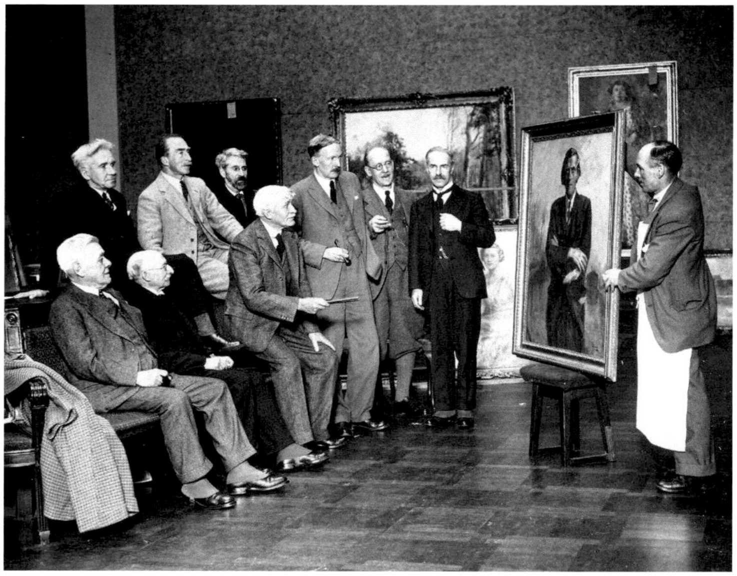

Plate 70 | Oppenheimer tees off at the Scottish Artists Society golf outing, courtesy of the Stewartry Museum, Kirkcudbright

Plate 71 | The Selection Committee of the Royal Scottish Academy, 1936, Royal Scottish Academy Archives. (*Portrait of James Maxton MP* by Sir John Lavery is the painting being viewed).

a wall in the house. It is reputed that the wall was covered by 1960.

It was not just a casual observation when Oppenheimer noted Woodlea's proximity to Kirkcudbright golf course in his letter to Mr J E McGill Duncan. Oppenheimer was a keen and proficient golfer, enjoying the sport as much as he did fishing. He participated with many contemporaries in the Scottish Artists' Golfing Society's outings [pl.70] and was Captain of Kirkcudbrightshire Golf Club in the 1936/37 season. He is said in the Club's 1993 Centenary booklet to have been generous giving both of 'his time and in other ways'. For example he donated a framed sketch plan of the course in 1928 and later, in his captaincy year, a case of King George VI silver coins as a trophy for a competition. Both have subsequently been lost. Renamed Kirkcudbright Golf Club in 1945, the course was frequented on Monday mornings by a regular four ball of Oppenheimer, Jim Williamson, the Procurator Fiscal, retired Chief Constable Alec Donald and Willie Raphael, the former station master.

Mary Evans recalled playing with Oppenheimer one day and taking a large divot out of the fairway. 'Och,dinna dunsh Scotland!' came the call from her uncle in an exaggerated accent from a short distance away.

Always prepared to encourage the young, Oppenheimer sent a postcard from Montrose in September 1954 to George Shamash who had just won a junior competition at the Club. 'News of your success has reached the east coast,' he said then extending his congratulations. The Shamash family from Kirkcudbright has subsequently included many low handicap and amateur champion golfers.

After his election to the Royal Scottish Academy in 1934, Oppenheimer advanced in seniority in artistic circles throughout the decade. He was respected among contemporaries not only as a co-founder of the Dumfries and Galloway Fine Art Association with Hornel, the Taylors and Chris Ferguson[80] but also through work for the Kirkcudbright Arts and Crafts Society. His RSA Committee commitments took him to Edinburgh a good deal in the six years from his election until war was declared.

Inevitably he also lost relatives, friends and colleagues along the way. Oppenheimer had been a pall-bearer at fellow artist William Hanna Clarke's funeral in Kirkcudbright in 1924 after the latter's untimely fatal accident at Campbell and Sons, a local joinery firm's workshop in Police Close. Oppenheimer's mother Susan died in Manchester in 1925. William Stewart MacGeorge succumbed after a short illness in November 1931 at the age of sixty. Oppenheimer's Italian companion had left Kirkcudbright for Gifford in East Lothian in 1929 shortly after his marriage partly as a result of a falling-out with Hornel supposedly over the latter's heavy drinking.[81] Hornel himself died in June 1933 having suffered a stroke the previous autumn. Nearly two years later in May 1935 Oppenheimer attended the ceremony at Kirkcudbright Academy at which a memorial oak-framed bronze plaque was unveiled in memory of Hornel, a long time benefactor of the school.

Oppenheimer was prominent amongst the mourners at David Gauld's funeral on 22 June 1936, which saw a large turnout of fellow RSA members and Scotland's art establishment. Gauld had been a frequent visitor to Kirkcudbright over many years and had shared a studio with MacGeorge in Castlemains for a time. 1935 Oppenheimer had joined Gauld on the RSA Hanging Committee and he was a member of the Council in 1935 and 1936 and the Selection Committee in 1936 and 1937 [pl.71].

In 1938 Oppenheimer suggested a significant improvement to the promotion of the RSA's annual exhibitions. In April he wrote to Sir George Pirie, the President and to members of the Council of the RSA proposing better advertising of the exhibition on the Mound galleries. 'I have been for a long time of the opinion that after the publicity of the opening week of our Exhibition, the passer-by in Princes Street seems to forget that the show is still open. This applies still more to the visitor to the city during the summer months, and I have known many cases of folk having missed the Exhibition, thinking the Gallery was closed.'[82] He put this down to the 'rather forbidding and gloomy façade of our building'. The entrance door was less than visible as were the two small notice boards. Accordingly the Council should invite 'a Leith sail-maker' to provide a large banner to be tied across the columns of 'the severe Doric portico'.

Oppenheimer submitted an illustration which he also described in some detail. 'To be in keeping with the architectural setting I think that

80 Christian Jane Ferguson, 1876–1957, a native of Dumfries, studied at the Glasgow School of Art becoming principal art mistress at Glasgow High School for Girls. She painted landscape and architectural subjects in both oil and watercolour.

81 MacGeorge married Mabel Munro a watercolourist and widow of artist Hugh Munro. Over twenty years his junior Mabel, the niece of the Earl of Minto obtained considerable notoriety by her first marriage to the penniless and hence unsuitable to contemporary eyes, Munro, and thereafter by leaving forty five of MacGeorge's paintings to the Town Hall in Haddington and not returning them to the Stewartry after his death in 1931.

82 Royal Scottish Academy archives, letter to the President and Council, 8 April 1938

the natural colour of sail-cloth should be retained, and I would like to have the upper inscription in gilt with black contours and the lower in red, also contoured in black. The lettering should be very carefully spaced and be an example of how an Academy thinks a public notice of this sort should be done.' Furthermore, it 'should be drawn by an expert and the painting and gilding could be requested of one of the better students in the Decorators Class at the College of Art.'

RSA's Secretary David Foggie's cold water reply later in the month explained that the Council thought that the Board of Trustees would object, especially to the size, but that nonetheless notices 'with exhibition in red painted on them' were being given serious consideration. (The RSA does now hang a banner between its portico columns and so Oppenheimer's advice was eventually heeded.)

The limited promotional ambition of his peers did not do too much harm to Oppenheimer's own sales from the Academy's exhibitions. Sixteen of his pictures were bought by patrons and the public between 1936 and 1950.

Oppenheimer received many favourable and honourable mentions in newspaper columns from his election to the RSA in 1934 through until the 1950s. *The Times* on 26 April 1935 reporting on the RSA exhibition, again bracketed George Houston and Oppenheimer.

> *'The Scottish landscapes of (Houston) are always notable and this year he is seen at his best. Charles Oppenheimer RSA is another painter of memorable Scottish scenes and in Harnessing the Dee, now the property of the Glasgow Corporation, he brings to the industrial scene the vision of a poet.'*

The Roman Wall painted in 1938 attracted much attention as did for example a watercolour of the same year entitled *A Moorland Road in Galloway*. 'There is the delicacy of poetry in this study. In the distance there are blue hills, and fronting them stretches of pleasant brown. A felicitous sky patterns the roadway with sun and shade.'[83] The picture was hung in an exhibition entitled *Art and Peace, Expression of the Nation's Cultural Attainments. The Studio* did not neglect Oppenheimer over this period. His 1937 Royal Academy entry *A street in old France* was handsomely featured under the title of *Cavée St Firmin, Montreuil-sur-Mer* in its edition of March 1940.[84] Another picture from this period is *The Old Lighthouse – Southerness on Solway* [pl.72] which was doubtless executed in combination with a golf outing. A similar painting hangs in the clubhouse of the nearby golf course.

Less than a year before the outbreak of war, Oppenheimer received an invitation for what would have been a further high accolade. Sir Henry Rushbury wrote on 12 November 1938[85] requesting Oppenheimer's

83 *The Scotsman*, 4 July, 1938

84 *The Studio*, Volume 119, March 1940, page 79.

85 The letter is in the archives of the Stewartry Museum in Kirkcudbright

86 In conversation with Joe Campbell, 13 June, 2007

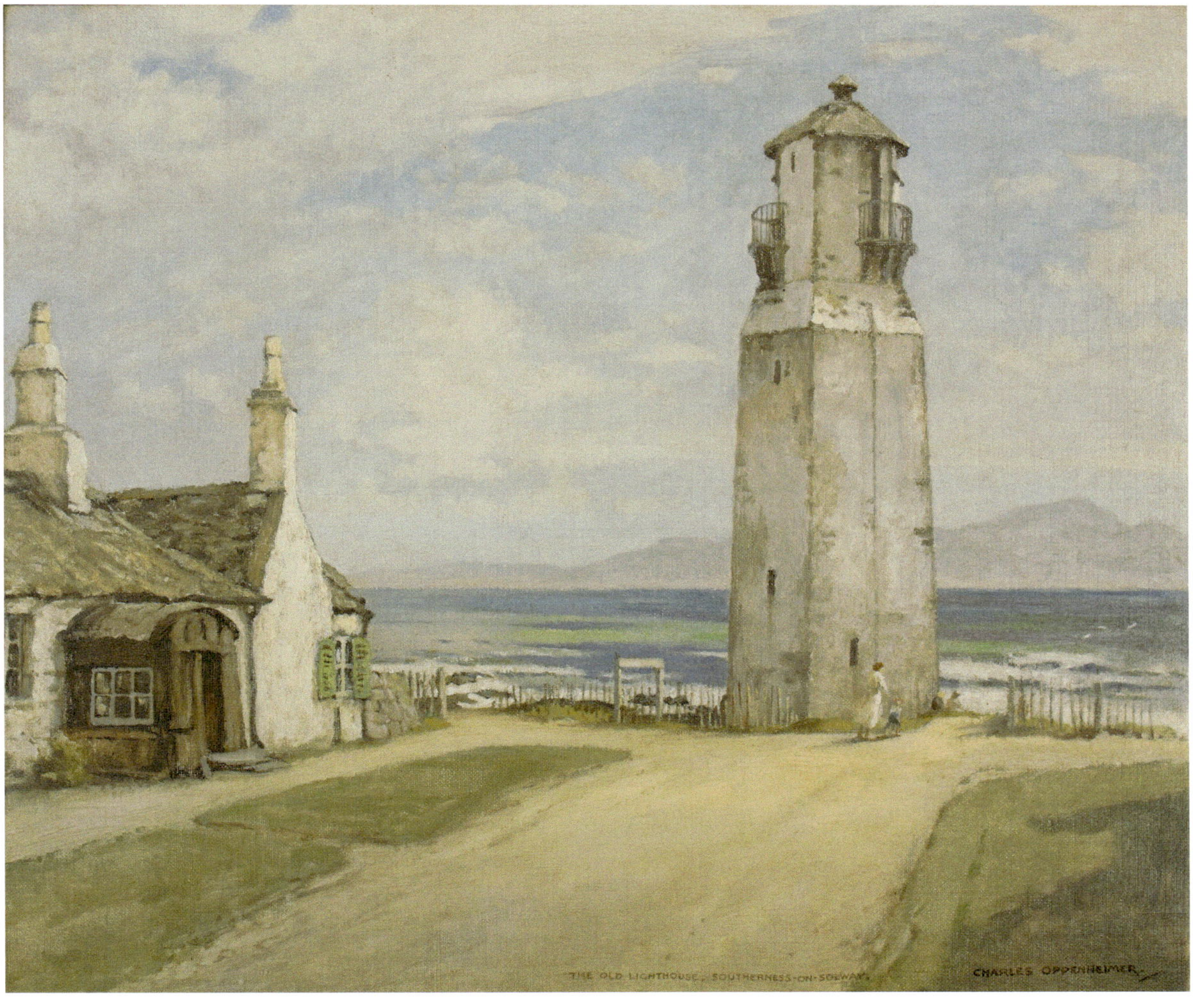

Plate 72 | *The Old Lighthouse – Southerness on Solway*, 1930s, Private Collection, oil on canvas, 19½ x 23½ inches

permission that he and a number of friends should nominate Oppenheimer for membership of the Royal Academy. Years later Connie Oppenheimer explained that apart from the toil of travelling to and from London more often, they could not easily have met the costs involved.[86] Rushbury and his friends were to be disappointed, but Oppenheimer continued to send his paintings to annual exhibitions in London for the next fourteen years and made special efforts to do so in wartime.

The Oppenheimers had little chance to enjoy their new home at Woodlea before the outbreak of war on 3 September 1939. At 64 and well beyond the age for call up, Oppenheimer became a voluntary special constable in 1941 and was to be seen on many occasions over the next four years going in uniform about his police duties in Kirkcudbright. Perhaps with half an eye on a revival of the anti-German sentiment of twenty five years previously, he was assiduous in his duties. 'We had a strenuous time here last week up all night for five consecutive nights on police work.' Kirkcudbright might not have been in the front line but the neighbouring

Tongland dam and military installations at Dundrennan perhaps were the targets for the German bombs that fell near the town in early May 1941. 'We had four bombs unloaded on open ground [at Ardendee] but no one was touched and no damage except broken windows'; he told RSA Assistant Secretary Henry Hastings in a letter dated 12 May.

> *I lost nine panes in my studio but they were small and are all in again. It left me too sleepy to work at any painting that week but am at it again now 'as fresh as paint' as the saying is.*

Bomb damage had been evident in his journey to support the Royal Academy annual exhibition earlier in the year. Oppenheimer was a regular visitor to the varnishing day and found 'four of the rooms are closed but the RA is better for it as it isn't so tiring with fewer pictures'. His three were 'very well hung'. As to London itself, it was 'still the great city, almost all of it standing intact, though of course where it has got it there is heavy damage. If they kept at it for another 10 years London would still be there and most of it looks quite normal but for broken windows which make a building look rather derelict but does not affect the structure'.

Oppenheimer's observations are not only interesting in the particular but also with regard to popular perceptions of people resident outside the capital. 'That won't win the war for them. I came away feeling much more satisfied after seeing what it was like instead of reading about it – for in reading one is apt to dwell on the ruins and to forget the great bulk of the city still standing firm.'[87] During the war years Oppenheimer was asked by the Pilgrim Trust to contribute a painting to the Trust's 'Recording Scotland' initiative. *White Gables, Kirkcudbright* joined other works in the final collection covering twenty four counties, the purpose of which to allow later generations to know something of how Scotland looked as the clouds of war had gathered.

The war years marked the end of Oppenheimer's involvement as an office-bearer with Scottish art institutions. Nevertheless he did achieve a further distinction when for the 1949–50 session, he became President of the Manchester Academy of Fine Arts to which he had first been elected thirty eight years previously. Oppenheimer kept almost a continuous relationship with the Manchester Academy, exhibiting a total of one hundred and twenty paintings, his last two being *The Old Tolbooth, Kirkcudbright* and *Lake Lucerne*. He did not send pictures after he was made an honorary member in 1952. *The Old Tolbooth* and *Evening, Lake Lucerne* were displayed on loan from Manchester Art Gallery to the centenary exhibition held at Manchester Town Hall in 1959 of work of both, then current and past members.

Wartime Special Constable Oppenheimer [pl.83] had at least one privilege accompanying his duties – an enhanced petrol ration. It allowed modest excursions to painting grounds nearby. On one occasion he found that the Duncan family had just missed Campbell's bus back to Edinburgh. Oppenheimer went to his car nearby, took off the petrol cap, stuck in his walking stick and withdrew it announcing that he could take the family as far as Knockbrex.[88]

In his later years Oppenheimer's driving was the cause of both amusement and concern. He had little idea of the requirements of other traffic. He drove slowly and would stop to look at a view without pulling to the side. He drove in daytime with headlights full on and on one occasion lost control of a car that he had newly acquired. Seemingly the gearing was difficult and to his discomfort, he came down the Puir Hoose Brae from Woodlea too quickly, shot across the main Tongland Road and hit the parapet of the railway bridge at the foot. No-one was injured.

James Campbell recalls encountering Oppenheimer when on the Post Office counter in Castle Douglas not long after the end of the war. Oppenheimer announced with some enthusiasm that he had a commission to paint Threave Castle and had come from Kirkcudbright in his new car at a top speed of 35mph.[89] Commenting in *The Scotsman* in 1961 after the artist's death, Wilfrid Taylor recalled how, until well into his eighties the Oppenheimers would leave Kirkcudbright for Edinburgh making their way 'slowly and sedately in an old fashioned car'. 'A serene man he saw no point in missing the glories of the countryside by driving at much more than 20mph. Sometimes he would drive on to Montrose, a town which he had known in his youth and of which he was very fond.'[90] Friends and colleagues 'worried about his safety but he managed the journeys and never came to harm'. Nor for that matter did other road users.

Oppenheimer retired as a Special Constable after the war. He is widely credited with the design of the Scottish police cap badge which includes the motto '*Semper Vigilo*'. His obituary in the Galloway News stated as much. In fact the badge was created in 1931 by Robert Dickie Cairns the art master at Dumfries Academy at the request of the then Chief Constable of the Dumfries County force.

The confusion seems to have occurred because Oppenheimer may well have been involved in the early design of the chequered bands worn on Police caps and uniforms in Scotland from the 1930s and now to be found worldwide. The so-called '*Sillitoe tartan*' was the inspiration of Sir Percy Sillitoe the Chief Constable of the City of Glasgow Police. He was responding to complaints from the public that Police officers were not readily recognisable in the dark because of the colour of their uniforms. Her Majesty's Inspector of Constabulary for Scotland at the time was

87 Oppenheimer to Henry Hastings, Assistant Secretary, 12 May 1941, RSA Archives

88 In conversation with Niall Duncan, June 2005. Knockbrex is a large mansion house situated at the entrance to Carrick Shore around five miles west of Borgue in the direction of Gatehouse of Fleet.

89 In conversation with Jim Campbell, 13 June 2007

90 'A Scotsman's Log', *The Scotsman*, 22 April 1961

Brigadier General Robert Maxwell Dudgeon DSO MC who was a friend and likely a patron of Oppenheimer. No direct evidence has yet been uncovered but Police historians believe, and Oppenheimer family tradition holds that Dudgeon asked Oppenheimer to make an initial drawing or design for the chequered band having first discussed the matter with Sillitoe probably during or after an inspection of the Glasgow force.[91]

Oppenheimer's work was in steady demand both during the war years and throughout the post-war period. 'I have been most fortunate in the RSA and any big painting seems to have attracted a good deal of attention. I have been lucky too in the RA where an oil and also a watercolour have found purchasers', he commented to one correspondent:

> *It is all very unexpected in war-time and I put it down partly to the black-out causing people to take more interest in their own houses to which they are more confined in the winter months. There is a decided trend towards a greater interest in all the arts and it is a healthy thing and a promise for the future.*[92]

The prediction held true for Oppenheimer in as far that he sold fourteen paintings from the RSA Annual Exhibition alone from 1945 to his death in 1961.

The post-war years brought change and loss as well as certainty and gain. Three constant Kirkcudbright artist friends died: Jessie King in 1949, Bill Robson in 1950 and E.A. Taylor, Jessie's husband, in 1951.

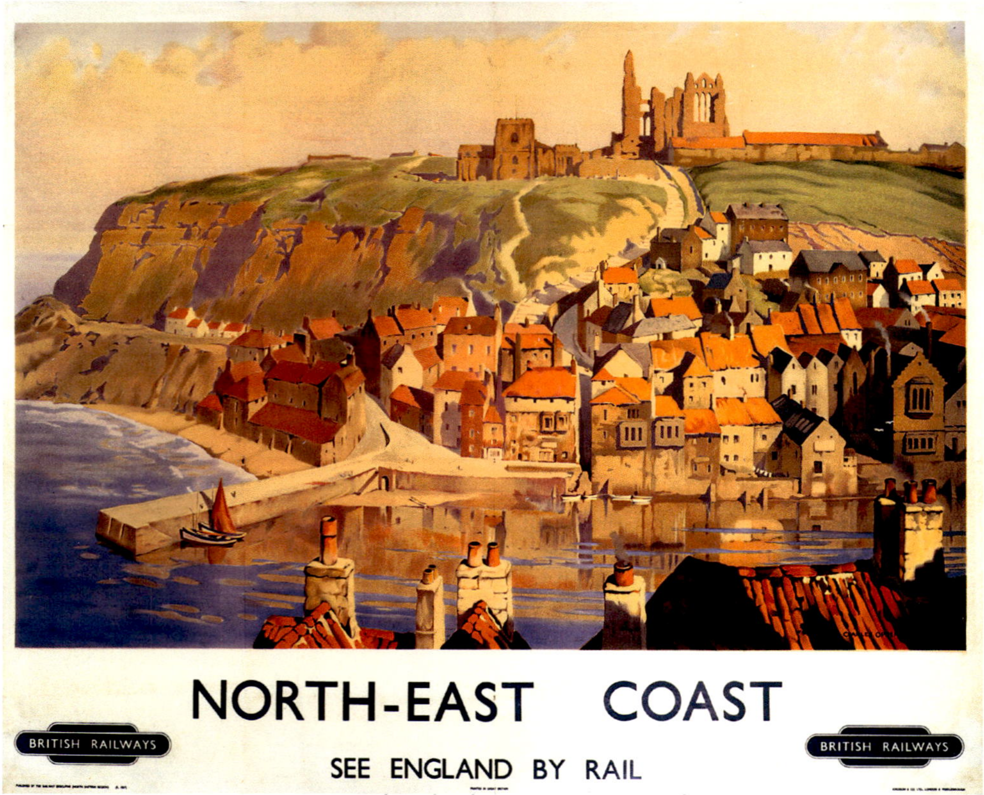

Plate 73 | *North East Coast (The Red Roofs of Whitby)* c.1950, railway poster, National Railway Museum Science & Society Picture Library, 39¼ x 49¼ inches

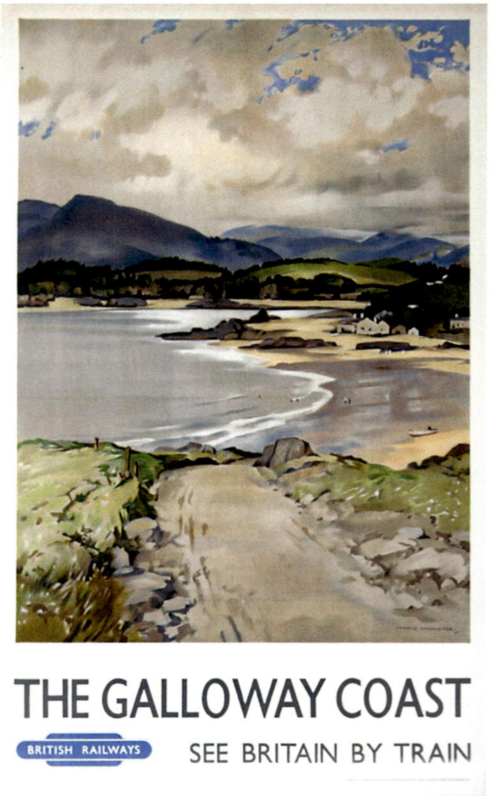

Plate 74 | *The Galloway Coast, Sandgreen Bay, Kirkcudbright,* 1955 railway poster, Private Collection, 49¼ x 24½ inches

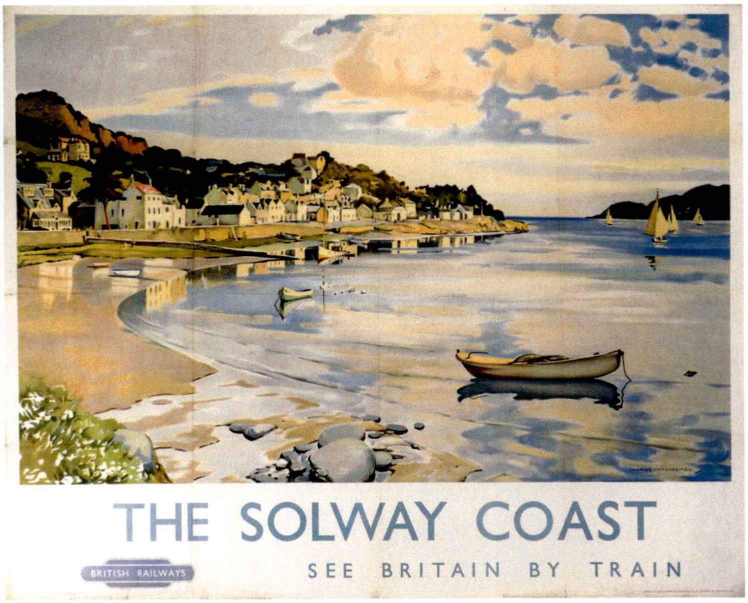

Plate 75 | *The Solway Coast, Kippford,* 1948 railway poster, National Railway Museum Science & Society Picture Library, 39¼ x 49¼ inches

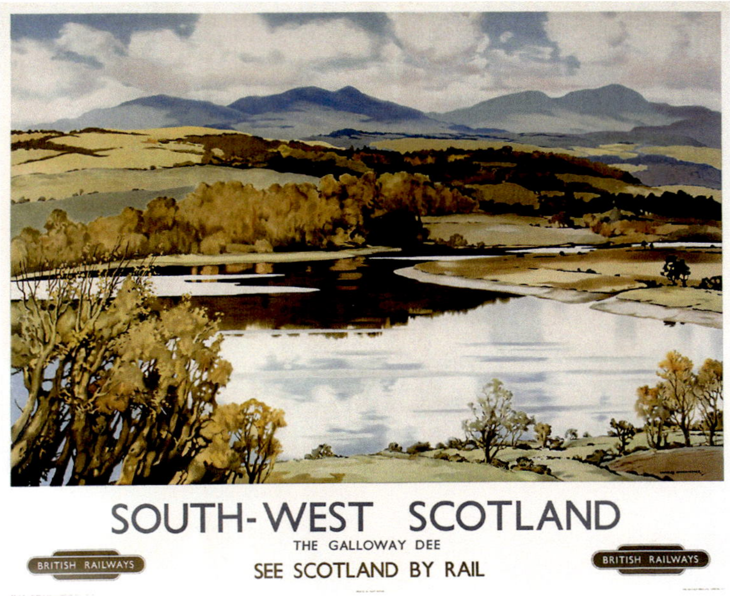

Plate 76 | *South West Scotland: The Galloway Dee*, 1950–1953, railway poster, Private Collection, 39¼ x 49¼ inches

Each was a grievous loss. Oppenheimer had known Taylor and King for nearly fifty years; he had spent his first weekend in Kirkcudbright as their guest at the time of his decision to leave Manchester. Bill Robson and the Oppenheimers were in each other's homes constantly over the duration of their acquaintance, a grand-daughter recalling how Oppenheimer would call to see her grandparents regularly when they were less able to get about in their later years. On a happier note, the Oppenheimers celebrated their Golden Wedding in 1953.

A loss of another sort occurred in 1952. Oppenheimer decided not to exhibit again at the Royal Academy. However it was not his age that led to the decision. He told friends and relatives that the Academy was giving too much wall space to poor or deliberately odd works. 'I agree with Munnings'[93] was his considered conclusion. He remained a stalwart of the RGA and RSA, his last pictures at their respective annual shows being exhibited in 1958 and 1960.

The Artist summarised Oppenheimer's position in these post-War years as that of 'a luminary of the Scottish constellation':

> *His fame has been won through the usual channel of exhibitions and acknowledgement of his gifts by public bodies, and better, through the recognition that has come to him from his fellow artists. His rise to fame has none of the hidden flash of the meteor. It has had the quiescent growth of those meadows and trees he loves so intimately and paints so well. He has risen with the steadfastness of a star.*

Retirement seems never to have crossed Oppenheimer's mind until he reached the age of eighty five in 1960. Indeed he had entered upon a new type of venture in the late 1940s when he became involved in the

91 I am indebted to Joe Craig the Curator of the Dumfries and Galloway Constabulary Police Museum for his help in clarifying these matters

92 Extracts from a letter to J. E. McGill Duncan Esq, 25 July 1942

93 Sir Alfred James Munnings KCVO, PRA (1878 – 1959) was known as one of England's finest equestrian painters and a stern and outspoken critic of Modernism.

production of railway posters. It is now unclear how this work came to him. Friends and family claim that he had to attend publishers to understand more about production techniques and what was expected of him. It is said that he recounted that a particular painting style was best which when enlarged from the original, served advertising purposes. *The Solway Coast, Kippford* [pl.75] is the best such example. Commissioned by LNER (London and North Eastern Railway) it was displayed by the newly nationalised British Railways in 1948.[94] Oppenheimer stands in front of it in his studio in a photograph taken in 1958 [pl.84].

Three more posters were produced for British Railways. Two, *South West Scotland: The Galloway Dee* [pl.76] and *North East Coast: See England by Rail: View of Whitby Harbour* [pl.73] can be dated to the 1950s whilst *The Galloway Coast: Sandgreen Bay* [pl.74] has definitely been ascribed to 1955 by railway historians. The income from these railway posters was said by Oppenheimer to be a welcome addition to his sales from exhibitions and commissions. Mystery however surrounds an allied area of endeavour, namely carriage prints. Relatives and friends recall seeing a number of these prints in train carriage compartments in the 1940s and 1950s. Experts in this form of ephemera or railwayana can find no trace of any such work either in extant examples or in the records of known printers. Everything may now be lost or waiting to be rediscovered somewhere.[95]

Oppenheimer remained a vigorous participant in Kirkcudbright life. In the autumn of 1955 the recently turned octogenarian wrote to the press as the elected Honorary President of the Kirkcudbright Harbour Cottage Fund. He explained that he was requesting donations to save the derelict eighteenth century harbour cottage which formed part of 'a notable group of buildings' beside Kirkcudbright harbour. 'All who have been charmed by this famous group, and the thousands of artists who have painted it, will agree that this disappearance of the cottage would be a calamity.' The subsequent donations and help from the National Trust for Scotland and the Historic Buildings Council for Scotland and the public were enough to ensure that the building was saved, restored and opened on 6 September 1957 as the Harbour Cottage Art Gallery. Oppenheimer's support for the cause had contributed significantly to the Fund's success. His prestige also helped when paintings by artists who had connections with the town were collected for the inaugural exhibition.

One of Oppenheimer's last letters in the Royal Scottish Academy's archives was written to Stanley Cursiter in September 1960. By now he was eighty five and his words summarise both the nature of the man and his outlook on life. There had been discussion about an Academy pension for Oppenheimer but he had 'second thoughts' and decided not to apply.

94 The Transport Act 1947 nationalised the railways from 1 January 1948

95 I am grateful to the UK's leading expert, Greg Norden of the Travelling Art Gallery for his advice on railway posters and carriage prints.

I have never placed the money side of a painter's life too highly and my wife and I have always lived quietly and my real rewards came when a City Art Gallery made a purchase for its permanent collection. Also I was brought up to 'put by for a rainy day' so when a sale came off I always did that. My friend and banker tells me that I have now got enough to allow me to go on in our old comfortable way. I have always told my wife that if ever she is in real need to ask you for your advice in any Academy matters, as one who knows the ropes. But there must be many artists in these difficult times who require the help of the pension fund much more than I do, so I am leaving it for them. I am ever thankful to have my wife still with me after 57 very happy years of married life. I have always been proud of my membership of the RSA and of the fact of you and I being elected together.

Charles Oppenheimer died in Kirkcudbright Cottage Hospital on the evening of Sunday 16 April 1961. He left his estate to Connie in 'love, favour and affection'.

In the *Sunday Express* of 25 May 1958 he had famously remarked that the Highlands were 'too sensational' to paint. 'Fine to visit. Fine to climb. But not adaptable enough for painting.' He had also lamented that contemporary 'Kirkcudbright is not what it was artistically'. 'Once there were great men here.' So indeed there were; and Charles Oppenheimer was one of them.

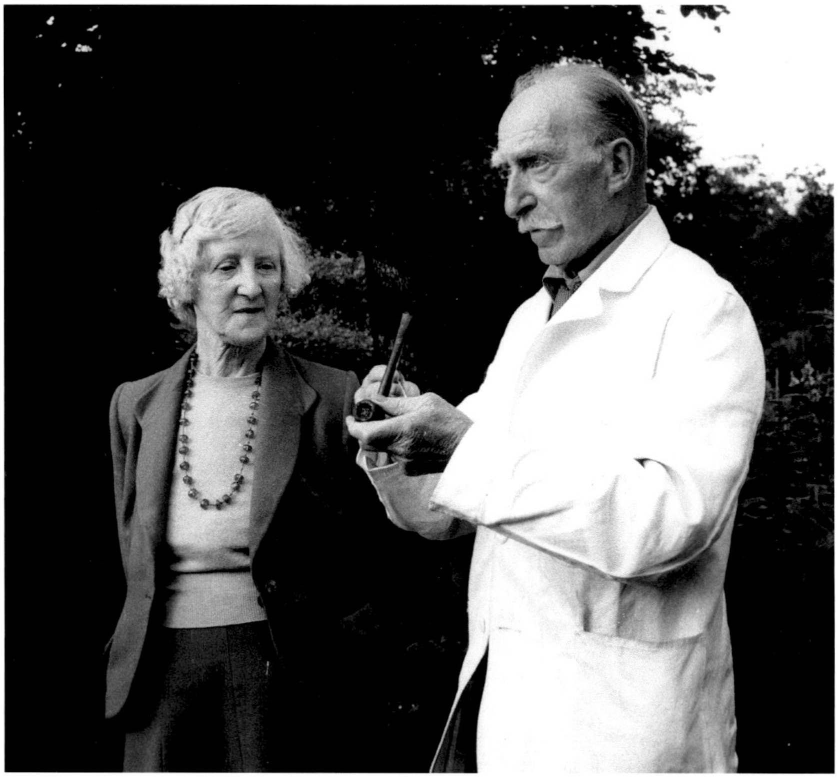

Plate 77 | Mr and Mrs Charles Oppenheimer, 1958, courtesy of the Stewartry Museum, Kirkcudbright

LUDWIG OPPENHEIMER LTD: A BRIEF HISTORY

CHARLES OPPENHEIMER'S FATHER Ludwig, commenced his business career in Manchester in 1865. Two other Oppenheimers appear in the 1865 edition of the city's Trade Directories. Joseph Oppenheimer, described as a merchant, conducted his business from 52 Brown Street in the city centre and James Oppenheimer, another merchant but of Leimnitz and Company, was recorded at York House in Oxford Road. Whilst there is no surviving record of any family relationship between Ludwig and his namesakes, it is a reasonable supposition that Joseph was an uncle, an older cousin or a more distant relation because Ludwig's first business address was 52 Brown Street, Manchester.

The development of Ludwig's business from its first mention can be charted in Trade Directory entries. By 1871 he is said to be an importer of parquetry and foreign floor tiles still in the Brown Street building. However by the time of Charles' birth, the 1875–76 Directory records that Ludwig had left Joseph behind and was now at 17 Cooper Street not far away and close to the Town Hall.

A reference, in the columns of *The Scotsman* on 9 June 1874 headed 'New Inventions' recorded the award of a patent in the previous week to 'Oppenheimer, tiles, & c'. The opening sentence of the patent describes its purpose. 'My (i.e. Ludwig's) invention consists of a method of producing ornamental tiles or slabs in geometrical forms so that they may be adapted to a floor or wall to fit each other according to any desired pattern or arrangement after the manner of ordinary tiles.'

By 1877–78 the business had moved to 64 Mulberry Street, Hulme. The 1881 Census confirms the successful progress of the Oppenheimer family business which had survived the economic depression of the late 1870s. A note by the compiler in the column headed 'Rank, Profession or Occupation' declares that Ludwig Oppenheimer employed thirteen men and fifteen women. It also curiously claimed that he was an 'embroiderer', a misunderstanding or honest mistake, which may have caused some amusement among family and friends.

Plate 78 | Promotional leaflet for Ludwig Oppenheimer Ltd, 1920s or 1930s. courtesy of the Oppenheimer family

Many Victorian businesses prospered because they had 'some degree of monopoly power … through patent exploitation, the possession of

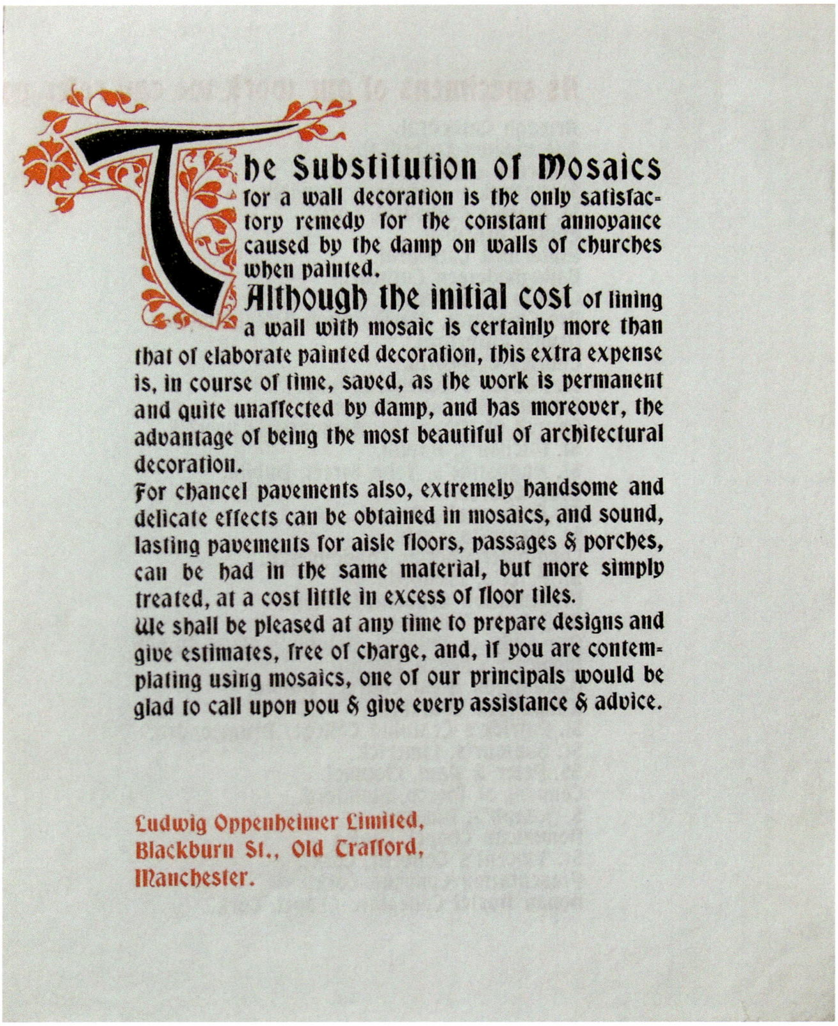

The Substitution of Mosaics for a wall decoration is the only satisfactory remedy for the constant annoyance caused by the damp on walls of churches when painted.
Although the initial cost of lining a wall with mosaic is certainly more than that of elaborate painted decoration, this extra expense is, in course of time, saved, as the work is permanent and quite unaffected by damp, and has moreover, the advantage of being the most beautiful of architectural decoration.
For chancel pavements also, extremely handsome and delicate effects can be obtained in mosaics, and sound, lasting pavements for aisle floors, passages & porches, can be had in the same material, but more simply treated, at a cost little in excess of floor tiles.
We shall be pleased at any time to prepare designs and give estimates, free of charge, and, if you are contemplating using mosaics, one of our principals would be glad to call upon you & give every assistance & advice.

Ludwig Oppenheimer Limited,
Blackburn St., Old Trafford,
Manchester.

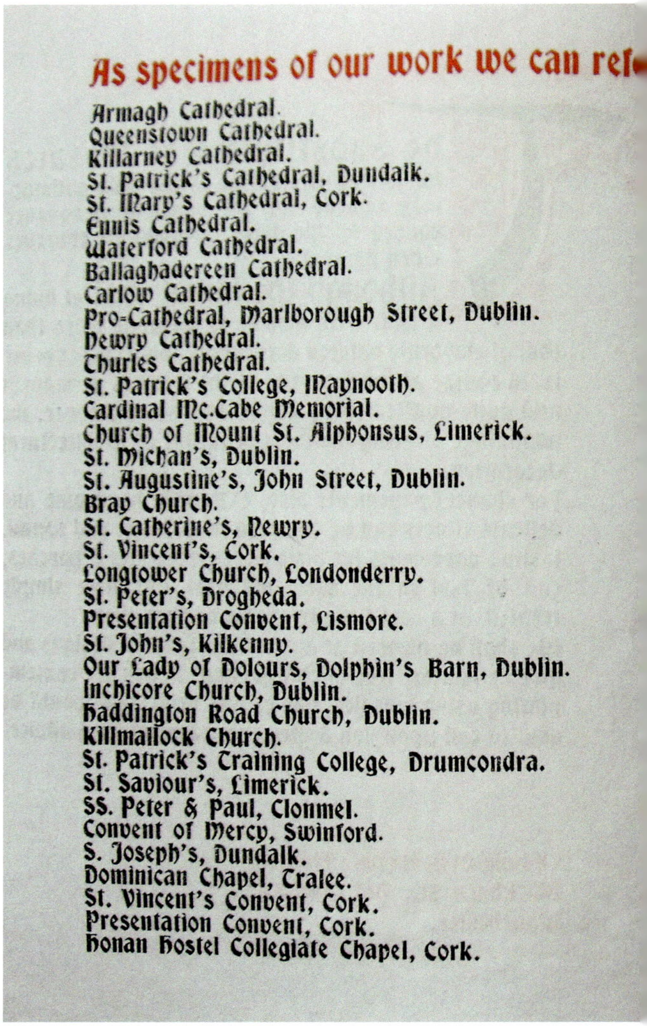

As specimens of our work we can ref

Armagh Cathedral.
Queenstown Cathedral.
Killarney Cathedral.
St. Patrick's Cathedral, Dundalk.
St. Mary's Cathedral, Cork.
Ennis Cathedral.
Waterford Cathedral.
Ballaghadereen Cathedral.
Carlow Cathedral.
Pro-Cathedral, Marlborough Street, Dublin.
Newry Cathedral.
Thurles Cathedral.
St. Patrick's College, Maynooth.
Cardinal Mc.Cabe Memorial.
Church of Mount St. Alphonsus, Limerick.
St. Michan's, Dublin.
St. Augustine's, John Street, Dublin.
Bray Church.
St. Catherine's, Newry.
St. Vincent's, Cork.
Longtower Church, Londonderry.
St. Peter's, Drogheda.
Presentation Convent, Lismore.
St. John's, Kilkenny.
Our Lady of Dolours, Dolphin's Barn, Dublin.
Inchicore Church, Dublin.
Haddington Road Church, Dublin.
Killmallock Church.
St. Patrick's Training College, Drumcondra.
St. Saviour's, Limerick.
SS. Peter & Paul, Clonmel.
Convent of Mercy, Swinford.
S. Joseph's, Dundalk.
Dominican Chapel, Tralee.
St. Vincent's Convent, Cork.
Presentation Convent, Cork.
Honan Hostel Collegiate Chapel, Cork.

some unique skill [or] the differentiation of their products.' Arguably, the Oppenheimer business had all three and was by then, outside Italy, a significant European mosaic manufacturing and design company.

The Oppenheimer mosaic business appears to have grown markedly in the 1880s to the extent that it moved premises to Blackburn Street off Stamford Street in Old Trafford in the either 1890 or 1891.

Ludwig's sons entered the business during these years. Lehmann and Charles became the designers and supplied the artistic input to the business whilst Ludwig Junior, Albert and William concentrated on the production, marketing and sales activities. Ludwig's youngest son Frank took no part in the business as he trained in medicine and eventually became an Army medical officer of senior rank.

As mentioned in the text the business became a limited liability company in 1901 after Ludwig's death. The eight shareholders were Lehmann and his wife Edith née Newton, Ludwig Junior and his wife Jessie née

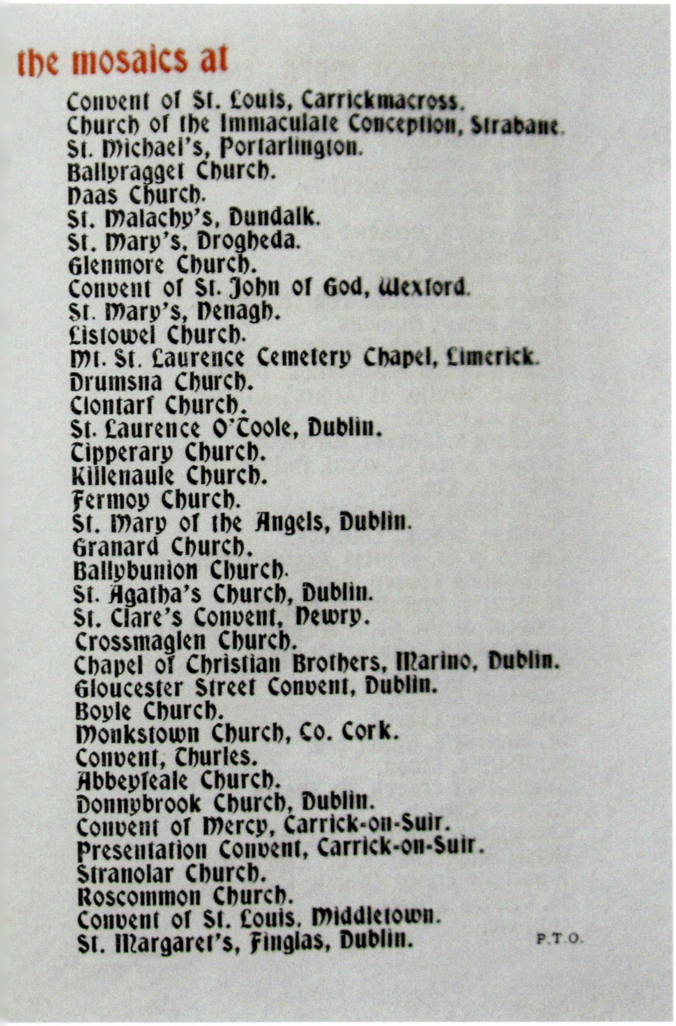

the mosaics at

Convent of St. Louis, Carrickmacross.
Church of the Immaculate Conception, Strabane.
St. Michael's, Portarlington.
Ballyragget Church.
Naas Church.
St. Malachy's, Dundalk.
St. Mary's, Drogheda.
Glenmore Church.
Convent of St. John of God, Wexford.
St. Mary's, Nenagh.
Listowel Church.
Mt. St. Laurence Cemetery Chapel, Limerick.
Drumsna Church.
Clontarf Church.
St. Laurence O'Toole, Dublin.
Tipperary Church.
Killenaule Church.
Fermoy Church.
St. Mary of the Angels, Dublin.
Granard Church.
Ballybunion Church.
St. Agatha's Church, Dublin.
St. Clare's Convent, Newry.
Crossmaglen Church.
Chapel of Christian Brothers, Marino, Dublin.
Gloucester Street Convent, Dublin.
Boyle Church.
Monkstown Church, Co. Cork.
Convent, Thurles.
Abbeyfeale Church.
Donnybrook Church, Dublin.
Convent of Mercy, Carrick-on-Suir.
Presentation Convent, Carrick-on-Suir.
Stranolar Church.
Roscommon Church.
Convent of St. Louis, Middletown.
St. Margaret's, Finglas, Dublin.

P.T.O.

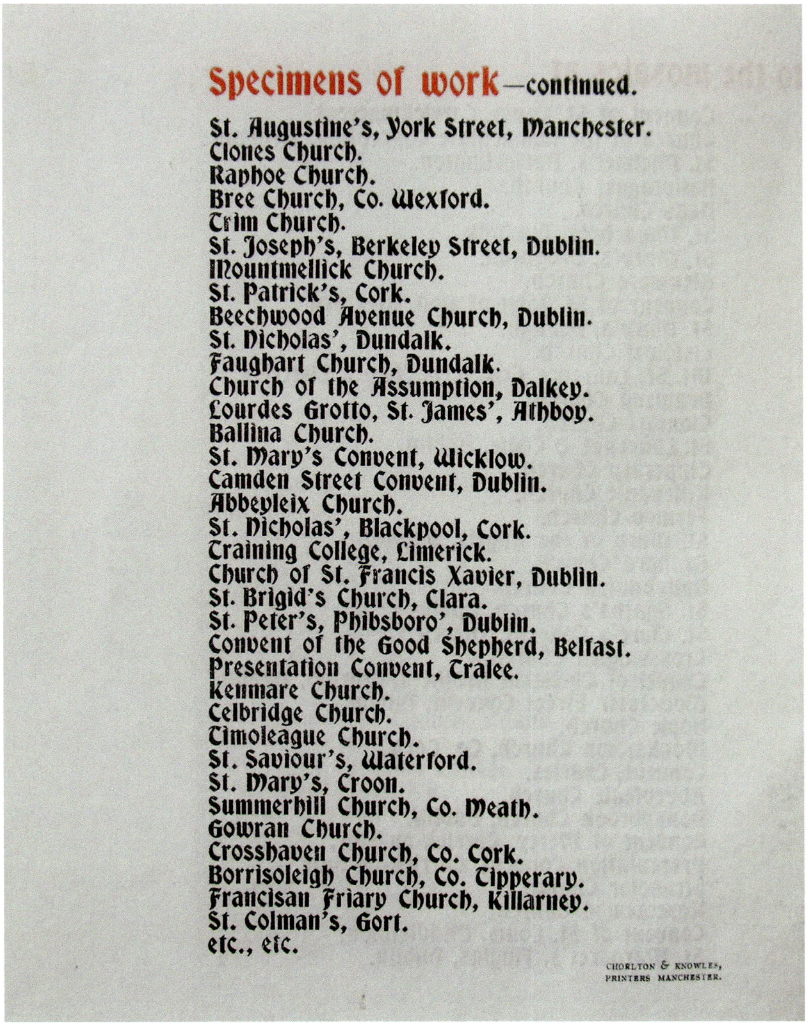

Specimens of work—continued.

St. Augustine's, York Street, Manchester.
Clones Church.
Raphoe Church.
Bree Church, Co. Wexford.
Trim Church.
St. Joseph's, Berkeley Street, Dublin.
Mountmellick Church.
St. Patrick's, Cork.
Beechwood Avenue Church, Dublin.
St. Nicholas', Dundalk.
Faughart Church, Dundalk.
Church of the Assumption, Dalkey.
Lourdes Grotto, St. James', Athboy.
Ballina Church.
St. Mary's Convent, Wicklow.
Camden Street Convent, Dublin.
Abbeyleix Church.
St. Nicholas', Blackpool, Cork.
Training College, Limerick.
Church of St. Francis Xavier, Dublin.
St. Brigid's Church, Clara.
St. Peter's, Phibsboro', Dublin.
Convent of the Good Shepherd, Belfast.
Presentation Convent, Tralee.
Kenmare Church.
Celbridge Church.
Timoleague Church.
St. Saviour's, Waterford.
St. Mary's, Croom.
Summerhill Church, Co. Meath.
Gowran Church.
Crosshaven Church, Co. Cork.
Borrisoleigh Church, Co. Tipperary.
Francisan Friary Church, Killarney.
St. Colman's, Gort.
etc., etc.

CHORLTON & KNOWLES,
PRINTERS MANCHESTER.

Plate 79 | Promotional leaflet for Ludwig Oppenheimer Ltd, c.1902, courtesy of the Oppenheimer family

Northrop, Albert and his wife Grace (who was Edith's sister), Charles and William.

At some time probably around 1897 or 1898, Eric, Lehmann and Edith's son joined the workforce. Albert left the business and became a farmer in Cheshire in the mid 1900s. Charles left for Kirkcudbright in 1909, the preparation for which included the alteration to the company's Articles of Association whereby shares could be sold in house or on the open market but only by the agreement of the other shareholders.

In 1915 Eric left the business after volunteering for active service. His father Lehmann did so simultaneously and was away from work from the end of 1915. However Charles returned from Kirkcudbright to take his place. Charles himself left together with his younger brother William at the end of 1916.

Family understanding is that Ludwig Junior asked Lehmann whether the business might be sold not long before the latter's death in hospital in

1916. However this did not happen and William and Eric resumed work on their return from the war. A recently uncovered letter places William in Ireland in December 1918 visiting clients in the Roman Catholic Church. Charles did not return to work with the business preferring his artistic career in Scotland.

Ludwig Junior was said not to be a particularly effective businessman and trade was also difficult during the war. At some time in the period 1919 to 1921 it seems that Albert decided to leave farming, bought out the other shareholders and ran the business with his son Fritz known as Geoff

Plate 80 | Verso of promotional leaflet for Ludwig Oppenheimer Ltd, 1920s or 1930s. courtesy of the Oppenheimer family

MOSAICS

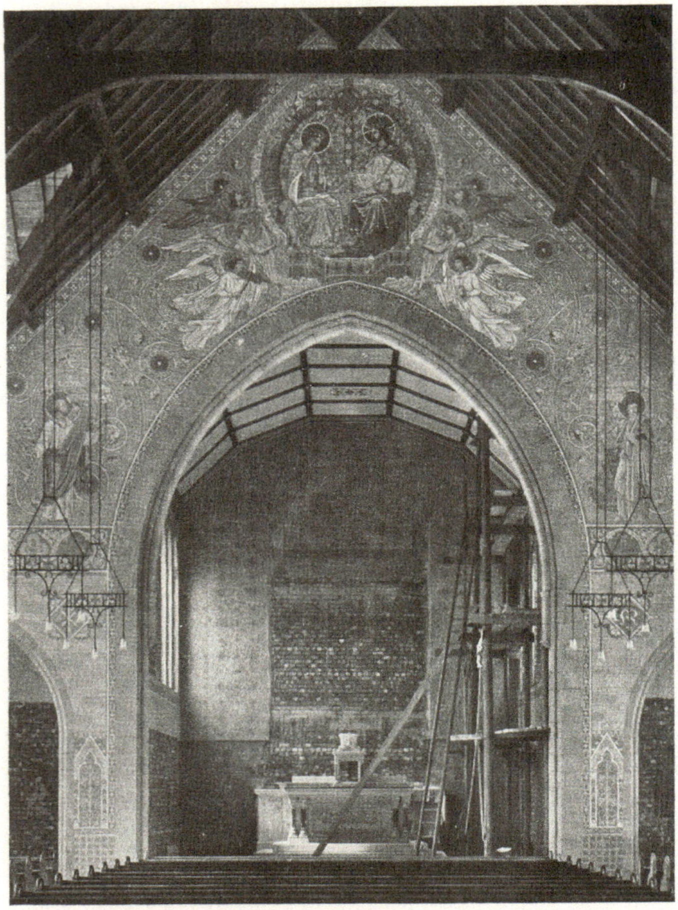

Photo by Cyril Foley, Wigan.

MOSAICS IN COURSE OF EXECUTION, ST. JOHN'S CHURCH, CHORLTON-CUM-HARDY.

L. OPPENHEIMER LTD.

MANCHESTER

P.T O.

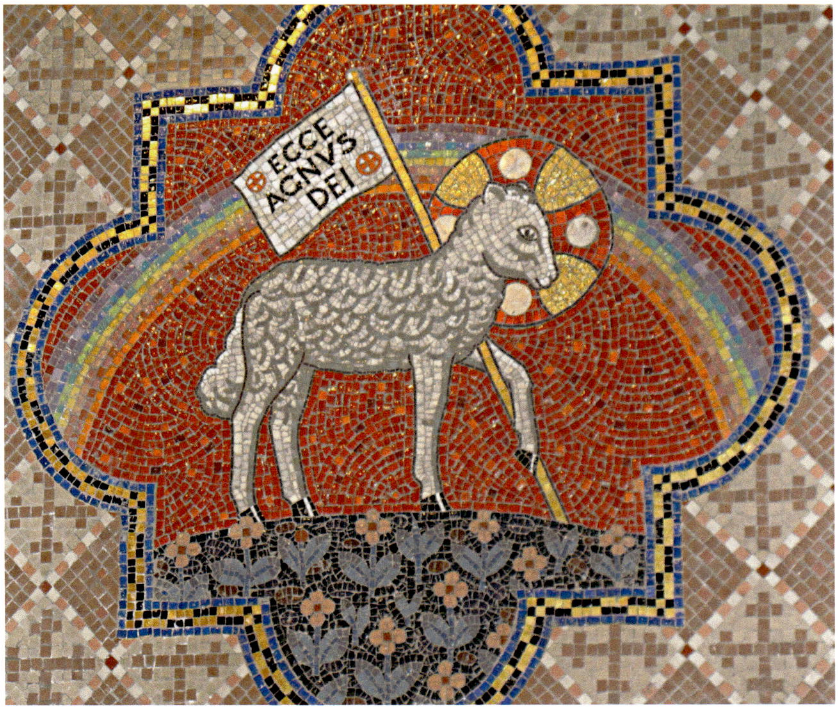

Plate 81 | *Ecce Agnus Dei*: detail from mosaic in the Sacred Heart chapel, Church of the Holy Cross, Charleville, Co. Cork, Ireland (1919–22), courtesy of Caroline M. McGee, Trinity College Dublin

and his nephew Eric who had changed his name to Newton, his mother's maiden name. Eric remained in the company until at least the end of the 1930s and eventually became an art critic of international renown (see footnote 40, page 51).

The company continued trading until 1965 when it closed as business had dried up. It appears that orders from Ireland in particular ceased when an indigenous mosaic and church decoration industry developed.

Fragments of information remain about Ludwig Oppenheimer Ltd. A colour illustrated catalogue from 1904 shows the type and scale of the company's products as shown in adjacent illustrations. A undated publicity leaflet [pl.79] that is probably from the early 1900s lists 110 buildings in which Oppenheimer mosaics could be found. These range from the Continent to Ireland but are predominantly Irish Roman Catholic religious buildings. The document is in lettering reminiscent of *The Eve of Saint Agnes* of 1901. Charles Oppenheimer may have written the text.

It has not yet been possible to ascribe particular mosaic work to him and that may never be possible. However the family until a few years ago kept a camera and lens which he designed to take photographs of the interior of buildings. Clearly this was used in the planning of work and possibly to capture intelligible images of the finished products.

Oppenheimer's business training and varied experiences doubtless contributed significantly to his success as an artist.

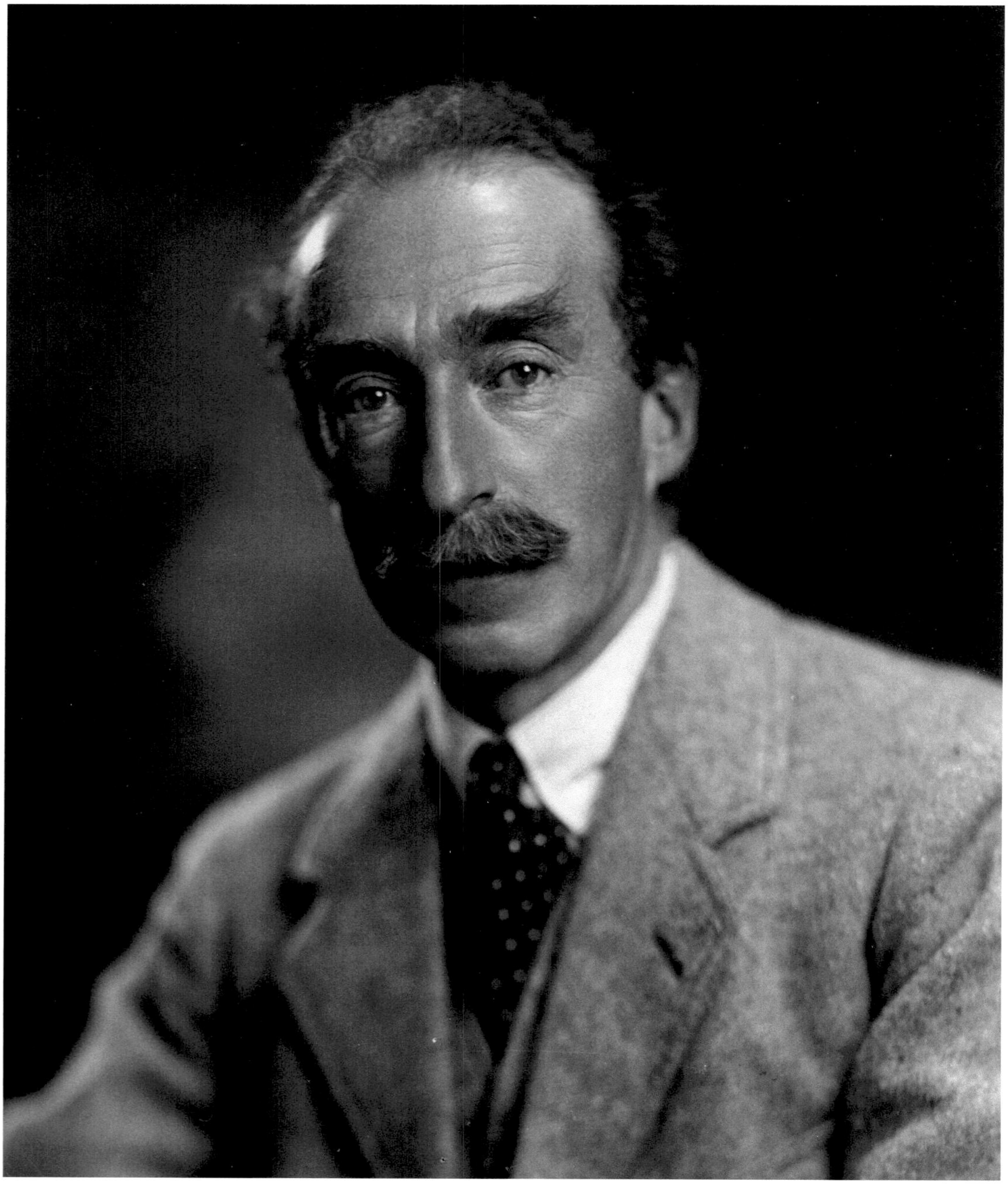

Plate 82 | Charles Oppenheimer, c.1927
courtesy of the Oppenheimer family

CHRONOLOGY

Plate 83 | Stewartry of Kirkcudbright Constabulary in 1945, by kind permission of the Dumfries and Galloway Constabulary Police Museum.
Back row: Sproat, A. Stewart, Grierson; 2nd Back Row: C. Oppenheimer (circled), H. McCorkindale, McDougal, Peacock, Marshall, Corrie, not known, Davidson, not known, not known, S. Seggie; Middle Row: not known, Graham Barley, not known, Hugh McDavit, not known, Austin, J. Hastings, Norman McMillan, Hughan, Irving, J. Crosbie; 2nd Front Row: Wallace, Hannay, J. Kerr, McClymont, Sheddon Tait, Sassoon, Laurimer, not known, Parker, not known,Thomson; Front row: Mcintyre, A.C. Brown, Milne, Gilmour, not known, Dudgeon, Wicham Weaks, not known, Hutchison, McCall.

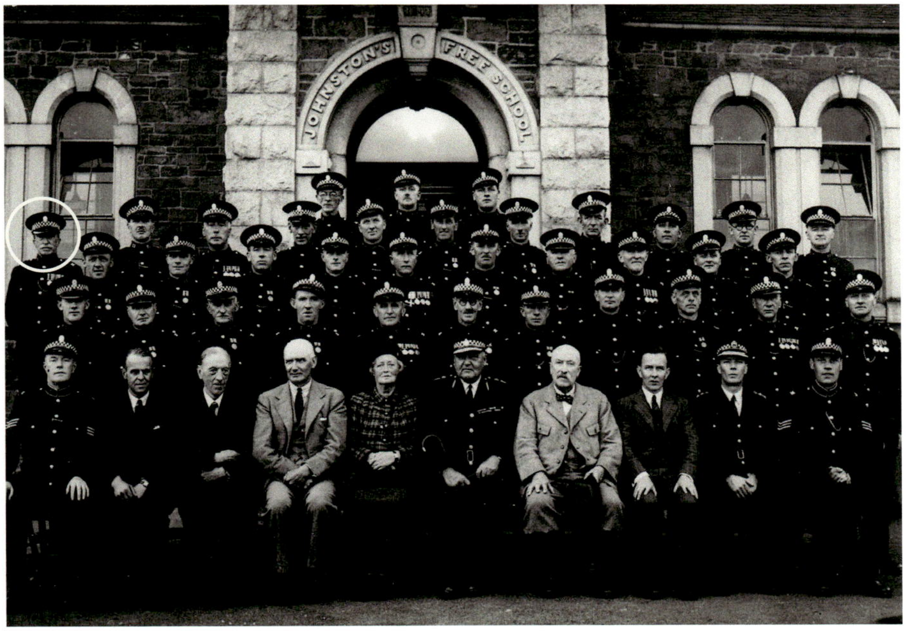

1875
Born 10 October at 58 Park Street, Greenheys, Chorlton-upon-Medlock, Manchester

1879
Moved to 102 Burlington Street

1887
Enrolled in the Manchester School of Art

1892
Awarded a Free Studentship at the School of Art

1892/3
Moved to 144 Withington Road, Whalley Grange, Manchester

1893
Won two Goadsby prizes at the School of Art

1894
First picture exhibited at the Manchester Academy of Fine Arts

1896
Wins prize and travels to Italy

1898
Returns to Italy

1900
Around turn of the century, joins 2nd Volunteer Battalion of the Manchester Regiment of Mounted Infantry

1901
8 January, death of father, Ludwig Oppenheimer Snr.

1901
Family business becomes Ludwig Oppenheimer Ltd

1903
28 May, married Constance Emily Taylor in St Margaret's Parish Church, Whalley Grange

1903
Resident at 197 Stamford Street, Old Trafford

1906
16 January, line drawing published in the *Manchester Guardian*

1906
First picture, 'Old Mills, Montreuil', exhibited at the Royal Academy

1906
Moved to 24 Athol Road, Alexandra Park, Manchester

1909
Moved to 14 High Street, Kirkcudbright in the summer or autumn

1909
Associate Member of the Manchester Academy of Fine Arts

1911
Elected a member of the Royal Scottish Academy of Painters inWatercolours (RSW)

1912
Travels to Italy with William Stewart MacGeorge

1913
First one man show in Glasgow at George Davidson Ltd's galleries in Sauchiehall Street

1913
November, elected to Kirkcudbright Town Council

1915
March, moved to 37 Mayfield Road, Whalley Grange, Manchester to assist in running Ludwig Oppenheimer Ltd

1915
December enlists in Royal Garrison Artillery

1916
Death of eldest brother Lehmann

1916
18 October, in the front line at Bethune in northern France

1917
4 January, transferred to 1 Corps Intelligence Section

1919
Returned to Kirkcudbright

1919
Chairman of the Kirkcudbright Post of the Comrades of the Great War (later The Royal British Legion

1919
13 September, resigned from the Town Council in a dispute over veterans' rights

1920
September, one man show at Taylor and Brown's gallery in 136 St Vincent Street, Glasgow

1924
Contributes panel to the Scottish Forestry Hall at the Wembley Exhibition

1927
March, elected an Associate Member of the Royal Scottish Academy (ARSA)

1934
14 February, elected full Member of the Royal Scottish Academy (RSA) and member of the RSA Selection Committee

1935/6
Council Member and Selection Committee, RSA

1936/7
Hanging Committee Member, RSA

1939
Moved to Woodlea, Kirkcudbright (in the spring of the year)

1941
Special Constable in local Police force

1949–55
Involved in the production of posters for British Railways

1955
Honorary President of the Kirkcudbright Harbour Cottage Fund.

1961
16 April died, Kirkcudbright

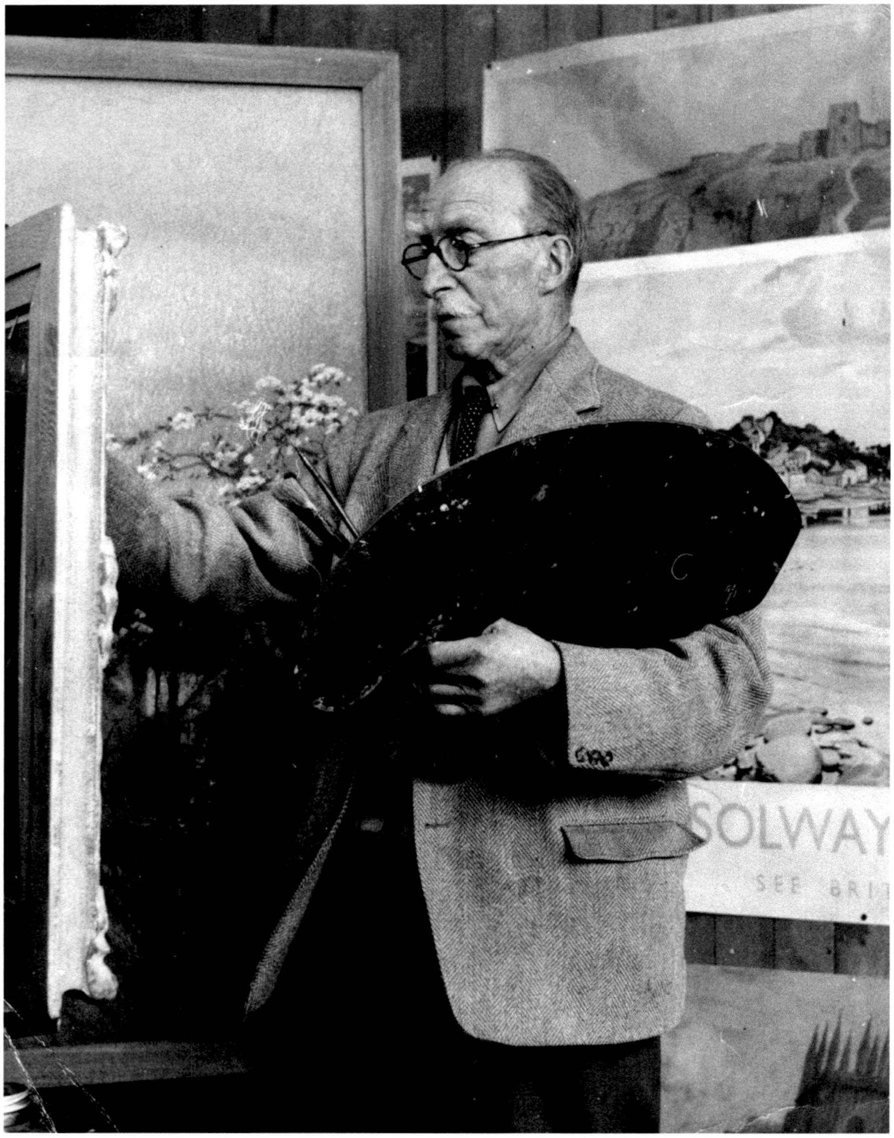

Plate 84 | Charles Oppenheimer in his studio, 1958.
Photograph courtesy of the Oppenheimer family

WORKS EXHIBITED BY OPPENHEIMER

Details of works exhibited by Oppenheimer at the Royal Scottish Academy and the Royal Glasgow Institute can be found in the relevant volumes listed in the bibliography

THE ROYAL ACADEMY

1906 No.997, Old Mills, Montreuil

1908 No.734, Early spring

1912 No.571, The Dee, Galloway
No.604, A Solway port

1913 No.142, Serenata
No.696, The Salute from San Giorgio
No.871, Old Whitby

1914 No.810, Verona

1915 No.26, Moonlit waters: Venice
No.424, San Marco

1916 No.441, Water-lilies
No.725, Piazetta

1917 No.879, A Galloway river

1918 No.173, Verona, 1912 guineas

1919 No.424, An evening sky, Venice

1920 No.354, Lily pool

1921 No.16, Water-lilies
No.328, Kirkcudbright: evening

1923 No.74, Winter time
No.90, Winter gloaming

1924 No.44, Pond lilies
No.308, Market Place, Verona

1925 No.561, Kirkcudbright: moonlight

1926 No.465, In my garden: twilight

1927 No.560, Italian Hill Village

1928 No.81, Frosty Morning
No.506, The old High Street

1931 No.427, Venice

1932 No.75, The morning sun
No.489, Monday morning

1933 No.668, Kirkcudbright under snow

1934 No.628, Midsummer twilight, Kirkcudbright
No.678, Hexham

1935 No.456, The Galloway Dam nearing completion
No.620, February sunshine, Kirkcudbright

1936 No.215, Sunshine and shadow, Assisi
No.594, Engineering in concrete

1937 No.149, An Edinburgh sunset
No.355, Early morning: a Solway port
No.408, A street in old France

1938 No.152, A Galloway landscape
No.425, From a tower, Kirkcudbright

1939 No.294, Galloway Woodlands in February
No.355, Red Roofs of Whitby

1940 No.197, Bridge of Dee, Galloway
No.718, Roman Wall, Northumberland

1941 No.103, Kippford
No.230, Evening glow, Galloway
No.458, A Galloway steading

1943 No.219, A relic of old Kirkcudbright
No.561, An old bridge in Galloway

1944 No.426, Winter time, Kirkcudbright

1945 No.214, Monastery of St. Francis, Assisi
No.433, On the Grand Canal, Venice

1946 No.432, Foundations of a dam

1948 No.339, Winter landscape, Galloway

1949 No.310, Galloway Woodlands in Winter
No.346, An Old Bridge in Galloway

1951 No.305, Road to the Hills, Cumberland

1952 No.116, A Winter Scene, Galloway

ROYAL SOCIETY OF WATER COLOUR PAINTERS IN SCOTLAND

1912 No.19, Kirkcudbright, 18 guineas
No.198, Runswick Bay, 8 guineas
No.210, St Marks, Venice – The Baptistry, 15 guineas

1913 No.145, Gandria – Lake of Lugano, 12 guineas
No.147, An Early Morning Sketch, Verona, 6 guineas
No.153, The Mischabel, £20
No.167, Ponte Vecchio, Verona, 12 guineas

1914 No.19, Evening Glow, Kirkcudbright, £20
No.47, The Market Place, Verona, 12 guineas
No.157, On the Dee Kirkcudbright, £80

1915 no exhibition

1916 No.93, At Nervi, Italian Riviera, £10
No.102, The Road to Lucca, £10
No.156, Ponte Vecchio, Florence, £10

1919 No.163, The Mill Race, 18 guineas
No.297, Whitby, 12 guineas

1920 No.20, Standard Rose, £20
No.52, Winter Landscape, £25
No.80, The Harvest Field, £25

1921 No.67, Allotments, £25

No.130, A Galloway Moor – Heather Burning, £50
No.150, A Lily Pool, £50
No.257, Galloway Uplands, £21

1922 No.2, Following the Plough, £18
No.77, Winter, £25
No.112, From San Miniato, £25
No.158, Woodcutters, £20

1923 No.104, The Farm Pool, £25
No.184, Clearing After Rain, 12 guineas
No.202, The Steading on the Hill, 12 guineas
No.259, A Visit from the Circus, £35

1924 No.66, Edinburgh, £40
No.104, Windsor, £40
No.113, Siena – Nightfall, £40
No.202, The Old Cornmill – Winter, 18 guineas

1925 No.51, San Pietro Pambio, 15 guineas
No.55, Tesserete, 15 guineas
No.157, Twilight Lake Lucerne, £21
No.222, Glendroit, 14 guineas

1926 No.11, Winter Evening Kirkcudbright, 12 guineas
No.89, On the Galloway Coast, 18 guineas
No.92, The Temporary Bridge, £21
No.231, Kirkcudbright, £30

1927 No.33, Head of Mosedale, 15 guineas
No.47, Vines at Gandria, 12 guineas
No.100, Gandria, £21
No.125, Scawfell, 15 guineas

1928 No.11, Alpine Mountain Road, 12 guineas
No.42, Study of a Glacier at Grindelwald, 12 guineas
No.72, Evening Light Lucerne, 15 guineas
No.122, Dalehead Cumberland, 12 guineas

1929 No.201, Arch of Titus, £21
No.209, Roofs of Assisi, 18 guineas
No.213, A Creek at Rimini, not for sale
No.275, Ponte Fabricio and the Palatine, 14 guineas

1930 No.176, Afterglow – Siena, no price
No.264, Isola dei Pescatori, no price
No.276, The Arno at Pisa, no price
No.317, A Creek at Rimini, no price

1931 No.17, Assisi, 16 guineas
No.265, Orvieto, 16 guineas
No.268, Discharging Cargo, 14 guineas
No.273, Hill Country – Umbria, 16 guineas

1932 No.2, Venetian Palaces, 12 guineas
No.7, Rainstorm in St. Gothard, 10 guineas
No.281, Drying the Nets, Chiogga, 16 guineas
No.306, A Sketch at Assisi, 10 guineas

1933 No.8, The Dee, Galloway, £25
No.134, The Cairngorms in Cloud, 14 guineas
No.138, Larig Ghru Pass, Cairngorms, 14 guineas
No.287, Passing Showers, Newtonmore, 14 guineas

1934 No.108, Speyside Evening, £14
No.115, A Galloway Glen, £25
No.118, Oxford from Magdalen Tower, £16
No.225, An Autumn Day – Galloway, £25

1935 No.110, Assisi, 10 guineas
No.139, The Road to the Hills, 10 guineas
No.186, On the Dee, Galloway, 10 guineas
No.209, The Head of the Glen, 10 guineas

1936 No.101, Autumn in Galloway, £20
No.226, Old Kirkcudbright, £15
No.234, A Galloway Glen, £20
No.323, The Road to the Hills £12

1937 No.65, Winter Landscape, £25
No.115, Evening Speyside, £10
No.150, Study Of Madonna Lilies, £15
No.296, Glen Banchor, Newtonmore, £21

1938 No.13, A Galloway Glen, £20
No.58, A Trout Stream, £20
No.316, Galloway Moorlands – Evening Light, £20
No.320, The White Cliffs of Dover, £25

1939 No.126 A Galloway Road, 13 guineas
No.144, Autumn Landscape in Galloway, £21
No.158, At the foot of the Merrick, 13 guineas
No.167, Among the Galloway Hills, £21

1940 No.5, Winter Landscape, Kirkcudbright, £21
No.16, Galloway Uplands under Snow, £21
No.114, Autumn Landscape in Galloway, £21
No.122, A Galloway Stream, 18 guineas

1942 No.133, The Wandering Stream, £21

1944 No.227, Speyside, Autumn Evening, not for sale
'IN AUSTRALIA' A Late Snowfall, not for sale

THE SOCIETY OF SCOTTISH ARTISTS

Oil if not otherwise stated

1922 No.164, Tidal Waters, £84
No.292, Kirkcudbright Evening £200

1923 No.19, Siena Nightfall £50, watercolour
No.75, Edinburgh, £40, watercolour
No.82, The Old Corn Mill – Winter, 18 guineas, watercolour
No.91, Windsor, £45, watercolour

1924 No.105, Lugano, £30
No.114, The Eiger Glacier, £70
No.206, The Jungfrau, £150

1925 No.2, Piazetta, £25, watercolour
No.189, Alpine Sunset, £80
No.196, Suidhe Fheargais, Arran, £40
No.228, In my Garden, Twilight, £40

1926 No.159, Cir Mhor, Head of Glen Sannox, 15 guineas, watercolour
No.151, An Old World Garden, £42
No.208, White Gables, £75
No.278, The Tolbooth, £42

1927 No.159, AD 1666 Study of an Old House, £40
No.232, Painted Sails, Venice, £50

1928 No.154, Boats at Rimini, £50
No.225, On the Venetian Lagoon, £25
No.235, Ponte di Canneregio, Venice, £25

1929 No.25, Water Lilies, £30
No.100, A Galloway Stackyard, £50
No.254, Palazzo Desdemona, Venice, £100

1930 No.73, Adriatic Fishing Boats, £50
No.121, The White Porch, £50
No.134, Study of Ducks, £20

1931 No.71, Springtime in Kirkcudbright, £50

1932 No.170, Glen of the Calder, Newtonmore, £20
No.210, Old Runswick, £20

No.247, Runswick Bay, £20
Whitby Old Town and Abbey, £20
No.167, The Calder at Newtonmore, £20

1933 No.48, A Spring Morning, £20
No.74, The Old Tolbooth, Kirkcudbright, £50
No.102, The Roman Wall, Northumberland, £50

1934 No.68, A Lily Pool, £80

1935 No.13, The Calder in Spate, £20
No.99, Whitby, £20
No.135, Venice, £50

WALKER INSTITUTE AND ART GALLERY, LIVERPOOL

Oil if not otherwise stated

1908 No.667, A Whitby View, 15 guineas, watercolour
No.993, The End of the Day, £52.10.00

1909 No.556, The Flood Sluice, 18 guineas, watercolour

1921 Kirkcudbright Evening, £250

1926 No.57, The Jungfrau, £200
No.991, In My Garden Twilight £50

1928 No.84, Venetian Shipping, £150

1929 No.906, Nocturne, Venice, £90
1930 to **1932** did not exhbit

1933 No.264, February Sunshine, Kirkcudbright, £125
No.300, Kirkcudbright Under Snow, £60

1934 No.47, Palazzo Desdemona, £75
No.1064, Florence, £75

1935 No.31, The Galloway Dam near completion, £350

1937 No.15, My Garden at Twilight, £120

1938 No.6, Cavée St Firmin, Montreuil sur Mer, £85

FINE ART SOCIETY EXHIBITION – OCTOBER 1930

Watercolours:
No.1, Santa Chiara, Assisi, 15 guineas
No.2, Discharging Cargo, 12 guineas
No.3, Seathwaite and Great End, 18 guineas
No.4, The Little Cornmill, 15 guineas
No.5, Franciscan Monastery, 12 guineas
No.6, A By-Road – Orvieto, 10 guineas
No.7, Assisi, 15 guineas
No.8, Glendroit, 15 guineas
No.9, Ponte Fabricio, Rome, 12 guineas
No.10, Olives, San Domenico, 10 guineas
No.11, A Creek at Rimini, 20 guineas
No.12, Arch of Titus, Rome, 20 guineas
No.13, A Summer Sea, 25 guineas
No.14, The Grand Canal, Venice, 18 guineas
No.15, The Arno at Pisa, 10 guineas
No.16, San Francesco, Assisi, 8 guineas
No.17, Orvieto, 16 guineas
No.18, Towards the Mischabel, 12 guineas
No.19, The Plain of Umbria, 10 guineas
No.20, Approach to Orvieto, 8 guineas

Oils:
No.21, Orvieto, 40 guineas
No.22, Low Tide – Kirkcudbright, 60 guineas
No.23, Tesserete, 25 guineas
No.24, Bridge of Dee, 40 guineas
No.25, Solway Shore, 18 guineas
No.26, Fishing Boats, 40 guineas
No.27, Spring Morning, 20 guineas
No.28, Winter Sunshine – Kirkcudbright, 100 guineas
No.29, San Vitale – Ravenna, 20 guineas
No.30, Boats at Rimini, 40 guineas
No.31, The Guidecca, Venice, 20 guineas
No.32, The Forum, Rome, 40 guineas
No.33, Washing Day, 20 guineas
No.34, Hadrian's Wall, Northumberland, 60 guineas
No.35, Craignair Granite Quarry, 18 guineas
No.36, Building the Stack, 50 guineas
No.37, Winter Gloaming, 45 guineas
No.38, Springtime, 15 guineas
No.39, Kirkcudbright at Sunset, 25 guineas
No.40, The Artist's Garden, 150 guineas
No.41, The Yair Net, 60 guineas
No.42, Study of Ducks, 15 guineas
No.43, The Old Town – Twilight, 25 guineas
No.44, Edinburgh Castle, 50 guineas
No.45, The Lily Pond, 50 guineas
No.46, The White Porch, 40 guineas
No.47, Rimini, 18 guineas
No.48, Venice at Sundown, 80 guineas
No.49, Kirkcudbright at Night, 50 guineas
No.50, Last Days of Winter, 45 guineas
No.51, Harvest Moon, 20 guineas
No.52, Old Olives – Assisi, 60 guineas
No.53, In spate, 20 guineas
No.54, Painted Sails – Rimini, 20 guineas
No.55, An Evening Sky, 12 guineas
No.56, The Piazzetta, Venice, 60 guineas
No.57, The Galloway Dee, 20 guineas
No.58, Palazzo Desdemona, 60 guineas
No.59, A Galloway Stackyard, 35 guineas
No.60, Florence, 50 guineas
No.61, A Tangle of Shipping – Chiogga, 20 guineas
No.62, On the Lagoon, 20 guineas

Watercolour Drawings:
No.63, In the Evening Light – Lucerne, 10 guineas
No.64, Rainstorm in St Gothard, 12 guineas
No.65, Near Rosthwaite, 14 guineas
No.66, A Mountain Torrent, 12 guineas
No.67, The Road to Buttermere, 15 guineas
No.68, The Galloway Coast, 15 guineas
No.69, Evening Light – Assisi, 15 guineas
No.70, Hexham, 10 guineas
No.71, Nightfall – Siena, 30 guineas
No.72, Bridge Builders, 18 guineas
No.73, Orvieto from the South, 12 guineas
No.74, The Head of Mosedale, 16 guineas
No.75, Hill Country – Umbria, 14 guineas
No.76, An Alpine Road, 12 guineas
No.77, Thun at Twilight, 10 guineas
No.78, The Hayfield, 12 guineas
No.79, An Italian Village, 10 guineas
No.80, Lifting Mists – Styhead, 15 guineas
No.81, A Vine Pergola, 12 guineas
No.82, Assisi from the Olive Groves, 15 guineas
No.83, Roofs – Assisi, 14 guineas
No.84, A Farm by the Sea, 18 guineas

THE MANCHESTER ACADEMY OF FINE ARTS

No.8, Blencathra from Druid's Circle, 10 guineas
The Lion of St Mark, Venice, £31.10/-

1910 An Old World Village, 15 guineas
A Spring Morning, Goring on Thames, 10 guineas
Cold February, 8 guineas
The Old Farmstead, 18 guineas
The Quiet Harbour, £52
By the River, 10 guineas
The Orchard, £21

1911 The Flood Sluice, £15
Last Days of Winter, £10

In Spate, £20
Autumn Morning, £25
The Lily Pool, £50

1912 The Harvest Field, £21
September's Garland, £25
The Last Hour of Toil, £150

1913 Goring Reach, 18 guineas
Kirkcudbright Harbour, 12 guineas
Piazza Erbe, Verona, £200
Old Whitby, £25

1914 At Sunrise, Lugano, £25
From a Verona Balcony, £50
St Mark's, Venice, £200

1916 A Galloway Salmon River, £50
Florence (Early Morning) without frame, £45
Verona, £21
Water Lilies, £21
Florence at Dusk, £21

1917 A Street in Florence, £15
A Spring Morning Italy, £10
The Thames Near Goring, £10
Harvest, £20

1920 Mrs R.L. Taylor, no price
Florence, £80
Duck Pond, £20
Autumn Gold, £20
Lily Pool, £60

1921 Harvest Moon, £200
A Passing Shower, £20
Waterlilies, £80
Still Waters, £20
Kirkcudbright: Evening, £250
Winter Gloaming, £100

1922 Little Water Mill, no price

1923 The Lone Pine, 12 guineas
A Spring Morning, 12 guineas
The Galloway Dee, £75
At the Gloaming, £25
Evening, Lake Lucerne, £75

1924 Florence from San Miniato, £30
Ebb Tide, £35
The Last of the Snow, £40
Windsor, £35
Breaking Seas, 12 guineas
Clearing After Rain, 12 guineas
At the Gloaming, £100,

1925 Evening, Altdorf, 12 guineas
Cortivallo, 15 guineas
Twynholm Braes, £21
The Jungfrau, £150
Kirkcudbright Moonlight, £42
Across the Estuary, £21

1926 Cir Mhor, Head of Glen Sannox, no price
Granite Quarry,Whitworth, no price
Frosty Morning, £42
Piazetta at Dusk, £84
In My Garden, Twilight, £42
At the Quayside, £21

1927 The Great Quarry, Craignair £60
Building the Stack, £45
The White Porch, £45
The Old World Garden, £45
Camp Fire, no price

1928 Flying Buttresses, 10 guineas
The Old High Street, £50
The Artist's Garden, £150

1929 Arch of Titus, 18 guineas
Ponte Fabricio and the Palatine, 12 guineas
Orvieto, £50

1930 Palazzo Desdemona, £100
Venice at Sundown, £105
Lily Pool, £75

1931 Low Tide, Kirkcudbright, £75
The Piazetta, Venice, £75
Washing Day, £25
Hadrian's Wall, Northumberland, £80

1932 Durham, £150

1933 Kirkcudbright under Snow, £50
Venice Asleep, £100
A Highland Burn, £150

1934 Midsummer Night, Kirkcudbright, no price

1935 A Lily Pool, £80
Old Edinburgh, £125
February Sunshine, Kirkcudbright, £100

1936 Engineering in Concrete, no price

1937 A Street in Old France, no price

1938 A Galloway Landscape, no price

1939 Fishermen's Houses, Runswick, £25
A Grey Morning, Runswick Bay, no price

1941 The Old Tolbooth, Kirkcudbright, £25
Apple Trees, £30

1942 Durham, £25

1944 From a Studio Window, not for sale

1945 Whitby, £175

1946 Foundations of a Dam, not for sale

1948 From My Studio Window, no price
Winter Landscape, Galloway, £80

1949 Cavée St Firmin, Montreuil-sur-Mer, £105

1950 Ponte San Trinita, Florence (destroyed 1944) £105

1951 The Port of Rimini, no price

1952 Winter Landscape, Galloway, no price

1959 The Old Tolbooth, Kirkcudbright, Loan
Evening, Lake Lucerne, Loan

BIBLIOGRAPHY

BAILE DE LAPERRIERE, Charles, *The Royal Scottish Academy Exhibitors 1826–1990*, Calne, 1991

BILLCLIFFE, Roger (editor), *The Royal Glasgow Institute of the Fine Arts 1861–1989: Dictionary of Exhibitors*, 4 vols, Glasgow, 1990–92

BOURNE, Patrick ed., *Kirkcudbright 100 Years of an Artists' Colony*, Atelier books, Edinburgh, 2000

CRAWFORD, Elizabeth, *Women's Suffrage movement: a reference guide. 1886–1928*, London: UCL Press, 1999

DAVIES, Peter, *A Northern School, Lancashire artists of the twentieth century*, Redcliffe, Bristol, 1989

GORDON, Haig, *From Capri to Kirkcudbright, The Life and Work of William Robson, (1863–1950)*, St Cuthbert Publications, 2005

GORDON, Haig, *Tales of Kirkcudbright Artists*, Galloway Publishing, 2006

NEWTON, Laura, (Editor) *Painting at the edge, British Coastal Art Colonies 1880 – 1930*, Sansom and Company Ltd, Bristol, 2005

NICHOL, Charles, *Leonardo da Vinci*, Penguin Books, 2004

O'NEILL, Morna, *Art and labour's cause is one: Walter Crane and Manchester, 1880–1915*, Whitworth Art Gallery, University of Manchester, Manchester, 2008.

O'NEILL, Morna, *Walter Crane: The Arts and Crafts, Painting, and Politics 1875–1890*, Paul Mellon Centre for Studies in British Art, Yale University Press, New Haven, 2010.

OPPENHEIMER, Sir Francis KCMG, *Stranger Within*, Faber and Faber, London, 1960

OPPENHEIMER, Lehmann, *The Heart of Lakeland*, Sherratt and Hughes, London and Manchester, 1908

PUGH, Professor Martin, *The Pankhursts*, Allen Lane, The Penguin Press, 2001

SAYERS, Dorothy L., *Five Red Herrings*, Victor Gollancz Ltd, 1931

INDEX

Alloway, Ayrshire, 41
Anti-German sentiment, 7, 43–46, 48, 51, 87, 107
Arras, France, 47
Arthur, Janet, (Fanny Parker) *suffragette*, 41
Artist, The, periodical, 15, 23, 31, 86, 96, 99, 111
Artists' Rifles, 23rd London Regiment, 47

Bacchus Marsh, Australia, 33
Baillie, William (Bill), 86
Balfour Arthur, Prime Minister, 27
Berkshire Downs, 30
Bethune, 48, 49, 122
Bismarck, Prince Otto von, 11
Blacklock, Thomas Bromley, *artist*, 33
Blewbury, Berkshire, 30
Bliss, Douglas Percy, *art critic*, 100, 101
Boer War, 25
Borthwick, Alfred Edward, *artist*, 56
Botanic Gardens Museum, Southport, 94
Broughton House, Kirkcudbright, 8, 9, 34, 69, 91
Brunswick, Germany, 11, 12
Burns, Robert, *artist*, 56

Cairns, Robert Dickie, 109
Campbell, James, 91, 109
Campbell, Joe, 8, 26, 39, 74, 79, 86, 87, 92, 106
Carson, Sir Edward, 45
Cheltenham Ladies' College, 25
Chorlton-upon-Medlock, 12, 40, 121
— *Board of Guardians*, 12
Churchill, Winston, as *MP for a Manchester constituency*, 27
Clarke, William Hanna, *artist, funeral of*, 105
Colbeck, Thomas William, *trading with the enemy case*, 43
Cooke, Geraldine Miss, *women's suffrage movement*, 40, 41

Country Life, 74
Crane, Walter, artist and Director of Manchester School of Art, 7, 17, 18, 56,
Crawford, William Caldwell, *artist*, 56
Cristol Military Hospital, Boulogne, 47
Cursiter, Stanley, 64, 112

'Derby scheme', 46
Disraeli, Benjamin, 13
Doig, Wilson and Wheatley's gallery, 65
Dudgeon, Brigadier General Robert Maxwell, DSO MC, 110
Dumfries Standard, 56
Dumfries and Galloway Fine Art Association, 105

Equal Franchise Act, (1928), 41
Evans, Miss Mary, 8, 21, 23, 26, 48, 70, 81, 82, 104
'*The Eve of Saint Agnes*', (by John Keats) illuminated manuscript, 18, 19, 119
Exposición de Artes e Industrias Británicas, Buenos Aires, 89

Falkner, John Meade, *novelist*, 85
Ferguson, Christian Jane, *artist*, 105
Findlay, James, 12
Foggie, David, *Secretary of the RSA*, 106
French, General Sir John, 25

Galloway Hydro-Electric Scheme, 97, 98, 99
Gauld, David, *artist*, 64, 105
George Davidson Ltd, Glasgow, *art dealers*, 34, 66, 122
Gibson, John, *Kirkcudbright Town Clerk*, 46, 47, 52
Gladstone, William Ewart, *statue of*, 27
Glasgow Art Club, 36, 67
Glasgow, Roberta, *art critic*, 58
Graphic Club, Manchester, 31

Guardian (The Manchester Guardian), 13, 20, 21, 27, 51, 54, 121

Hanover, Germany, 11
Harbour Cottage Art Gallery, Kirkcudbright, 112
Hastings, Henry, *Assistant Secretary to the RSA*, 108, 109
'*The Heart of Lakeland*' (by Lehmann Oppenheimer), 18, 20, 21, 127
Hornel, Edward Atkinson, *artist*, 33,
— *Oppenheimer as tenant*, 34,
— *encourages Oppenheimer to stand for Council*, 38,
— *relationship with MacGeorge*, 64, 105
Houston, George, *artist*, 55, 100, 101, 106

Intelligence Section, 1 Corps, 44, 48, 49, 122
Isaacs, Rufus, *Attorney General (later Marquis of Reading)*, 45

Jackson, Charles Arthur, *brother of Frederick William*,
— *art dealer and picture framer*, 29
Jackson, Frederick William, *artist*, 7, 28, 29, 30, 103,

Keats, John, *poet*, 18
King, Jessie Marion, *artist*, 33, 86, 110, 111
Kirkcudbright Advertiser, 36, 39, 40, 46, 67,
Kirkcudbright Town Council election 1912, 38, 39
Kirkcudbrightshire Golf Club, 104
Knight, Harold, *husband of Laura*, 30, 31
Knight, Laura, *artist*, 29, 30, 31

La Thangue, Henry Herbert, 37, 38
Lens, 42, 43, 47, 48, 49,
Liverpool Courier, 29, 30, 36
Lloyd George, David
— *birth place*, 12,
— *extension of franchise*, 41
— *social legislation*, 45
Lorimer, John Henry, *brother of Robert, artist*, 56
Lorimer, Sir Robert, *artist*, 56

MacGeorge, William Stewart, *artist*, 7, 33, 64, 65, 69, 105, 121
Manchester, *radical nature of*, 12–13
Manchester City News, 36, 38, 58, 67
Manchester Municipal School of Art, 7, 9, 15, 17, 28, 40, 121
Manchester Regiment of Mounted Infantry,
— *2nd Volunteer Battalion*, 24, 31, 121
Millburn Street, Kirkcudbright, 34
Montrose, 7, 12, 18, 33, 54, 104, 109
Mories, FG, *art critic*, 15, 86, 89, 99,
Moultrie, Beryl, 8, 26
Mouncey, William, *artist*, 33, 103,
Munnings, Sir Alfred, *artist*, 111

The Nebuly Coat, 85
Newnham College, Cambridge University, 25
Newton, Edith, 15, 24, 47, 116, 117
Newton, Grace, 24, 117
Newtonmore, Inverness-shire, 54, 124, 125
Neilson, Henry Ivan, *artist*, 34
Nixon, William, 12

Oppenheimer, Albert, 13, 15, 17, 20, 24, 51, 116, 117, 118,
Oppenheimer, Charles
— *birth*, 13
— *early years and education*, 15
— *Manchester School of Art and tutors*, 16–18
— *close relationship with eldest brother, Lehmann*, 20–21
— *first paintings*, 23
— *business like attitudes of*, 13, 82–85, 103
— *mounted infantryman*, 24–25
— *engagement and marriage to Connie*, 25–26
— *1906 election cartoon and free trade*, 26–28
— *friendship with Fred Jackson*, 28–29
— *moves to Kirkcudbright*, 30, 33
— *first one man show and critical attention*, 34–36
— *election to Town Council*, 39
— *and women's suffrage*, 39–41
— *returns to Manchester*, 46
— *goes to war*, 46–49
— *argues for veterans*, 51–52
— *and angling*, 53, 54
— *and Speyside*, 54
— *with MacGeorge in Italy*, 64–65
— *Italian pictures praised*, 67
— *friendship with William Robson*, 64, 70, 111
— *Scottish Forestry Hall, Wembley Exhibition*, 56, 58
— *criticism of Fine Art Society show*, 72–75
— *and Dorothy L Sayers*, 81–85
— *dislike of being observed at work*, 86
— *and Harbour Cottage Art Gallery*, 112
— *helps a student*, 87
— *difficulty in dating paintings of*, 92
— *full member of the RSA*, 96
— *attitude to buildings in the landscape*, 99
— *comparison with George Houston RSA*, 55, 100–101, 106
— *moves to Woodlea*, 103, 107
— *and golf*, 103, 104, 106
— *proposes better advertising of the RSA*, 105–106
— *as a Special Constable*, 107–109, 121
— *invitation to join Royal Academy*, 106
— *and railway posters*, 112
— *and the Lilies series of pictures*, 92–93
— *death*, 113
— *his style*, 7, 53, 56, 69–70, 84, 92, 112
— *agrees with Munnings*, 111
Oppenheimer, Constance Emily (Connie) (née Taylor), 23, 33, 46, 85, 91, 107
— *engagement and marriage*, 25–26
— *at Cambridge*, 25
— *teaching*, 25
— *and Jackson's portrait*, 29
— *and women's suffrage*, 39, 41
— *and anti-German sentiment*, 45
— *in Italy*, 64, 74, 75
— *about MacGeorge*, 64
— *a kind hostess*, 81
— *inherits estate*, 113
Oppenheimer, Ethel, 47
Oppenheimer, Eric (son of Lehmann James) 47, 117, 119
— *changes name*, 51, 118
Oppenheimer, Sir Francis Charles, 45, 127
Oppenheimer, Ernest, 45
Oppenheimer, Frank, 13, 15, 116
Oppenheimer, Julius, *trading with the enemy case*, 43
Oppenheimer, Lehmann James, 15, 17, 18, 23, 24, 51, 61, 116, 117, 122,
— *exhibits at same time as Charles at RA*, 21
— *relationship with Charles*, 20, 21
— *age on enlistment and military career*, 46, 47
Oppenheimer, Ludwig Snr, 11, 12, 13, 15, 16, 24, 61
Oppenheimer, Ludwig Jnr (Louis), 13, 15, 20, 23, 116, 117, 118
Oppenheimer, Ludwig Ltd, 8, 9, 27, 28, 43, 51, 52, 121, 122
— *patent*, 115
— *Articles of Association*, 24, 27, 117
— *wartime letter*, 44
Oppenheimer, William Renwick, 13, 17, 20, 47, 48, 116, 117, 118
Oppenheimer, Susan McCulloch (née Findlay), 12, 13, 16, 105

Palazzo Mafia, Verona, 69
Pankhurst, Christabel, 12, 40
Pankhurst, Emmeline, 12, 39
Pankhurst, Richard, 12, 39
Pankhurst, Sylvia, 12, 40
Paterson James, *artist, President of the RSW*, 71
Police cap badge, '*Semper Vigilo*', 109
Poucher, Walter Arthur, 20
Pugh, Professor Martin, 13, 127
Puir Hoose Brae, Kirkcudbright, 85

Reekie, William Maxwell, *artist*, 82
Robson, Carmella, 61, 64, 70
Robson, William (Bill) *artist*, 33, 41, 61, 70, 103, 110, 111, 127
Royal Astronomical Society, 11
Royal British Colonial Society of Artists, 89
Royal Garrison Artillery, 180 Siege Battery, 47
Royle, Herbert, *artist*, 36, 38
Runswick Bay, Whitby, 30, 31
Rushbury, Sir Henry, 106, 107
Russell-Cotes Gallery, Bournemouth, 92

St Margaret's Parish Church, Whalley Grange, Manchester, 26
Sayers, Dorothy L,
— *rents 14A High Street*, 81
— *Five Red Herrings*, 81, 82, 83
— *The Nine Tailors*, 86
Schleswig Holstein war, 1864, 11
Scotsman, The, 34, 36, 38, 49, 53–56, 72, 74, 81, 89, 91–94, 96, 106, 109
Shamash, George, 104
Shaw, George Bernard, 29, 30
Sheffield Daily Telegraph, 29
Sillitoe, Sir Percy and the '*Sillitoe tartan*', 109
Smith, William (Bill), 9, 86
Studio, The, 17, 21, 96, 106
Sunday Express, 113

Taylor and Brown Gallery, 54, 122
Taylor, Ernest Archibald, *artist*, 31, 33, 96, 105, 110
Taylor, Robert Llewellyn, FIC, FCS, 25

Venice, 23, 28, 40, 61, 64, 65, 66, 67, 70, 74
Verona, 38, 64, 65, 66, 67, 69,
Da Vinci, Leonardo, *solitary nature of an artist*, 87

Wainwright, Alfred, 20
Waverley railway line, 18
Willis, Richard Henry Albert, *artist and teacher*, 17, 56

Zulu, (a yacht), 94